To Herb and Barbara,
with much love.
ARON

D0849685

Images of Sephardi and Eastern Jewries in Transition

The Teachers of the Alliance Israélite Universelle, 1860–1939

Images of Sephardi and Eastern Jewries in Transition

The Teachers of the Alliance Israélite Universelle, 1860–1939

ARON RODRIGUE

University of Washington Press

Seattle & London

Library of Congress Cataloging-in-Publication Data
Rodrigue, Aron.
    Images of Sephardi and eastern Jewries in transition : the teachers of
the Alliance israélite universelle, 1860–1939 / Aron Rodrigue.
    p. cm.
    Includes bibliographical references and index.
    ISBN 0–295–97281–5
    1. Jews—Islamic countries—Correspondence.   2. Jewish teachers—
Islamic countries—Correspondence.   3. Jews—Education—Islamic
countries.   4. Islamic countries—Ethnic relations.   5. Alliance
israélite universelle.   I. Title.
DS 135.L4R63   1993   93–15121
909'.04924—dc20   CIP

Contents

List of Illustrations   *vi*
Acknowledgments   *viii*
A Note on the Documents   *ix*
Map   *x*
Introduction   *3*

  1. An Overview of the Alliance's Activities   *7*

Part I: THE SCHOOLS AND TEACHERS OF THE ALLIANCE
          ISRAÉLITE UNIVERSELLE   *23*
  2. Instruction in the Alliance Schools   *25*
  3. The Alliance Teaching Corps   *34*

Part II: THE DISCOURSE OF THE ALLIANCE TEACHERS AND
          THE "CIVILIZING" OF THE JEWISH COMMUNITIES OF
          THE LANDS OF ISLAM   *69*
  4. The Moralizing Agenda   *71*
  5. The Emancipation and Reformation of Women   *80*
  6. The Transformation of the Social Structure of the Jewish
      Community   *94*
  7. The Critique of Traditional Judaism   *105*
  8. The War of Languages   *125*
  9. A Portrait of the Communities   *135*
10. The Impact of the West and the Alliance Schools   *179*

Part III. THE ALLIANCE TEACHER AS POLITICAL ACTIVIST
          AND POLITICAL OBSERVER   *201*
11. The Task of Protection   *205*
12. The Teacher as Patriot and Advocate of the Jews   *217*
13. The Age of Nationalism   *245*

Conclusion   *287*
Glossary   *293*
Bibliography   *295*
Index of Personal Names   *304*
Index of Place Names   *306*

Illustrations

All photographs are courtesy of the Alliance Israélite Universelle

following page 148

The school in Tunis, Tunisia, end of the nineteenth century

Prize day at the school for boys, Tangier, Morocco, 1928

Jewish refugees from the city of Settat in front of one of the Alliance schools in Casablanca, Morocco, April 1904

A sewing class in Constantine, Algeria

A class at the school on Meschnaka Street, Tunis, Tunisia, 1886

A Jew of Bou-Saada, Tunisia

A Jewish woman of Tunis, Tunisia

Teachers and rabbis in Tunis, Tunisia, 1886–87

The personnel of the schools for boys and girls in Monastir (Bitola), Ottoman Empire (Macedonia), 1912

Students of the school for boys, Monastir (Bitola), Ottoman Empire (Macedonia), 1912

Students of the school for boys in Salonica, Ottoman Empire (Greece), end of the nineteenth century

Students of the school for girls, Rustchuk (Ruse), Bulgaria, 1902

Students in the vocational program, Samacoff, Bulgaria, 1892

Orphans at the Alliance school in Tchorlu (Çorlu), Turkey, 1921

The personnel of the schools for boys and girls in Beirut, Lebanon, 1909

Advanced class, Beirut, Lebanon, 1909

Scouts from the Alliance schools in Damascus, Syria, 1933

The Jewish quarter in Damascus, Syria, 1920s

Students of the school for boys, Baghdad, Iraq, 1898

Students of the Laura Kadoorie school for girls, Baghdad, Iraq

Laura Kadoorie school for girls, Baghdad, Iraq

Students of the school for girls, Baghdad, Iraq, 1900

A girls' class, Laura Kadoorie school for girls, Baghdad, Iraq, 1925

School recess, Yezd, Iran, 1925

The first communal committee of the Alliance in Teheran, Iran, 1898

A boys' class, Isphahan, Iran, 1925–26

Students of the Laura Kadoorie school for girls, Teheran, Iran, 1938

Acknowledgments

This is an expanded, updated, and revised version of a book that appeared in Paris in 1989 under the title *De l'instruction à l'émancipation: Les enseignants de l'Alliance Israélite Universelle et les Juifs d'Orient, 1860–1939,* published in the Diaspora series of Editions Calmann-Lévy. My thanks go to Bernard Lewis for initially suggesting the idea of this project.

I would like to thank Georges Weill for allowing me access to the archives of the Alliance Israélite Universelle and Yvonne Lévyne for making my work in these archives particularly pleasant. I am grateful to Esther Benbassa, who read and commented upon the various drafts of the French version.

The research for this book has benefited from the support of the Memorial Foundation for Jewish Culture and from a Summer Faculty Fellowship from Indiana University, and I thank both institutions. I am grateful to the American Friends of the Alliance Israélite Universelle, whose grant enabled me to undertake the translation of the documents printed in this volume. My thanks go to Barbara Pieroni, who did the first draft of the translations, and to my research assistant, Joan Clinefelter, for typing and retyping the various versions of the manuscript.

A Note on the Documents

All the documents reproduced here are from the archives or the publications of the Alliance Israélite Universelle and are translations of French originals. Hebrew, Turkish, Arabic, and Persian words that appear in the texts have been transliterated in a simplified manner to conform to English transliteration usage; no diacritical marks have been used. The meanings of non-European words are explained in the notes or supplied by me in the letters at their first occurrence.

In order to convey as closely as possible the original flavor of the texts, the place names in the documents have not been modernized. Widely accepted nineteenth-century versions in the English-speaking world have been used throughout. Hence, for example, Smyrne in the original appears as Smyrna, but not as İzmir. Table 2 gives the nineteenth-century versions along with the modern names.

Map by Corinna Campbell

Locations of schools of the Alliance Israélite Universelle, 1910

Images of Sephardi and Eastern Jewries in Transition

The Teachers of the Alliance Israélite Universelle, 1860–1939

Introduction

The irruption of Europe into the economy, politics, and culture of the Middle East and North Africa in the course of the nineteenth and twentieth centuries constitutes a watershed in the history of this region. European domination, whether military, economic, political, or cultural, altered conclusively most aspects of life that it touched. Indeed, if one focuses on the issue from the perspective of the East itself, it becomes quite clear that the burning question of the day was not the "Eastern Question," the central preoccupation of a Europe obsessed with the vacuum created by the decline in Muslim power, but the "Western Question." It was the triumphant and triumphalist West with its newly acquired economic and military might fueled by the Industrial Revolution that posed the main challenge to the rest of the world.

One of the most important consequences of the incorporation of the Middle East and North Africa into the European sphere of influence was the process of westernization that was set in motion. It began as a primarily defensive stance. If Western military might could be defeated only through the adoption of European armaments and warfare tactics, then such a borrowing was clearly in order. The Ottoman as well as the North African states began their reforms in this domain. European-style warfare was learned from European military officers, who trained and remodeled the local armies. However, in order to learn the new techniques, European languages also had to be acquired. Gradually an elite of military officers and bureaucrats emerged, proficient in European languages as well as familiar with European ideas and ideologies. They became convinced of the necessity of transforming not only the military but also the state apparatus and indeed eventually civil society as well. The model for reform was to remain the European one. This process was fully and radically completed most notably in the case of Turkey with the advent of the Turkish republic in 1923.[1]

1. For Turkey see, e.g., Bernard Lewis, *The Emergence of Modern Turkey*, 2d ed. (London: Oxford University Press, 1968); and Stanford J. Shaw and Ezel K. Shaw, *History of the Ottoman Empire and Modern Turkey*, 2 vols. (New York: Cambridge

However, the European powers themselves were far from taking a disinterested attitude toward the process of reform and westernization. They were not above strongly suggesting and indeed imposing theoretically far-reaching constitutional change, as with the Reform Decree of 1856 in Turkey and the Fundamental Pact of 1857 in Tunisia. And of course, in the case of direct European colonial rule in Algeria after 1830 or mitigated colonial rule as in Tunisia and Egypt after 1881 and 1882, Morocco in 1912, and the Fertile Crescent after World War I, the full weight of the West was brought to bear in most areas of life. Europe not only was the superior power but was also fully convinced of its own superiority. Since it was deemed to have reached the most advanced stage of civilization, all other cultures and societies had to follow its lead and, whether willingly or not, adopt its ways and undergo the reforms it suggested or imposed. This perspective lay at the heart of the triumphalist prism through which all non-European reality was refracted and was to guide European "civilizing" missions, most notably that of the country which made a special cult of its mission, France.

Westernization emerged as an open-ended phenomenon of mimesis, emulation, adoption, or adaptation of European ways. It represented the kaleidoscope of responses based on the reorientation around the central referent, a reified "West." At its core lay a profound inequality of power and the attempt by the powerless to transcend their position of inferiority even while internalizing the perception of Western superiority. As a rule, the appropriation and co-optation of the culture arriving from the metropole and its mixture with elements of the home culture accompanied the confrontation with the West as it manifested itself in the locality.[2] The non-West never transmuted itself into the West but created a new, hybrid reality that was nevertheless overdetermined by European superior power.

European domination of the Middle East and North Africa and the process of westernization that accompanied it form the general context in which the modern encounter between the West and the Sephardi and Eastern Jewish communities of the Muslim world took place, an encounter that decisively marked the last century of Jewish existence in the lands of Islam. Sephardi and Eastern Jews did not, of course, remain immune to the demands and attractions of the West. However, one crucial difference distinguished their experience from that of their Muslim neighbors. For

University Press, 1976–77). For a provocative analysis of westernization see Theodor von Laue, *The World Revolution of Westernization* (New York: Oxford University Press, 1987).

2. For the latest discussion of this phenomenon of "transculturation," see Mary Louise Pratt, *Imperial Eyes: Travel Writing and Transculturation* (London: Routledge, 1992).

the Sephardim and Eastern Jews the most important and central impetus for cultural westernization came in most areas from their coreligionists in the West, especially the French Jews working through the Alliance Israélite Universelle with its vast school network in Muslim countries. An added twist was supplied by the militantly westernizing teaching corps of this society. These teachers, primarily Middle Eastern and North African Jews trained by the organization in Paris, returned to spread their newly adopted culture with all the zeal of neophytes.

The central focus of this study is the Alliance teachers and their activities. The aim is to illuminate the problematic nature of Middle Eastern and North African Jewry's encounter with the West through the presentation of the rich correspondence of the teachers with the Alliance Central Committee in Paris. The teachers supplied the Alliance not only with frequent information about matters concerning schooling and education but also with extensive details about the life of the local Jewish community, its communal and social structure, its customs and mores, its relationship with the surrounding non-Jewish population and the authorities, and the changes it underwent as a result of political, social, and economic developments. The teachers were both participants in and observers of an era of rapid change, and their correspondence drew a distinct picture from a unique vantage point.

I have made no attempt to be exhaustive in the selection of texts included in this volume, as such a task is beyond the capacity of any one researcher. The decision to end this work with the year 1939 has been dictated by the fact that the archival material after this date is not available. Furthermore, the ideological realignment of the Alliance after World War II merits a full study on its own.

I have chosen to present some of the representative documentation that best conveys the full range of ideas and activities of the Alliance teachers and their gaze on the Sephardi and Eastern Jewish communities. Their letters form a distinctive genre and are often self-referential, pointing to a common discursive framework shared by all the writers. My purpose in this book is not to produce a reader on the history of the Jews of Muslim lands in modern times. Rather, I aim to explore the ways these Jewish communities were perceived by a radically westernizing group among them.

This study is conducted in two registers. One is that of textual representation, the constructed image of the Jews of the lands of Islam as it is represented in the letters by the Alliance teachers, an image refracted through the looking glass held to the observing eye of the radical westernizer. The observer and the observed are both protagonists in the same process, and the authors themselves, far from being outsiders, are an integral part of the phenomenon that they depict. The second register is that of the information about the sociopolitical transformation of this Jewry and the world in which it lived that is embedded in the picture created by the texts. The two registers are closely intertwined. The site of representation here is the shifting sands of a Middle East and North Africa engaged with the challenge from the West, and the letters are revelatory of a context that eventually was to prove extraordinarily corrosive to the position of the Jews in Muslim lands.

The richness of this source and my concern to convey its full flavor have led me to somewhat mute my own authorial interventions in the texts. Nevertheless, a distinct argument about westernization, the Alliance teachers, and their relationship with Sephardi and Eastern Jewries runs throughout the book. I proceed through the letters, drawing with them a composite picture, a mosaic. I introduce and elaborate upon each theme of the discursive universe of this correspondence. Then I let the letters that follow each of these introductions further illustrate, explicate, and demonstrate the argument. My ultimate aim has been to reveal the "voice" of the Alliance teacher and through his or her words not only understand all the modulations of this "voice" but also comprehend the ironies, contradictions, and dissonances of the process of Sephardi and Eastern Jewish westernization embedded in it.

1
An Overview of the Alliance's Activities

The Alliance Israélite Universelle was founded in Paris in 1860 with the aim of fighting for Jewish rights throughout the world and defending Jews wherever they were persecuted. As its statutes proclaimed, the Alliance sought

1. to work throughout the world for the emancipation and the moral progress of the Jews;
2. to help effectively all those who suffer because they are Jews;
3. to encourage all publications designed to achieve these results.[1]

The origins of the Alliance and the forces leading to its creation have been the subject of many studies and need not detain us here.[2] Suffice it to say that the founders, deeply imbued with the liberal ideals of the age and inspired by the principles of the French Revolution, all subscribed to the emancipation ideology so dominant among West European, especially French, Jewry of the time.[3] For them, the emancipation of the Jews, the granting of equal rights and full citizenship first begun in France in 1790–91, was a process destined to spread throughout the world and transform all Jewish communities. Antisemitism and persecution were relics of the past destined to disappear as modern civilization destroyed superstition and prejudice. However, the process was not as yet complete, for many countries had still not given full rights to the Jews and bigotry still reared its ugly head. The Damascus blood libel of

1. "Appel à tous les Israélites," in Alliance Israélite Universelle (AIU), *Alliance Israélite Universelle* (Paris, 1860), 39. The statutes and the changes they underwent can be found in André Chouraqui, *Cent ans d'histoire: L'Alliance Israélite Universelle et la renaissance juive contemporaine (1860–1960)* (Paris: Presses Universitaires de France, 1965), 412–16.

2. The most thorough account is in Michael Graetz, *Les Juifs en France au XIXe siècle: De la Révolution française à l'Alliance Israélite Universelle,* translated by Salomon Malka (Paris: Seuil, 1989). See also Narcisse Leven, *Cinquante ans d'histoire: L'Alliance Israélite Universelle (1860–1910),* vol. 1 (Paris: Félix Alcan, 1911).

3. For the ideology of the founders, see Georges Weill, "Emancipation et humanisme: Le discours idéologique de l'Alliance Israélite Universelle au XIXe siècle," *Les Nouveaux Cahiers* 52 (Spring 1978): 1–20.

1840, which accused the Jews of the ritual murder of a Capuchin monk,[4] and the Mortara affair of 1858, in which the Catholic church in Italy had refused to return to his parents a Jewish boy secretly baptized by the maid of the house, were only the most recent examples. The duty of emancipated Jewry vis-à-vis its persecuted coreligionists, as well as Jewish solidarity,[5] called for the creation of a Jewish organization to fight for Jewish rights in the international arena. The Alliance Israélite Universelle, with its talmudic motto "All Jews are responsible for each other,"[6] was the first international Jewish body founded for this purpose.

However, in the classic spirit of the emancipation ideology, the Alliance was also convinced, just like those who had debated Jewish emancipation at the time of the French Revolution, that the Jews themselves had to change if they were to merit emancipation. They had to transform themselves into enlightened, modern citizens, abandoning their particularistic habits and attitudes. Again, in the classic terminology of the Enlightenment, the Jews had to be "regenerated" in order to show themselves worthy of emancipation and citizenship. Hence, to extend emancipation and equal rights successfully, Jewish solidarity called for a concerted effort of regeneration among Jewish societies that were "backward," societies that had yet to benefit from the age of progress.

It was this concern with regeneration that was behind the creation of the vast network of Alliance schools in the Middle East and North Africa.[7] This consideration was already evident in the *appel* of the new organization:

> . . . If you believe that a great number of your coreligionists, overcome by twenty centuries of misery, of insults and prohibitions, can find again their dignity as men, win the dignity of citizens;
>
> If you believe that one should moralize those who have been corrupted, and not condemn them; enlighten those who have been

4. The latest analysis of the blood libel of 1840 is to be found in Tudor Parfitt, "'The Year of the Pride of Israel': Montefiore and the Blood Libel of 1840," in Sonya Lipman and Vivian D. Lipman, eds., *The Century of Moses Montefiore* (Oxford: Oxford University Press, 1985), 131–48.

5. On this theme see the article by Phyllis Albert, "Ethnicity and Jewish Solidarity in Nineteenth-Century France," in Jehuda Reinharz and Daniel Swetschinski, eds., *Mystics, Philosophers, and Politicians: Essays in Jewish Intellectual History in Honor of Alexander Altmann* (Durham, N.C.: Duke University Press, 1982), 249–74.

6. *Babylonian Talmud,* Shavuot 39a.

7. On regeneration and the Alliance's ideology, see Aron Rodrigue, *French Jews, Turkish Jews: The Alliance Israélite Universelle and the Politics of Jewish Schooling in Turkey, 1860–1925* (Bloomington: Indiana University Press, 1990), 1–8. Regeneration is discussed extensively in Jay R. Berkovitz, *The Shaping of Jewish Identity in Nineteenth Century France* (Detroit: Wayne State University Press, 1989).

blinded, and not abandon them; raise those who have been exhausted, and not rest with pitying them; defend those who have been calumnied, and not remain silent; rescue all those who have been persecuted, and not only talk about the persecution . . .

If you believe in all these things, Jews of the world, come hear our appeal, join our society and give us your help.[8]

The ideological specificity of this program of regeneration notwithstanding, there were other reasons why Western Jewry was increasingly conscious of the Jewish communities around the Mediterranean basin. The growing Western penetration of the economy of the Middle East and North Africa, the introduction of the steamboat, and the rapid increase in trade were accompanied by an influx of Europeans—merchants and others—into the ports around the Mediterranean. The ease of transportation and communication was reflected in the extraordinary increase of reports on the Middle East and North Africa in the European press. The nascent Jewish press also began to write extensively on the Jews of Muslim lands from the early 1840s onward, usually in an extremely unfavorable way, accusing these Jews of ignorance, superstition, and fanaticism.[9] It is undoubtedly true that this was in part a reflection of the generally negative perception of non-Western societies so prevalent in nineteenth-century Europe, a perception that European Jewry shared in full. But there was an added dimension. For a recently emancipated Western Jewry with a tenuous hold on its newly gained equality, and with its goals of integration and assimilation, the Jews of Muslim lands were clearly a source of deep embarrassment. The Jews of the West feared that the Gentiles would tar them with the same brush as their unenlightened coreligionists of the East.

By the middle of the nineteenth century, Eastern Jewry had come to constitute a "Jewish Eastern Question"[10] for the leadership of Western Jewish communities. Both a genuine and deeply felt solidarity with Jews in distress and embarrassment and distaste when faced with "uncouth" coreligionists suffused the discourse of Western Jewry and later that of the Alliance. This also contributed to the deep ambivalence toward the local communities which pervaded all the correspondence of the teachers with the Alliance Central Committee.

8. "Appel à tous les Israélites," in AIU, *Alliance Israélite Universelle,* 10–11.
9. Rodrigue, *French Jews, Turkish Jews,* 8–17; Michel Abitbol, "The Encounter between French Jewry and the Jews of North Africa: Analysis of a Discourse (1830–1914)," in Frances Malino and Bernard Wasserstein, eds., *The Jews in Modern France* (Hanover, N.H.: University Press of New England, 1985), 31–53.
10. See the series of articles by Ludwig Philippson in *Allgemeine Zeitung des Judenthums* 18 (1854): 152–54, 189.

Unlike Russia, which barred Western Jewish interference with its Jewish subjects (who were perceived in the same negative light by Western European Jewry as Sephardi and Eastern Jews), the Muslim powers were relatively nonchalant about such efforts, or were too weak to offer much resistance. This fact, together with Western penetration into the area, facilitated considerably the activities of an organization such as the Alliance.

It would be easy to see in the Alliance's efforts a Jewish variant of French colonialism, with its theories of "assimilation." However, although the colonialist context is crucial for understanding the larger dynamic of domination of the non-European with which the Alliance inevitably became associated, it does not explain adequately the ideology and self-representation of the organization. The Franco-Jewish leadership of which the Alliance was an integral part saw itself in a continuum with the rest of the Jewish people. The act of emancipation and the accompanying process of "regeneration" had allowed French Jewry to enter "civilization." Eastern Jewries were not perceived as distinctively different, as "other," but as essentially extensions of "self," and it was only a matter of time before they underwent the same process in the face of advancing "civilization." Solidarity dictated that they be helped along this path. The very process of emergence from servitude and "obscurantism" that French Jewry was seen to have undergone thanks to the French Revolution had to become the normative route to be followed by traditional, nonemancipated Jewish communities. Hence the self-legitimizing drama of emancipation/regeneration had to be enacted over and over again.

The ideology of the Alliance, deeply marked by the integration and acculturation of French Jewry but also imbued with a great sense of international Jewish solidarity, was not, however, as contradictory as a more nationalist Jewish historiography following the Holocaust has described. The identity of nineteenth-century emancipated and emancipationist Jewry, especially French Jewry, was a complex one that cannot be reduced to the paradigm of "assimilation."[11] What appeared as Jewish in this identity—such as solidarity—was not a "remnant" from an all-encompassing preemancipation "tradition" or a "persistence" of ethnicity. Jewish ethnicity in the postemancipation era was not a survivor but a dynamic reconstruction that rearticulated the old and the new and reached a new configuration that needs to be understood on its own terms. Emancipation and the challenge of integration that it brought

11. See the articles in Pierre Birnbaum, ed., *Histoire politique des Juifs en France* (Paris: Presses de la Fondation Nationale des Sciences Politiques, 1990).

with it redrew the boundaries of Jewish ethnicity and created a new identity that took fierce pride in being French while maintaining pride in and a strong sense of belonging to the Jewish people as a collectivity throughout the world. The new Jew, the citizen-Jew, represented a break with a past full of suffering and became the model to be exported, to be universalized. This new Jewish ethnicity in France, already in evidence in the first decades after the Revolution, eventually found its natural home in the Third Republic, creating what can be called a "republican Judaism" that pervaded all aspects of French Jewish life until Vichy.[12]

It became the duty of the Alliance to ensure that the rest of world Jewry followed in the footsteps of French Jewry to enter the new age— hence the depth of the engagement with Jewish communities elsewhere. Ethnic boundaries had shifted and had not created a "lesser" Jew but simply a "different" Jew, a distinctive, modern Jew. This was the new model that had to be exported.

The general context of French imperialism within which the Alliance operated should not obscure the fact that the relationship between the organization and the Quai d'Orsay was a complex one. In spite of the fact that the Alliance rendered invaluable service to the cause of French linguistic expansion, the political relationship between the Alliance and the French Foreign Ministry was not particularly strong until the first decades of the twentieth century.

Although the leadership and the ideology of the Alliance remained distinctively Franco-Jewish, members of the society were to be found in all corners of the globe. The composition of the Alliance, as well as its audience, was an international Jewish one. Too close an association with French interests would have run the risk of alienating its non-French members. Indeed both the Quai d'Orsay and the Alliance took this international nature of the society seriously. In fact, only the *Ecole Normale* of the Alliance was registered as an official body in Paris. Otherwise, the Alliance as an institution had no legal French status until 1975. As a result, in the first decades of its existence, it asked for and received no subsidies from Paris, and its schools were not put under official French protection in the Levant and North Africa. They benefited only from *de facto* protection in the localities when the need arose. In 1868 and in 1879, at the request of the Alliance Central Committee, the French Foreign Ministry asked its consuls to protect the Alliance

12. Aron Rodrigue, "L'éxportation du paradigme révolutionnaire: Son influence sur le Judaïsme sépharade et oriental," in ibid., 185. This new ideology is very much in evidence among the Jews holding various state offices during the Third Republic. See Pierre Birnbaum, *Les fous de la République: Histoire politique des Juifs d'Etat de Gambetta à Vichy* (Paris: Fayard, 1992).

institutions. This was left to the discretion of the individual consul and did not carry the weight of juridical protection.[13]

The entry of most of the Maghreb into the sphere of French control led to greater contact between the Quai d'Orsay and the Central Committee, which sought to promote its schools. In North Africa, the Alliance teachers and French officials collaborated closely. The erosion of French power in the Middle East by the early twentieth century and conflicts between the Alliance and new, rival Jewish movements such as Zionism led to further consolidation of the ties between the organization and the French government. World War I constituted a turning point in the relationship. The Alliance, much impoverished by the war, began to receive regular subsidies from the French Foreign Ministry.[14]

The Alliance was not founded to serve and aid French influence. Nevertheless, the primacy given by the organization to the teaching of French and its missionary zeal to westernize, which in this case often meant to Gallicize, led inevitably to a convergence with the aims of French foreign policy, especially that of spreading the use of the French language to gain adherents to its cause. As a result, their juridical status notwithstanding, the Alliance schools eventually became, intentionally or not, allies of French interests abroad.

The Alliance grew rapidly. Anyone could become a member by paying a subscription of six francs a year. The membership increased from 850 in 1861 to 3,900 in 1865, to 13,370 in 1870, to over 30,000 in 1885. By 1880, 349 local committees had been established in various parts of the world. Of these, 56 were in France (including Alsace-Lorraine), 113 were in Germany, and 20 were in Italy. The French membership declined from 80 percent of the total in 1861 to approximately 50 percent in 1864 and less than 40 percent in 1885.[15] However, the leadership (the Central Committee) remained firmly French.

The first Alliance school opened in Tetuan in Morocco in 1862. It was followed by schools in Damascus and Baghdad in 1864, in Volos (in present-day Greece) in 1865, and in Adrianople (Edirne, in Turkey) in 1867. Even though the Central Committee had launched an appeal for funds to support its educational work in 1865,[16] the financial resources of the organization were not sufficient for the large-scale expansion of the fledgling school network. Expansion was made possible only by the

13. On this topic see Rodrigue, *French Jews, Turkish Jews,* 148–49.

14. Ibid. See also Joan G. Roland, "The Alliance Israélite Universelle and French Policy in North Africa, 1860–1918" (Ph.D diss., Columbia University, 1969), 334–35.

15. Georges Weill, "The Alliance Israélite Universelle and the Emancipation of the Jewish Communities of the Mediterranean," *Jewish Journal of Sociology* 24 (1982): 119–21.

16. AIU, *L'oeuvre des écoles* (Paris, 1865).

munificence of the noted philanthropists Baron Maurice de Hirsch and his wife. The baron endowed one million francs to the Alliance in 1873 for its work in the Ottoman Empire, covered its yearly deficits, and in 1889 gave it an endowment of ten million francs.[17] His wife, Clara, was particularly active in the creation in 1897 of an *oeuvre de nourriture,* which dispensed free lunches to the poor in the schools. With the help of these two eminent personalities and other leading Jewish philanthropists such as the Goldschmidts and the Bischoffsheims, the Alliance was put on a secure financial footing.

However, the organization did not perceive itself as a philanthropic body, although when disaster struck a Jewish community, it was at the forefront of the help that arrived from abroad. Many questions had to be answered before a school could be established. The Alliance was very eager to resolve certain issues before it accepted responsibility for the new institution. The active support of a group of local notables had to be guaranteed. It was hoped that the supporters of the new schools would have sufficient influence to neutralize any possible opposition. Once the demand from a locality was established, local financial support had to be secured. The Central Committee would consent to send a director only after this condition was met. This director would more often than not take over an already existing school, earmarked by the local notables and community as a potential Alliance establishment, and transform it into a full-fledged Alliance institution. Local financial resources would consist of a subvention from the community and a minimal tuition fee to be paid by those students who could afford it. Of course, there were wide variations from school to school in this respect, and many institutions were closed and reopened because of problems with local financing. There was, however, one constant. The schools were totally independent of the supervision of the local communities and local Alliance committees, and the salary of the school director was always paid by the Alliance.[18]

The years between 1880 and 1914 constituted the golden age of the organization. Alliance schools for boys and girls were established in all the major Jewish centers in an area ranging from Morocco in the west to

17. Paul Silberman, "An Investigation of the Schools Operated by the Alliance Israélite Universelle from 1862 to 1940" (Ph.D. diss., New York University, 1973), 63–64. For the life and activities of Maurice de Hirsch, see Kurt Grunwald, *TürkenHirsch: A Study of Baron Maurice de Hirsch, Entrepreneur and Philanthropist* (Jerusalem: Israel Programs for Scientific Translation, 1966). On the philanthropic activities of the de Hirsch family, see Sarah Leibovici, *Si tu fais le bien* (Paris: AIU, 1983), 11–24.

18. For an example of the founding of an Alliance school and its functioning, see Aron Rodrigue, "Jewish Society and Schooling in a Thracian Town: The Alliance Israélite Universelle in Demotica, 1897–1924," *Jewish Social Studies* 45 (Summer–Fall 1983): 263–86.

Iran in the east, and lesser communities were joining the school network in increasing numbers. From 1872 on, upon the suggestion of David Cazès, the director of the Volos school,[19] apprenticeship programs were created to complement the work of instruction, and a trades school was founded in Jerusalem in 1882. In 1870, *Mikweh Israël,* the first modern agricultural training school in Palestine, was established by Charles Netter, one of the Alliance founders, on the outskirts of Jaffa. Other agricultural schools were instituted in Djedeida in Tunisia in 1895 and in Asia Minor in 1900.[20] Two short-lived rabbinical seminaries were created by the Alliance, one in Turkey and the other in Tunisia.[21] By 1914, 43,700 students were attending 183 Alliance institutions. As can be seen from table 1, the Alliance underwent a dramatic growth in the decade before World War I, especially with the extension of the network to Iran in 1898 and to the smaller centers of the Sephardi and Eastern Jewish diaspora. Table 2 lists all the Alliance schools founded from 1862 to 1935.

World War I inaugurated a period of crisis, with grave financial and logistical problems. The real challenge—which in the end would lead to the dismantlement of the network—was the intransigent nationalism that began to appear in the immediate aftermath of the war. Turkey and Greece, with their populous Judeo-Spanish communities, which had hitherto constituted the focus of the Alliance's educational system, gradually nationalized the schools, which then had to break their ties with the Central Committee in Paris. However, the loss was made up by new schools opened in the interior of Morocco, where security had improved with the "pacification" undertaken after the French Protectorate was established in 1912.

World War II was the real watershed for the Alliance. The Holocaust and the founding of the state of Israel led to a complete revision of the ideology of the organization and to the adoption of a more pro-Zionist stance. The process of decolonization after World War II and the mass migrations of Jews from Arab countries altered the school network be-

19. Cazès, 31 Oct. 1872, Archives of the AIU, Grèce XX.E.251.

20. For the foundation of *Mikweh Israël,* see Georges Weill, "Charles Netter ou les oranges de Jaffa," *Les Nouveaux Cahiers* 21 (Summer 1970): 2–36; see also Leven, *Cinquante ans,* 2:265–319. For the Djedeida school see Leven, *Cinquante ans,* 2:319–32. On Asia Minor see Rodrigue, *French Jews, Turkish Jews,* 273–75.

21. On the rabbinical seminary in Turkey, see Aron Rodrigue, "The Alliance Israélite Universelle and the Attempt to Reform Rabbinical and Religious Instruction in Turkey," in S. Schwarzfuchs, ed., *L'"Alliance" dans les communautés du bassin méditerranéen à la fin du 19ème siècle et son influence sur la situation sociale et culturelle* (Jerusalem: Misgav Yerushalayim, 1987), liii–lxx.

yond all recognition. The Alliance of the post–World War II era was a
very different organization from the Alliance of the period from 1860 to
1939.

TABLE 1
The Growth of the Alliance Educational Network

Year	Number of schools	Number of students
1865	3	680
1871	14	2,365
1880	43	5,910
1891	55	12,400
1901	109	29,000
1909	149	41,000
1913	183	43,700
1922	112	35,426
1931	126	43,708
1939	127	47,746

SOURCES: Data taken from the *Bulletin semestriel de l'Alliance Israélite Universelle* 34
(1909): 108–9; G. Weill, "L'action éducative de l'Alliance Israélite Universelle de 1860
à 1914," *Les Nouveaux Cahiers* 78 (1984): 51–58; *Paix et Droit* 2 (Oct. 1922): 16; *Paix
et Droit* 11 (Mar. 1931): 8; *Paix et Droit* 19 (Mar. 1939): 12.

TABLE 2
Alliance Schools Founded from 1862 to 1935

Country[a] and town	Type of school	Date of foundation
ALGERIA		
Algiers	*Talmud-Torah,* co-ed	1900
Constantine	*Talmud-Torah,* co-ed	1902
Oran	*Talmud-Torah,* co-ed	1907
BULGARIA		
Burgas	primary, girls	1896
Phillipopolis (Plovdiv)	primary, boys	1881
	primary, girls	1885
Rustchuk (Ruse)	primary, boys	1879
	primary, girls	1885
Samacoff	primary, co-ed	1874
Shumla (Shumen)	primary, boys	1870
	primary, girls	1874
Silistria	primary, boys	1897

TABLE 2.—*Continued*

Country*a* and town	Type of school	Date of foundation
BULGARIA (*cont.*)		
Sofia	primary, boys	1887
	primary, girls	1896
Tatar-Bazardjik	primary, boys	1880
	primary, girls	1883
Varna	primary, co-ed	1880
Widdin	primary, boys	1872
	primary, girls	1880
Yamboli	primary, co-ed	1881
EGYPT		
Alexandria	primary, boys	1897
	primary, girls	1897
Cairo	primary, boys	1896
	primary, girls	1896
Abassieh	primary, boys	1902
	primary, girls	1902
Tantah	primary, boys	1905
	primary, girls	1905
GREECE		
Cavalla	primary, boys	1905
	primary, girls	1905
Demotica (Didymotikhon)	primary, co-ed	1897
Gumuldjina (Komotini)	primary, co-ed	1910
Janina	primary, boys	1904
	primary, girls	1904
Larissa	primary, boys	1868
Preveza	primary, co-ed	1908
Rhodes	primary, boys	1901
	primary, girls	1902
Salonica	primary, boys	1873
	primary, girls	1875
	for the poor, boys	1897
	for the poor, girls	1897
Serres	primary, co-ed	1901
Volo (Volos)	primary, boys	1865
IRAN		
Burugerd	primary, co-ed	1913
Hamadan	primary, boys	1900
	primary, girls	1900

TABLE 2.—*Continued*

Country[a] and town	Type of school	Date of foundation
IRAN (*cont.*)		
Isphahan	primary, boys	1901
	primary, girls	1901
Kermanshah	primary, boys	1904
	primary, girls	1911
Keshan	primary, co-ed	1929
Seneh	primary, boys	1903
	primary, girls	1905
Shiraz	primary, boys	1903
	primary, girls	1903
Teheran	primary, boys	1898
	primary, girls	1898
Yezd	primary, boys	1928
	primary, girls	1930
IRAQ		
Amara	primary, boys	1910
Baghdad	primary, boys	1864
Kadoorie	primary, girls	1893
Noam	for the poor, girls	1927
Nouriel	for the poor, boys	1902
Saleh	for the poor, boys	1905
Basra	primary, boys	1903
	primary, girls	1913
	for the poor, boys	1913
Hanekin	for the poor, co-ed	1911
Hille	primary, boys	1907
	primary, girls	1911
Kerkuk	primary, boys	1912
Mossul	primary, boys	1907
	primary, girls	1912
ISRAEL		
Caiffa (Haifa)	primary, boys	1881
	primary, girls	1895
Jaffa	primary, boys	1892
	primary, girls	1894
Mikweh Israël	agricultural, boys	1870
Jerusalem	primary, boys	(1868) 1897[b]
	primary, girls	1906
	vocational, boys	1882

TABLE 2.—*Continued*

Country[a] and town	Type of school	Date of foundation
ISRAEL (*cont.*)		
Safed	primary, boys	1897
	primary, girls	1897
Tiberias	primary, boys	1897
	primary, girls	1900
LEBANON		
Beirut	primary, boys	1869
	primary, girls	1878
Saida	primary, co-ed	1902
LIBYA		
Tripoli	primary, boys	1895
	primary, girls	1898
MACEDONIA		
Monastir (Bitola)	primary, boys	1910
	primary, girls	1903
Uskub (Skopje)	primary, boys	1902
	primary, girls	1905
MOROCCO		
Agadir	primary, co-ed	1935
Azemmour	primary, co-ed	1911
Benahmed	primary, co-ed	1929
Beni Mellal	primary, co-ed	1927
Berrechid	primary, co-ed	1927
Boujad	primary, co-ed	1927
Casablanca		
N. Leven	primary, boys	1897
	primary, girls	1900
M. Nahon	primary, co-ed	1933
Verdun	primary, boys	1933
Demnat	primary, co-ed	1929
El Ksar	primary, co-ed	(1879) 1911
Fez		
S. Lévi	primary, boys	1881
	primary, girls	1899
Ville Nouvelle	primary, co-ed	1934
Kasbah Tadla	primary, co-ed	1932
Larache	primary, boys	(1873) 1901
	primary, girls	(1874) 1901

TABLE 2. — *Continued*

Country[a] and town	Type of school	Date of foundation
MOROCCO (*cont.*)		
Marrakesh	primary, boys	1892
	primary, girls	1901
Mazagan	primary, boys	1906
	primary, girls	1906
Meknes	primary, boys	(1901) 1910
	primary, girls	(1901) 1910
Midelt	primary, co-ed	1928
Mogador	primary, boys	(1867) 1888
	primary, girls	1908
Of the *Mellah*	primary, boys	1906
Oued Zem	primary, co-ed	1935
Ouezzane	primary, co-ed	1926
Oujda	primary, co-ed	1926
Rabat	primary, boys	1903
	primary, girls	1910
Safi	primary, boys	1907
	primary, girls	1907
Saleh	primary, boys	1913
	primary, girls	1913
Sefrou	primary, co-ed	(1911) 1914
Settat	primary, co-ed	(1910) 1927
Tangier	primary, boys	(1865) 1889
	primary, girls	(1874) 1881
Taourirt	primary, co-ed	1927
Taroudant	primary, co-ed	1929
Tetuan	primary, boys	1862
	primary, girls	(1868) 1882
Tiznit	primary, co-ed	1934
SYRIA		
Aleppo	primary, boys	1869
	primary, girls	(1872) 1911
Bahsita	for the poor, boys	1910
	for the poor, girls	1910
Djemilie	primary, girls	1889
Damascus	primary, boys	(1864) 1880
	for the poor, girls	1883
TUNISIA		
Djedeida	agricultural, boys	1895

TABLE 2.—*Continued*

Country[a] and town	Type of school	Date of foundation
TUNISIA (*cont.*)		
Sfax	primary, boys	1905
	primary, girls	1905
Sousse	primary, boys	1883
Tunis		
Hafsia	primary, boys	1910
Malta Srira	primary, boys	1878
	primary, girls	1882
Rabbinical	boys	1907
TURKEY		
Adrianople (Edirne)	primary, boys	1867
	primary, girls	1870
Aydin	primary, boys	1894
	primary, girls	1904
Bursa	primary, boys	1886
	primary, girls	1886
Cassaba (Turgutlu)	primary, co-ed	1897
Constantinople (Istanbul)		
Balat	primary, boys	1875
	primary, girls	1882
Daghamami (Dağhamamı)	primary, boys	1875
	primary, girls	1880
Galata	primary, boys	1875
	primary, girls	1879
Goldschmidt	primary, boys	1876
Haskeuy (Hasköy)	primary, boys	1874
	primary, girls	1877
Tseror	primary, boys	1908
Haydar Pasha (Haydar Paşa)	primary, co-ed	1893
Kuzgundjuk (Kuzguncuk)	primary, boys	1879
	primary, girls	1880
Ortakeuy (Ortaköy)	primary, boys	(1882) 1901
	primary, girls	1882
Rabbinical	boys	1897
Dardanelles (Çanakkale)	primary, boys	1878
	primary, girls	1888
Gallipoli (Gelibolu)	primary, boys	1905
	primary, girls	1913
Kirklisse (Kırklarelı)	primary, boys	1913
	primary, girls	1911

TABLE 2.—*Continued*

Country[a] and town	Type of school	Date of foundation
TURKEY (*cont.*)		
Magnesia (Manisa)	primary, boys	1892
	primary, girls	1896
Pergamon (Bergama)	primary, co-ed	(1896) 1908
Rodosto (Tekirdağ)	primary, co-ed	1904
Smyrna (İzmir)	primary, boys	1873
	primary, girls	1878
	for the poor, boys	1898
Karatash (Karataş)	primary, co-ed	1895
Tchorlu (Çorlu)	primary, co-ed	1911
Tireh (Tire)	primary, boys	1897
	primary, girls	1910

NOTE: This is an amended and corrected version of a table compiled by Paul Silberman, "An Investigation of the Schools Operated by the Alliance Israélite Universelle from 1862 to 1940" (Ph.D. diss., New York University, 1973), 248–54. The towns listed are Anglicized versions of the names used in the Alliance publications. The names in parentheses are the ones in current use. See also *Bulletin Semestriel de l'Alliance Israélite Universelle* 38 (1913): 122–58. The table excludes all institutions that received subsidies from the Alliance but were not directed by Alliance teachers or did not follow the Alliance curriculum.

[a]According to present borders.

[b]Founded in 1868, closed, and reopened in 1897.

PART I

THE SCHOOLS AND TEACHERS
OF THE ALLIANCE ISRAÉLITE UNIVERSELLE

2
Instruction in the Alliance Schools

All Alliance establishments began as institutions of elementary education. In the first years, the directors exercised considerable freedom of action and, while always fulfilling the wishes of the Central Committee in Paris, could supervise the teaching in the manner they saw fit. This changed in 1883–84 when the school program was set by the Central Committee.[1] According to the new instructions sent to the teachers, there were to be four classes corresponding to the four years that the students were supposed to attend the school. There could be two additional classes for the young children, which would constitute a kind of kindergarten. The subjects taught were written and spoken French, arithmetic, geography, general history, the rudiments of the physical and natural sciences, French calligraphy, Hebrew, biblical and postbiblical Jewish history (the latter added during the 1892–93 school year),[2] Jewish religious instruction, and a "useful language," such as the language of the country or English, German, or Spanish (see table 3). The time devoted to Hebrew in the girls schools was considerably shorter, the additional time taken by the teaching of needlework. All the courses except religious instruction, Hebrew, and biblical history, which were taught by local rabbis, were given by the Alliance-trained director and his assistants. As in the system employed in France, the subjects were treated in a concentric fashion. All the subjects were covered in the first year and then studied in greater depth and detail in each following year.

Although the Alliance establishments were fashioned after elementary schools in France, these were no ordinary French institutions. The attention given to numerous languages at a very early stage and the emphasis upon Jewish subjects, as well as the considerable variation in the number of classes in each school, made them unique. It proved difficult to regulate the students' age of entry, which could range from six to seven in some schools to ten to eleven in others. In certain institutions in Salonica, Constantinople, and Casablanca, the programs were expanded over the

1. "Instructions pour les professeurs," Archives of the AIU, France XI.E.1.
2. Fresco, Haskeuy, annual report 1892–1893, Archives of the AIU, France XVIII.F.29.

TABLE 3
The Curriculum in the Alliance Schools
A. Boys

Subjects taught	1st and 2d classes: Hours per week		3d and 4th classes: Hours per week	
	Minimum	Maximum	Minimum	Maximum
Postbiblical Jewish history	1	2	—	—
Biblical history and religious instruction	1	2	1	2
Hebrew	5	10	5	10
Reading in French	5	8	6	10
French language	5	6	6	6
Arithmetic	3	4	2	3
Geography	2	3	2	3
History	2	2	1	2
Sciences	1	2	1	1
Elementary applied sciences	2	3	2	3
Calligraphy	2	2	2	3
Language other than French	5	10	5	10
Singing	1	1	1	1
Drawing	1	2	0	0
Physical education	2	2	1	2

B. Girls

Subjects taught	Hours per week	
	Minimum	Maximum
Jewish history	1	2
Biblical history and religious instruction	1	2
Hebrew	2	2
Reading in French	4	5
French language	4	4
Arithmetic	2	2
Geography	1	1
History	1	1
Sciences	1	1
Elementary applied sciences	2	2
Calligraphy	2	2
Language other than French	4	5
Sewing	7	10
Singing (1st and 2d classes)	1	1
Drawing	1	1
Physical education	1	1

C. *5th and 6th Classes, etc.*

Subjects taught	Minimum	Maximum
Religious instruction and Hebrew	7	10
Reading in French	5	10
Calligraphy	5	5
Elementary applied sciences	8	10
Language	4	6

SOURCE: AIU, *Instructions générales pour les professeurs* (Paris, 1903), 63.

years with the addition of classes such as accounting, these four-year schools becoming seven- or eight-year ones and receiving recognition as state-approved secondary institutions. But the overwhelming majority of the institutions dispensed an extended elementary education that today would probably be considered the equivalent of a middle secondary-level education.

The programs of individual schools varied due to the lack of qualified teachers in certain subjects and the personal interests of the directors. These factors played an important role in determining the quality of instruction offered in the various subjects. In spite of this, however, the highly centralizing Central Committee in Paris managed to maintain a remarkable degree of uniformity in the network.

The teaching of the French language remained the cornerstone of the Alliance schools. They were popular precisely because of this fact. In an age when French colonialism held sway in North Africa and the French language had become the lingua franca *of trade and commerce in the Levant, the acquisition of French was first and foremost of practical utility for the Jews of the area.*

In 1903, the Central Committee published its circulars on educational matters for its teachers together with the program of 1883–84 in a manual entitled Instructions générales pour les professeurs.[3] *These* Instructions, *which, with minor modifications, remained in effect until World War II, provide a good insight into the type of education offered in the Alliance schools:*

CLASSES

In the Alliance schools there are four classes, which correspond to the four years of the program of study.

3. AIU, *Instructions générales pour les professeurs* (Paris, 1903).

The most advanced class is called the 1st class, the next 2d, and so on in descending order.

In the schools with high enrollment, one class may be divided into two or more divisions, which would then be called Division A, Division B, etc., of the nth class. The program of study is exactly the same for every division of the same class. The divisions are created because it is impossible for a single instructor to teach effectively a class of more than forty or fifty students. In no way are the divisions established to make distinctions among the students of the same class. Each division must include at least thirty students.

In addition to the four classes defined above, the school may include one or more classes for younger children. These would be called the 5th and 6th classes (even in cases where there is no 4th class) . . .

DETAILED PROGRAM OF STUDIES

Some of the subjects taught will be compulsory, others optional.

The compulsory subjects are those which must be included in the program of study and which may not be eliminated.

The optional subjects are those which may be eliminated from the program according to time, place, and circumstances.

The compulsory subjects are:
a. Religious instruction.
b. Biblical and postbiblical Jewish history.
c. Hebrew (reading, writing, translation, grammar).
d. Oral reading in French and analysis of texts.
e. Spoken or written exercises in French (grammar, dictation, composition, memorization exercises).
f. Arithmetic, the metric system.
g. Local geography (province, country, neighboring countries), world geography, physical geography.
h. Local history (province, country, neighboring countries), world history.
i. Elementary physical and natural sciences.
j. Elementary applied natural sciences.
k. Calligraphy.
l. A language of practical application in the country (Turkish, Bulgarian, Greek, Arabic, Spanish, English, German).
m. For the girls, sewing and handwork.
n. Linear drawing

Optional subjects are:

o. Singing.

p. Free-form drawing.

q. Physical education.

Optional subjects may be taught only in those schools in which classes meet for more than six hours per day.

No subject other than those outlined above may be included in the curriculum without the prior authorization of the Central Committee.

In the classes for young children, the curriculum includes:

—Religious instruction, Hebrew, Jewish history.

—Reading exercises and text analysis, the number system, counting exercises.

—Calligraphy on slate tablets (which may be accompanied by drawing exercises).

—Lessons on things [*Leçons de choses*], with the particular goal of familiarizing pupils with everyday French vocabulary.

—A language of practical application in the country.

It is particularly recommended to the directors and to the Committees that great emphasis be placed on the teaching of the language of the country (Turkish, Arabic, Bulgarian, etc.); if this teaching were neglected, the school would not be able to produce the results expected by the parents.

The criterion for study of additional languages must above all be that of utility. The director will see to it that this teaching is performed in accordance with sound pedagogical principles. Each teacher should, as much as possible, conduct class and communicate with his students in the language he is responsible for teaching.

For the teaching of German and English, it is recommended that only teachers who have lived in Germany or England and who speak the language properly and have a suitable accent be employed.

[. . .]

CURRICULUM—GENERAL GUIDELINES

The general rule for the program of studies is that the material covered in each class must form a complete unit, independent of the material to be covered in the following classes. Each year, the student must complete the entire program. The following year, he will continue, quickly reviewing what he has already learned, expanding and developing the concepts already acquired in the previous year with the acquisition of new facts and details.

In order to implement this program effectively, teachers must not lose sight of the goal of the elementary school. The goal is not to provide students with technical instruction, to prepare them for particular careers, as, for example, a career in business. Language teaching is not the goal of the school. This is an all too widespread misconception in the East, which is disastrous for education. A language is a means, not an end in itself, a form of thought and of knowledge, not the thought or knowledge itself.

The director should, then, be careful not to distort the true nature of the primary school by making it a language school or a technical school whose teaching is aimed at the immediate utilitarian application of acquired knowledge in the form of wage-earning tools or skills . . .

Each year's teaching should in itself form a complete unit. The programs outlined below apply, except where otherwise indicated, to each of the four classes and should be covered in their entirety in one year in each of these classes. The only difference among the classes is that the teaching becomes more complete and encompasses a wider range of concepts with each successive year. The teacher in the upper classes should quickly review what the students have already mastered and should spend more time on those topics that have been touched on only briefly in the previous classes.

The one-year program is divided into ten months, beginning with the start of the school year after the holiday of *Sukot* [Tabernacles]. These months are represented in the schedule that follows by the numbers 1, 2, 3 . . . 10.

In a school whose 4th class is too weak academically for the successful implementation of the outlined program of study, this program may be implemented in the 3d class . . .[4]

The overriding importance given to the teaching of French in colonial North Africa is clearly in evidence in the letter by Albert Saguès underlining the purpose of good instruction in this subject in Tunisia, "pays français." Saguès echoed the injunctions of the Instructions *to go beyond the utilitarian: the acquisition of French would lead to the assimilation of the French mentality, which would bring with it "clarity and concision" in thought and counteract, through the reading of the textbooks, the negative influence of the Eastern surrounding:*

4. Ibid., 23–29, 49–50.

Tunis, 19 February 1914

[. . .]

The Jews of Tunisia—a French country—can benefit from the development of an understanding of French customs, mentality, and character, and from the assimilation of what appears to be good; to facilitate this, it will be enough for us to cultivate their faculty of judgment.

This being said, I would like to attempt to define with precision the role of reading in our teaching. Reading is intended to develop an accurate, intelligible, and fluent diction in our students, to expand their vocabulary so that they may express all of their thoughts with clarity and concision, and, finally, to enable them to acquire a significant mastery of the French language, whether French be the goal or the means of our teaching.

However, the utility of reading is not limited only to this; even as it takes on an instructive role, it assumes an educative function which is not without importance. From a good reading textbook we should expect twofold results. On the one hand, it should foster the growth of the goodness that is inherent in all children and inhibit the baser instincts which are either innate in them or acquired in disreputable company. At the same time, a good reading textbook should diminish the effects of the countereducation which children are given both in the streets and in the tainted atmosphere in which they live. In order to obtain these positive results, it would seem imperative that we instill a love of reading in our students.

Yet, reading manuals, even those adapted to the level of our students, are never so easy that some word, expression, or turn of phrase does not call for explanation from the teacher. Therefore, the results obtained by the teacher of reading depend as much on the teacher's method as on the textbook. I would even say that the method is more important than the choice of the book. A good teacher can make good use of any book, from the most intimidating to the most tedious. To do that, it is essential that the teacher apply himself to the careful preparation of a minutely detailed daily lesson. This is my understanding of such a lesson:

1. Recount to the students the narration that constitutes the subject of that day's reading, and have them summarize it. This should be done even before opening the book.

2. Explain difficult words or expressions found in the text and verify that students have understood all explanations. Only then read the text. Once the students are familiar with the subject, the words, and the expressions, no difficulty will stop them, and they will read with both ease and pleasure. The children will begin to enjoy reading, which, rather than seeming tedious, will become a recreation in which

they will indulge whenever time and means permit. Readings should
be selected in such a way as to inspire in our students the desire to do
good. They should develop sensitivity in the children without being
dogmatic (such dogmatic readings do not generally produce appreciable results): these carefully selected readings would fulfill our ideal of
teaching in this discipline . . .
[. . .]

A. Saguès

Archives of the AIU, Tunisie XXXIV.E.198a.

*The enthusiastic description below of the day of registration and admis-
sion is one echoed in tone in many letters by Alliance teachers once the
schools were well established and had attained great popularity:*

Tunis, 20 December 1912

[. . .]
    12 October 1912. El-Meschnaka Street, ordinarily so quiet and iso-
lated, with the only sign of life being the chatter of little girls on their
way to school, has taken on a strange appearance today. Since five
o'clock this morning, groups of women and children have been pour-
ing in from every direction and gathering here. They line the side-
walks, forming clusters which multiply and expand by the minute . . .
    Good heavens! What can be happening? The crowd swells and
thickens. There can be no doubt. We are besieged! The assailants'
intentions cannot be mistaken: they would take our building by
storm. The police must be summoned without delay. Three officers
arrive, out of breath. They have been forced to struggle their way
through the rising tide. They station themselves in front of the school
entrance. The concierge is trembling in fear; for a moment he feared
the crowd would force its way in. Fortunately, the gates are strong.
    From our vantage point not a single paving stone is visible. We see
only darting, bobbing heads. Curses and cries pierce the air. There is
a rumbling in the crowd; El-Meschnaka Street is no place for the
levelheaded this morning.
    The women of the *Hara* [the Jewish quarter], in spite of their size,
worm a sinuous path through the crowd toward the sacred gate. It is
a *marabout* which all seek to touch; once they have reached it some
cling to it fiercely.
    The more rational or more cautious hold back, as reluctant to deal
blows as to receive them. They prefer to wait their turn. Fools!
    Eight o'clock: The entrance gate is haltingly opened a crack. The
frightened headmistress casts an imploring glance at the police offi-

cers. Surrounded by this rabble, she would be too easy a prey in the hands of these *tricoteuses*.[5] But what can three policemen do to hold at bay a crowd with no sense of order or discipline? It is obvious they will be unable to enforce any semblance of order.

The rush toward the gaping hole is uncontrollable. The floodgates burst open and the wave of humanity, all the stronger for having been so long contained, pours into every corner of the school, rises up stairs, inundates corridors, overruns classrooms. The ill-fated headmistress and her heroic assistant are at the mercy of the crowd. They lose their footing and are tossed about in the storm until they suddenly feel the grip of strong hands and find themselves, as if by miracle, shut into the head office. They have bumps and bruises; their poor feet are beaten to a pulp. Yet, feeling this is a small price to pay for having escaped the threatening crowd, they breathe not a word of complaint.

A passerby, intrigued by this mad scramble, asks what is the reason for it. Someone says in reply, "Today is the day registration forms are distributed at the Alliance school for girls."

[. . .]

A. Saguès

Archives of the AIU, Tunisie XXIV.E.198a.

5. Women who knitted while watching the guillotine at work during the French Revolution.

3
The Alliance Teaching Corps

The Ecole Normale Israélite Orientale

During the 1860s, the teaching corps of the Alliance was composed of
young men recruited from the graduates of Jewish schools in France and
the Rabbinical Seminary in Paris. Most of them were Alsatian in origin.
Some of these teachers had long careers with the Alliance. Men like Félix
Bloch[1] and Maurice Marx[2] were important leaders and founded some of
the most important and successful of the Alliance schools, such as the
ones in Adrianople, Baghdad, and Salonica. However, as the school
network expanded, it became impossible to recruit teachers in France in
sufficient numbers to meet the demand. It was especially difficult to recruit
female teachers, to whom careers in the Middle East and North Africa did
not appear very attractive.

A series of debates among the Alliance leadership in the mid-1860s
finally resolved this issue.[3] The best graduates of Alliance institutions in
the Middle East and North Africa would be brought to Paris, trained as
teachers, and then sent to teach in and direct Alliance schools. The establishment to train the male teachers, the Ecole Normale Israélite Orientale
(ENIO), opened in Paris in 1867. The first students arrived in the same
year. Two of them, David Cazès from Tetuan, Morocco, and Nissim
Béhar from Jerusalem (by way of Istanbul, where he had been educated in
a Jewish school that taught French), were to have distinguished careers
with the Alliance.[4] The same was to be true for Fortunée and Rachel
Béhar, the sisters of Nissim Béhar, who arrived in 1872, the first Sephardi
women to be trained by the Alliance as teachers.[5]

1. A. H. Navon, *Les 70 ans de l'École Normale Israélite Orientale* (Paris: Durlacher,
1935), 111.
2. Ibid., 112. For a list of AIU teachers not trained at the ENIO, see ibid., 111–14.
3. Ibid., 14–18.
4. The careers of these two teachers merit monographs in themselves. For brief accounts of their trajectories, see ibid., 117. For Béhar, see also the obituary note by Jacques
Bigart in *Paix et Droit* 11 (Jan. 1931): 6–9, as well as Shelomo Haramati, *Three Who
Preceded Ben Yehudah* (in Hebrew) (Jerusalem: Yad Ben-Zvi, 1978), 84–125. No compara-
ble study exists on David Cazès.
5. Silberman, "An Investigation," 132.

The ENIO led a peripatetic existence until 1889. First housed in the Ecole de Travail, *the Jewish trade school in the Marais, it was located in the Rabbinical Seminary from 1872 to 1876 and then returned to the* Ecole de Travail. *Finally, with a gift from Baroness de Hirsch, a mansion at Auteuil was purchased in 1889 to house the school.[6] The Alliance normal school for the female teachers had to wait until 1922 to have its own building, purchased at Versailles with a gift from a wealthy Alliance alumnus from Baghdad, Ezechiel Schamoon. Before World War I, the young women were taught at the* Institut Bischoffsheim, *at Mrs. Isaac's, and at Miss Weill-Kahn's, all of them Jewish boarding schools in Paris.[7]*

*The ENIO received state accreditation (*reconnue d'utilité publique*) in 1880.[8] Unfortunately, information on the content of the education it provided is extremely scant. Initially, it offered a three-year program, similar to the French normal schools. At the end of this period of study, the students had to pass the French national examination for the* brevet élémentaire, *the diploma needed by all French elementary-school teachers in order to teach. In addition, the students had to study Hebrew, Jewish history, the Bible, and other Jewish subjects.*

The program was extended to four years in 1876, and eventually the students were expected to take the state brevet supérieur, *an examination required by the French educational system for all elementary-school teachers.[9] Leading intellectuals such as Joseph Halévi, the famous Orientalist, Isaïe Levaillant, the future Prefect and Director of Safety at the Ministry of the Interior, and I. Carré and Ferdinand Buisson, leading French educators, taught at the school.*

The program of studies consisted of the following in 1886–87:

> *First and second years:* 38 hours of instruction: French grammar and literature, 9 hours; English language, 2 hours; history, 4 hours; geography, 1 hour; arithmetic and geometry, 5 hours; physics and natural history, 2 hours; drawing, 4 hours; calligraphy, 1 hour; biblical history, 1 hour; Hebrew grammar, 1 hour; biblical exegesis, 3 hours; Mishna and Hebrew composition, 1 hour; singing, 2 hours; physical education, 2 hours.
>
> *Third and fourth years:* 31 hours of instruction: educational methods, 1 hour; French grammar and literature, 5 hours; English language, 2 hours; history, 3 hours; geography, 1 hour; algebra and geometry, 3 hours; accounting, 1 hour; physics and chemistry, 3

6. Navon, *Les 70 ans,* 18–21.
7. Silberman, "An Investigation," 132–33.
8. Navon, *Les 70 ans,* 24. For the statutes of the school, see ibid., 106–7.
9. Silberman, "An Investigation," 125.

hours; drawing, 2 hours; biblical history, 1 hour; Talmud, 1 hour; biblical exegesis, 3 hours; Hebrew composition, 1 hour; singing, 2 hours; physical education, 2 hours.[10]

There is no similar information about the subjects taught to the women, though it is safe to assume that they followed a curriculum broadly analogous to that of the ENIO.

The above program devoted about 15 percent of the time to Jewish subjects. This figure was around 10 percent in 1935.[11] The ENIO had to give more time to certain other subjects to ensure that the students would be able to pass the new brevet *examinations instituted by the French educational system after 1902.[12] However, the Jewish classes were of paramount importance, as one of the principal aims of the school was "to forge in each student a Jewish heart, a Jewish soul. Their great task ahead would be to inculcate in their future students the same principles that they will have absorbed during their years of study."[13] Nevertheless, the issue of the teaching of Hebrew and Jewish subjects at the ENIO and in the Alliance schools remained problematic, with both the traditionalists and later the Zionists criticizing the organization for laxity in this matter.*

The Alliance attempted several times to reform the teaching of Hebrew subjects in its schools and at the ENIO. One such attempt was outlined by A. H. Navon, the director, in 1913:

Paris, 30 October 1913

An outline of projected modifications to the Hebrew Studies program at the *Ecole Orientale* . . .

[. . .]

Subjects to be added to the program and assignment of responsibilities.

a. Jewish history (biblical times) in the context of ancient civilizations. We do not mean by this biblical history.

We believe that a course on the history of the Jews, beginning with the time of Joshua, should be developed at the *Ecole Orientale* . . .

The course that we propose to develop is designed to provide our future teachers with the means to teach this history, in their turn, without falling into either of two extremes: a blind acceptance of all

10. AIU, *Ecole Normale Israélite Orientale: Rapport sur l'année scolaire 1886–1887* (Paris, 1887), 2.
11. See the table showing the numbers of hours devoted to each subject taught at the school in the academic year of 1934–35 in Navon, *Les 70 ans,* 104–5. See also Silberman, "An Investigation," 137.
12. Silberman, "An Investigation," 134; Navon, *Les 70 ans,* 28.
13. Navon, *Les 70 ans,* 32.

that is contained in the "biblical histories" or contempt for these same events. There is an intermediate position to be taken based on respect for both tradition and reason . . .

b. Biblical exegesis (only in the 4th year): It is good to introduce our future teachers to these questions for they will later be drawn to them. More than that, it is necessary to prepare them for exegesis. What better direction to take than to interest them in Jewish studies? Here, guidance is everything . . .

[. . .]

c. History of modern literature (4th year): Mr. Slousch is the professor of modern Hebrew at the school . . .

In the new project, Mr. Slousch's goal is to render our young people capable of understanding and using modern Hebrew when the need arises. By "modern Hebrew" we do not mean "Neo-Hebrew" [Hebrew as it was then emerging as a spoken or written language in Palestine] but the language of our fine contemporary authors: Mappo, Javetz, Gordon (Leib), Calmann Schulman, etc. Our teachers must be familiar with the ideas expressed in contemporary Jewish literature. I therefore believe that a few lessons in literary history, supported by some of the best-known texts, are necessary.

In addition, pedagogical journals written in Hebrew for the teaching of Hebrew are currently being published, especially in Russia. These are a matter of real interest. I remember having read in one of them not long ago about a lesson given to students on "irony in the Prophets," which displayed a rare pedagogical talent on the part of the author. Mr. Slousch would, then, along with introducing them to Jewish literature, provide his students with pedagogical lessons on the teaching of Hebrew and would demonstrate the necessary methods. I could profitably assist him in this part of his undertaking.

d. Hebrew grammar, or, more accurately, "the Hebrew language": We must abandon the method according to which the teaching of Hebrew grammar is seen only as a collection of abstract theoretical rules with no practical aspect, constituting a kind of mental gymnastics devoid of application. This method has run its course even in the dead languages of Latin and Greek. We must head straight toward our true goal, the mastery of a language. This does not come from grammar but from reading, practice, and vocabulary. The rules, by which I mean those pertaining to the grammatical system, must be derived from real and concrete expressions . . .

[. . .]

A. H. Navon

Archives of the AIU, France IV.E.4a.

*The attempt to straddle the realms of both tradition and reason men-
tioned by Navon in the above letter was at the heart of the ambivalence of
the Alliance on matters that related to religion, an ambivalence shared
fully by its teachers. The true essence of Judaism was held to be in complete harmony with the principles of "modern civilization," which the
Alliance schools were designed to disseminate. In practice, among the
Jewish communities of North Africa and the Middle East, imbued with the
Jewish tradition, the Alliance teachers found themselves in the position of
being missionaries for modern Western civilization only. When faced with
the full weight of popular religion and tradition among the local Jews,
they were either unwilling or incapable of trying to synthesize modern
European notions of tradition and reason. Indeed, it is doubtful whether
such a synthesis, whose classic expression was the Reform Judaism of the
mid-nineteenth century, was ever really feasible for the Jews in the lands of
Islam, who lived under very different conditions.*

*The ENIO and its counterpart for the female students were highly
successful institutions and succeeded in providing excellent training to
generations of students, who moved on to become important figures in the
Sephardi and Eastern Jewish world. Of course, right from the beginning,
these teacher-training schools dealt with an elite student body composed
of the best students from the Alliance schools. The procedure for the
selection of the students was as follows:*

CANDIDACY FOR THE PREPARATORY SCHOOL

The teaching personnel of the Alliance are generally recruited from
among the Alliance schools themselves.

Around the month of May of each year, the Secretariat sends to all
the schools copies of the examinations which the students must take.
These examinations include a dictation, a composition written in
French, mathematics problems, one translation from Hebrew and one
translation into Hebrew. Needless to say, the candidates may not be
helped in any way and are not allowed to communicate with each
other during the tests . . .

Selected candidates must be no less than fourteen and no more
than fifteen years of age.

The director's responsibility in the selection of candidates is a serious
one, for the level of our personnel rests on this choice. He must make
his recommendations, therefore, only after considerable reflection and
with the interest of the work of the Alliance as his sole motivation.

Prior to his recommendation, the director must observe the candidates he wishes to select over a long period in order to be certain that
they have the qualities necessary to become teachers.

First, the student must have a sturdy constitution and be in good health, of average build, neither too tall nor too short, with no physical defects and no illnesses. Pronunciation should be clear, elocution should be fluent; the slightest vision or hearing defect is immediate and final cause for rejection. The respiratory tract, the larynx, and the lungs must be particularly strong and healthy in light of the strain these organs will be required to undergo later when the student becomes a teacher. In the course of this observation, hereditary tendencies must be given careful consideration, and the director must check whether the student's family is subject to instances of abnormal development, physical illness, tuberculosis, mental illness, epilepsy, and so forth.

The director, after having made the necessary observations and inquiries himself, will have the student undergo a medical examination, for which the family will incur the expense. A letter recording the results of the examination (preferably drafted by the physician) will be sent by the director to the Central Committee along with the director's own observations as outlined above.

An examination of the student's and family's morals equally demands the special attention of the director. It is important that the student and his family be well-mannered. All things being equal, a well-mannered and pleasant student will be preferred to an ill-mannered or vulgar student, or to one with an unpleasant physical appearance.

As to intellectual considerations, the director will be less concerned with the present level of the student's knowledge than with the faculties of his intellect. In making a comparison among the candidates he would like to propose, the director should study their strength of character, their perseverance, their assiduity, their sense of responsibility, and their punctuality. He will contrast the ease and quickness of understanding in some with the slower thinking of others, and the sometimes superficial brilliance with true depth of thought . . . By reflecting on these various issues, the director will discover a sufficient number of factors to give a reasoned and complete evaluation of his candidate.

The Central Committee informs the directors of the decisions made regarding their candidates. Admissions take place around the month of July . . .[14]

Two of these students eventually became directors of the ENIO themselves. Both were Turkish Jews from the town of Edirne (Adrianople)

14. AIU, *Instructions*, 75–78.

*who had served at various Alliance schools in the Middle East and North
Africa before being called to head the institution. Israël Danon occupied
the position from 1898 to 1911.[15] He was replaced by A. H. Navon, who
directed the school until his retirement in 1935.[16] The principle of recruit-
ing the personnel of the Alliance teaching corps from among the ranks of
those who had been the audience of the organization had been extended to
the position of the director of the ENIO himself.*

*The following portrait of the typical ENIO student was drawn by one of
the teachers in 1935:*

In spite of the diversity in the origins of our students, who come to
us from Jerusalem, Salonica, or Marrakesh, a certain number of common traits can be found among them. This allows the drawing of a
sketch of their collective "psychology" and their intellectual and ethi-
cal evolution. Such a sketch is based, of course, on the majority of
our normal school students—not taking into consideration a few elite
students who are far above the average and a few mediocre ones, far
inferior to what had been expected of them.

Let us first make mention of the fact—for their extreme ease in
adapting to an entirely new physical life is as fortunate as it is
unexpected—that after only a few weeks, these young people, transplanted into a rather rigorous environment, changing their nutritional
as well as their disciplinary routines, living in an unfamiliar world,
function quite well in that world, feeling no less at ease in it than in
their new uniforms. Rarely does a health problem interfere with their
schoolwork, which contributes to the satisfactory results of their studies. After four years, they will have become quite sufficiently Parisian
without having lost for that the sense of their original background.

Upon their arrival in Auteuil, they show themselves to be intelligent, curious, and anxious to learn: it is their intelligence which convinced their first teachers to encourage them to enter the normal
school; it is this intelligence, rather than the sum of their knowledge,
which the committee of admissions seeks to discern among the candidates; curiosity is natural in boys of this age, who are beginning vast
programs of scientific and literary studies. This curiosity often takes
them far. They want to profit most fully from their teachers; they ask
questions and discuss issues with an evident eagerness and interest.
The newness of the teaching does not fail to surprise and even over-
whelm them—they face complicated schedules, different teachers, ex-

15. For his career, see Navon, *Les 70 ans,* 119.
16. Ibid., 126–27. See also *Paix et Droit* 16 (Mar. 1936): 4.

ercises unlike those they were used to. Fortunately, they are good-natured and, especially at the beginning, their passive deference and timidity facilitate the task of those who must ask so much of them.

Getting started is rather difficult, however, for the qualities we have mentioned are hampered by certain regrettable inclinations: first, a certain lethargy for the kind of real studying that demands effort, concentration, reflection, and research; second, a complete lack of order and method, which is all too easily explained by their upbringing; finally, a tendency to be self-satisfied, an easily pardonable fault in a child who until now has succeeded easily and has not yet tackled any truly difficult study.

In spite of all this, their early work generally produces good results, and they make rapid and appreciable progress. But as they enter into the true heart of our teaching and the level rises a little, real difficulties are experienced. In fact, this is a question of crossing the gulf that separates a "slightly higher" education from the elementary education that our students have received. Because of the conditions under which it takes place, their elementary education tends necessarily to be oversimplified, to remain concrete and rather narrow. This is also linked to the denominational quality of their education and to the races and countries of the context. One would be tempted to say that we must "westernize" this too exclusively Eastern education. This must be done while in no way compromising the very clear task undertaken by the Alliance and while respecting all that is good, productive, and original in these schoolchildren. It is a delicate undertaking to open their minds to abstraction, a kind of thinking that does not easily take root in them, and to liberate them from the verbal formalism in which they indulge through habit and natural inclination, to instill in them the critical tools they will need to protect themselves against the facile and superficial kinds of reasoning that may cloud their judgment, and to provide them with the real moral discipline and the intellectual probity required in any school of higher education and in any undertaking of serious study.

These obstacles have nonetheless been overcome, as is attested by official results. At the examinations for the *brevet élémentaire* as well as for the first part of the *brevet supérieur,* our students generally succeed on their first attempt. They do as well as, if not better than, the Parisian candidates. It is appropriate to focus our attention on these results. These boys, who upon their arrival know only rudimentary science and for whom French is almost a foreign language, establish that they are capable of reasoning in depth over a geometry problem or an algebraic theory. They are able to organize and to write an acceptable composition on a moral or literary question, not to mention their performance in the other tests. In these two years alone, they have progressed to the point reached by the more privileged students in the French schools only after a period of three or four years.[17]

The aim of "westerniz[ing]" this too exclusively Eastern education" was the crux of the matter and constituted a further extension of the whole mission of the Alliance, now reaching the final stage of transforming the objects of its endeavors into active propagators of its message.

The arrival of the students in the ville lumière *and their life in the school constituted, of course, quite a cultural shock, but most seem to have adapted quite well, as the two following recollections indicate:[18]*

I left Adrianople in September of 1872. After a long voyage by *britchca* (coach) and a nine-day crossing, I arrived in Paris, at night, exhausted. An employee of the Central Committee, Mr. Weill, came to meet me at the station and took me to the hotel (*rue de Trévise*) where I was to spend the night before being taken to the boarding school the following day. As soon as I was alone in my room, I locked myself in, put the table against the door and did not open it again in spite of the repeated pleas of the staff and the owners, who gently tried to coax me into having a little something to eat. Again and again, I responded in my limited French: "Thank you, I am not hungry, I want to and I have to sleep."

I neither undressed nor slept.

The next day, recognizing Mr. Weill's voice, I let him in. He put me in a coach and took me to the *place de l'Arsenal,* where the Bischoffsheim boarding school was located at that time. As he introduced me to the director, I think I heard him whisper: "Intelligent but stubborn."

I still have wonderful memories of my stay at the Bischoffsheim, in spite of the anxiety I experienced for a while due to a misunderstanding.

Order, cleanliness, scrupulous moral standards, hygiene, abundant and well-balanced meals, enlightened supervision, all of these things along with good courses contributed to making the Bischoffsheim a model institution. This was all due to the tireless activity, the affectionate care, and the wise counsel of the late Mr. and Mrs. Bloch. He

17. Navon, *Les 70 ans,* 33–36.
18. Ibid., 77–79, 81–85.

was so like a father and she like a mother. The administration of this boarding school remained in their family down to the third generation and rightly so.

But how can I express the *savoir-faire,* the ardent charity, the loving severity, the vast erudition, and the spirit of devotion of their daughter, our dear Miss Florentine Bloch? Her father was the director, and her mother, the heart and soul of the Bischoffsheim. She supported them both in everything they did. She was good, sympathetic, and had a truly maternal heart. Miss F. Bloch was a friend, a sister, and a benefactress to all her students, but especially to the *"orientales,"* who were in the beginning the victims of the *"occidentales."* Miss F. Bloch had the talent of correcting this fault and of pointing out their error to the Parisian girls, who were mischievous and sly, and for whom everything about the *"petites orientales"*—this is how they contemptuously referred to the sisters of the late Nissim Béhar [one of the first Alliance teachers] and myself—was shocking. After a few months' time, Mr., Mrs., and especially Miss Bloch had succeeded in establishing a spirit of comradeship, of sisterhood, and of understanding among all of the students. The *"petites orientales"* were thankful for this. Thus, the foreign students still treasure a feeling of strong and affectionate gratitude toward the Bloch family and the institution. I would have led a tranquil and happy life there if my poor distraught mother had not written me shortly after my arrival in Paris: "I have been told that you are not in a school; leave everything and come home as soon as you have received my letter." Then I received a letter from one of my uncles, who was in India at the time: "I am sending you 600 francs but use only 100 francs and keep the rest to pay for your return trip; your mother writes me that you are not in a school but in a disreputable place. Before leaving Paris, write to me describing in detail the place in which you live, your schedule, if you go out often, the people you meet, etc. If you are in a respectable home, notify your poor mother immediately. People have been telling her that in Paris vice is around every corner and that young girls there are living in filthy districts full of debauchery." These two letters disturbed me greatly; I was 14 years old at the time. I hastened to send my family a detailed description of the boarding school, our daily routine, the course of study, the kindness of our teachers, etc. I then spent two anxious months until my family had made further inquiries and was more accurately informed, especially through the kind Mr. Félix Bloch, who was at that time the director of the boys' school in Adrianople, for it was he who had recommended me to the Alliance. My family gave me permission to continue my studies and set aside 500 francs to pay for my return trip if and when I so desired.

In general, life at the school was very pleasant. Once a week we were taken to the temple, where the eloquence of Chief Rabbis Isidor and Zadoc-Kahn went straight to the hearts of their listeners, lifting their spirits and comforting their souls. Once or twice a week, there was a walk, single file, chaperoned by one of the teachers, to the *Jardin des Plantes* or the Luxembourg. The students were always chaperoned, even when they went to the eye doctor. Still, there was a great deal of confidence placed in the *"orientales,"* and we were allowed to spend the day with the families of our Parisian friends, who would invite us for holidays, on our days off, and even at night to go to the theater. Had it not been for the burning desire to see our families again, life at the boarding school would have been untroubled, thanks to the Alliance. I would feel remiss were I not to mention the tender encouragement and the friendliness of the charitable women and the other people who made up the Supervisory Committee of the institution: Mr. and Mrs. Bischoffsheim, its founders, whose kindness and gentleness gladdened our hearts; their daughter, Mrs. Beer, and her prudent guidance; Mrs. Cahen d'Anvers, Mrs. Zadoc-Kahn, and their constant goodwill; Mrs. Eugène Manuel, the poet's wife. Mr. Manuel came often to the school, along with Mr. J. Derenbourg (a member of the *Institut*) and Mr. Rosenfeld, to give us tests, to encourage us, and to note our progress.

My examination—the first taken by an *"orientale"*—turned into quite an event when the jury learned from Chief Rabbi Zadoc-Kahn, who was present for the examination in religious instruction, that I was from Turkey and had been studying in Paris for only three years.

Mrs. Weismann

[. . .]

. . . The seminary building was quite large, set between the courtyard and the garden. One wing was assigned for use by the preparatory school. The dormitory, on the first floor, was quite spacious and well ventilated. The room used for classes and study on the ground floor was small, but as it looked onto the garden and had a southern exposure it had a bright and happy air. It was modestly furnished. A large square table with drawers was in the middle of the room, and the students would sit along one side and the teachers on the other.

When I arrived in September of 1875, there were 16 students: 4 were in their third year, 5 in their second, and 7 in their first. They

came from Tetuan, Volo, Baghdad, Smyrna, Salonica, Constantinople, Shumla, and Rustchuk.

The Eastern students and the seminarians prayed together in the
same oratory and took their meals together in the same refectory.
Here, a digression. I confess that, for my part, having come from
Rustchuk, a city serving as a link between the West and the Black
Sea, with a population in constant communication with Bucharest and
Vienna, the term "*orientaux*" used to refer to us seemed odd to me at
first, if not pejorative.

From the first moment of contact, I noticed that the future rabbis
considered us with a sometimes embarrassing curiosity. In this vein,
one of our group was asked if people ate with a fork in his country
and if they even knew what it was for. Perhaps they expected us to be
like the savages of the Far West, but it did not take long for them to
notice that among us there were some who were quite modernized
and not at all naive. Still I must admit, to be perfectly honest, that
one of our classmates drew attention to himself the day he arrived by
making a most extraordinary entrance. As he had found the main
door locked and was probably unaware of the use of a bellpull, and
having knocked in vain at the door, he scrambled over the fence, to
the great astonishment of the concierge . . .

When I add that the meals were excellent and that the Alliance
provided us with a five-franc monthly allowance, I can certainly say
that we spent a delightful year at the seminary.

I do have, however, some reservations to express about the way
our studies were run. Mr. Trenel seemed to take no interest in them
as he was so entirely absorbed in directing the seminary. There was
no lack of good teachers. Mr. Lemoine was very competent in the
teaching of history and geography; Captain Aron, the engineering instructor from the *Ecole Polytechnique,* was responsible for mathematics. Dr. Dépasse provided us with a clear and pleasant introduction to
the physical and natural sciences, Mr. Loeb gave us lessons in Hebrew grammar and exegesis, and for a time Mr. Ferdinand Buisson
captivated us with his discussions of pedagogy.

For my part, I enjoyed my teaching career as much as I did because I had had a natural inclination for teaching from the time I was
a child. I further developed this inclination by reading pedagogical
texts and journals and by consulting the *Dictionnaire encyclopédique
de pédagogie,* which had been published under the direction of Mr.
Ferdinand Buisson.

All the students, old and new, attended all of the courses and made
sure they took notes.

A few months before leaving, the graduating students began their training in the primary schools of the consistory[19] while the younger students prepared for the *brevet élémentaire*. The older students willingly helped them by giving them dictations, working on problems in mathematics with them, and suggesting appropriate texts for the preparation of other subjects.

The library was open to us and we read a great deal. We even had a group subscription to a daily newspaper, *La France*.

Alas, this happy, easy life only lasted one year. At the end of 1876, we were transferred to the *Ecole de Travail* on the *rue des Rosiers*, where we were set up in the wing that faces the street. Our new home was large, tall, and spacious, but I think it was imprudent to effect the transfer before the new director had arrived. In the meantime, we took our meals in the refectory of the *Ecole de Travail* with the apprentice workers. The food was mediocre and little appreciated by either the old or the new students. The former had been spoiled by the meals in the seminary and the latter were used to Eastern dishes.

We were placed under the supervision of medical students in training. We looked like exiles and were miserable. There were grumbles and complaints about the food. One day, we refused to try certain dishes. The next day, we received a visit by Mr. Netter, who sharply admonished us.

Finally, Mr. Marx arrived and everything was restored to order, but a strict, precise, overmeticulous order. We passed from one extreme to the other.

The new director overdid it. He imposed uniform dress and we only left the building in single file.

The Central Committee, for its part, was to put an end to its generosity by cutting our monthly allowance in half and then canceling it altogether. We rarely went to the theater. A number of assistant monitors were named, some of whom betrayed the administration and sided with the students, inciting them to insubordination.

In spite of the action of Mr. and Mrs. Marx, who tried to be in all places at all times for the students, the revolt which had been brewing finally broke out.

It was a short-lived rebellion. A delegation of the Central Committee arrived. After listening to the grievances of the malcontents, who claimed they were "abandoned like a shepherdless flock," it severely reproached them for their ingratitude and threatened to make an ex-

19. The state communal administrative body.

ample of them at the first sign of insubordination by sending the instigators home. The warning was effective and calm was restored.

After the graduating students had left, there was no further cause
for disciplinary action.

Mr. Marx also implemented an excellent practice. In order that
they might become more at ease in their future role as teachers, students who had received the *brevet* took turns presenting certain
courses to their classmates.

There were very good teachers in history and geography, mathematics, physics and natural sciences, French literature and composition,
and Hebrew and Jewish history. Drawing, singing, and physical education were also taught with care and attention, but there was no course
in pedagogy.

Grades were given by the teachers but there were no other examinations or evaluations, and no exam at the end of the year.

It was when I was at the end of my fourth year that the Central
Committee considered preparing students for the *brevet supérieur* for
the first time. On a trial basis, these were limited to in-house, rather
than official, exams.

That same year, Mr. Marx came to the realization that his constant
contact with the students was undermining his authority.

He decided to delegate a portion of his duties to a trustworthy fourth-
year student and to give him the title of head monitor. He chose me for
this position as I appeared to be more responsible than the others.

This position gave me the opportunity to act as a mediator between the
director and the students and to gain experience and authority. It also
afforded me the privilege of being named immediately upon the completion of my studies director of a school the Alliance was about to open.

Pau, 25 March 1935
Loupo

*In ways strongly reminiscent of many newly westernized "natives" in co-
lonial contexts, the Alliance teachers' self-identification with the West was
to be nearly total. The defensiveness about their Eastern origins so much in
evidence in these two letters would deeply mark their actions and attitudes.*

The Backgrounds and Careers of the Teachers

Algiers, 12 October 1932

[. . .]

I have just returned from my trip to Bulgaria and I am anxious to
get back to my work.

How right I was to undertake this trip, which I had been postponing from year to year, balking in the face of the expenses it would entail. My father was still alive when I arrived, he had been bedridden for two months, and I had the great consolation of talking with him for two precious weeks and for being with him during his last moments. My father was one of the last men of that generation who held firmly to ancient traditions yet vaguely sensed that those traditions were destined to fade away sooner or later and that a new world would suddenly appear. In this world, with the help of the Alliance, education would play a preponderant role in the East. My father's generation somehow understood that children must take advantage of the education offered them if they were not to be handicapped in their struggle in life. This is why my father did not hesitate a moment to sacrifice himself to remain alone in Karnabat, a small, lost village in Bulgaria where his work kept him, while he sent his children to Adrianople. It is there that my brothers and I began to study the most basic elements of the French language under the direction of Abraham Cazès at the Alliance school. And so, what little I am I owe to my father and to the sacrifices he chose for himself that we might receive an education. For this I shall be eternally grateful to him.
[. . .]

A. Confino

Archives of the AIU, Algérie II.F.1e.

This letter, by a leading Alliance educator, provides a rare insight into the family background of an Alliance teacher. Like the author above, most recruits to the Alliance teaching corps appear to have come not from the upper classes of the Jewish communities of the Middle East and North Africa but from the less well-to-do strata. The sons of the merchants and businessmen who made up the commercial and financial elite of these communities usually followed their fathers into business. However, for the bright and upwardly mobile offspring of the middle classes, especially in the provinces, a teaching career in the service of the Alliance was often an attractive means of quickly transcending the hierarchies of the locality and, above all, of moving into a status group that had great prestige. The male Alliance teacher was, almost by definition, catapulted into the notable class. He socialized with the notables, took part in local communal affairs, and was one of the leaders of the community. The source of his authority was his association with a Western organization that appeared to be very rich and powerful. The aura that everything Western began to acquire in the Middle East and North Africa in this period increased, by association, the prestige of the Alliance teacher. Indeed, the glittering prizes of a triumphant

*Western society, including the opportunity to spend four years in one of its
leading centers, the* ville lumière *itself, were powerful sources of attraction.*

*For the local Jews, whether opponents or supporters of westernization,
the Alliance teacher was the concrete and very real incarnation within the
Jewish community of the all-powerful West. As such, he or she was an
important personality who had to be reckoned with.*

*There was, of course, an added dimension in the case of the female
teachers. A teaching career within this organization was, until the early
twentieth century, the only career open to young Jewish women who
wanted to lead an independent existence and have a profession. The status
of women in the Middle East and North Africa was still bound by rigid
conventions. The father or brother controlled all aspects of a woman's life
until his role was supplanted by the husband upon marriage. In these
societies, a woman's decision to become an Alliance teacher was a revolutionary act in and of itself.*

*Indeed, the emergence among Sephardi and Eastern Jewry of such a
westernized elite as the Alliance teaching corps strongly suggests that
Jewish traditional society in these communities was already in relative
decline even before the full impact of the work of the Alliance had made
itself felt. In a vibrant, traditional Jewish society where the perennial
verities of revealed religion remained intact and in which the rabbinical
elite still enjoyed great prestige because of its command of them, the
Alliance with its alternative and dramatically different set of values could
never have succeeded in gaining adherents and recruits. The schools and
the Alliance teachers were themselves the symptoms as much as the causes
of the decline of tradition among Sephardi Jewry.*

*From which countries did the Alliance teachers originate? The bio-
graphical information about the teachers supplied by A. H. Navon in his
book celebrating the seventieth anniversary of the ENIO presents a
unique data base which allows us to calculate their distribution by place of
origin (see table 4).*

*The majority of the teachers were born in the Ottoman Empire, primar-
ily in the Judeo-Spanish culture area, which comprises present-day Turkey, Greece, and Bulgaria. These three countries alone seem to have
provided close to 60 percent of the teaching corps. This figure offers a
great contrast to the 9.9 percent represented by Morocco, the country in
which the Alliance maintained a presence the longest.*

*Many factors explain the remarkable domination of the teaching corps
by the Judeo-Spanish–speaking element. The Judeo-Spanish culture area,
more open to European influences, was more predisposed to the work of
the Alliance than the Arab world. It is noteworthy that twenty-two of the
thirty-one male graduates from Morocco and all nine of the female gradu-*

TABLE 4

The Graduates of the ENIO according to Country of Birth
(Present Borders), 1869–1925

Country	Males		Females		Total	
	No.	%	No.	%	No.	%
Turkey	85	34.4	73	46.8	158	39.2
Bulgaria	25	10.1	15	9.6	40	9.9
Morocco	31	12.5	9	5.8	40	9.9
Israel	30	12.1	11	7.0	41	10.2
Syria	18	7.3	10	6.4	28	6.9
Greece	14	5.7	14	9.0	28	6.9
Iran	7	2.8	—	—	7	1.7
Tunisia	6	2.4	—	—	6	1.5
Iraq	6	2.4	—	—	6	1.5
France	—	—	8	5.1	8	2.0
Romania	5	2.0	—	—	5	1.2
Algeria	4	1.6	—	—	4	1.0
Lebanon	4	1.6	2	1.3	6	1.5
Russia	3	1.2	2	1.3	5	1.2
Libya	3	1.2	2	1.3	5	1.2
Poland	—	—	2	1.3	2	0.5
Hungary	1	0.4	1	0.6	2	0.5
Egypt	—	—	1	0.6	1	0.2
Macedonia	1	0.4	2	1.3	3	0.7
Gibraltar	1	0.4	—	—	1	0.2
Unknown	3	1.2	4	2.6	7	1.7
Total	247		156		403	

SOURCE: A. H. Navon, *Les 70 ans de l'Ecole Normale Israélite Orientale* (Paris: Durlacher, 1935), 117–83.

NOTE: Although these are not definitive figures (Navon was unable to obtain information on some ENIO graduates), they are complete enough to give us a good indication of the distribution by country of origin of the Alliance teaching body.

ates came from Tangier or Tetuan. The Jewish communities in these two cities had direct contact with Europe and were Judeo-Spanish speaking.[20] Many of the teachers' reports indicate that the students whose mother tongue was Judeo-Spanish, with its Romance-language base, found it much easier to learn French than the others, who had to struggle considerably. Because a thorough command of French was a sine qua non *for admission to the ENIO, it is clear that the students of Judeo-Spanish*

20. The Judeo-Spanish dialect spoken in northern Morocco, called Haketia, differed slightly from the ones spoken in the Levant.

origin had a headstart over the others. Also, by World War I, the majority of the schools of the Alliance were in the Ottoman Empire, most in Judeo-Spanish communities. Consequently, this region supplied more teachers, while areas such as the interiors of Morocco and Iraq proved to be more difficult for the Alliance to penetrate.

Seventy-two of the 247 male (29.1 percent) and 23 of the 156 female (14.7 percent) graduates of the ENIO resigned within ten years of graduation. On the other hand, 112 male graduates (45.3 percent) and 67 female graduates (43 percent) served in the organization's schools for more than twenty years. The female teachers seem to have had a tendency to retire earlier than their male counterparts: 58 male teachers (23.5 percent) and 19 female ones (12.2 percent) served for over thirty years.[21]

The teachers who served for twenty years or more constituted the backbone of the school network. Often having started out as assistants under more senior directors or having inaugurated institutions in the smaller communities, they moved on to become the directors of the major Alliance establishments in the large centers, where they played a crucial role in the activities of the organization. Figures such as Béhar, Cazès, Arié, Fresco, and Sémach among the men, and Ungar, Salzer, Sémach, and Lévy among the women, were the solid foundation on which the whole Alliance edifice rested.[22]

Many teachers also published textbooks, memoirs, studies on particular communities, histories, novels, and plays, and were active in journalism.[23] Their work was recognized by the public authorities of the countries in which they served and by the French consuls and colonial administrators. Forty-nine male teachers (19.8 percent) and sixteen female teachers (10.2 percent) received official honors, such as the palmes academiques *and, in a few cases, even the* Légion d'honneur *from France, as well as the orders of the* Nishan-i iftihar *and the* Mecidiye *from Muslim rulers.*

Relations between the Teachers and the Alliance Central Committee

Frequent tours of inspection by trusted Alliance teachers were the principal means for the Central Committee to oversee the smooth functioning of

21. Navon, *Les 70 ans*, 117–83.

22. For a study of the career and life of one such Alliance teacher, see Esther Benbassa, with Aron Rodrigue, *Gabriel Arié: Une vie judéo-espagnole à l'Est* (Paris: Cerf, 1992).

23. Most notable for their writings are David Cazès, Jacques Loria, Moïse Fresco, Gabriel Arié, Joseph Sabbah, Moïse Franco, A. H. Navon, Moïse Nahon, Joseph Nehama, and Rachel Lévy.

its work. The details provided by such inspectors also offer a distinctive view of the activities and characters of the teaching personnel. A. Confino, then the director of one of the Alliance schools in Constantinople, rendered judgment on his colleagues in 1908 while inspecting the recently founded schools in Iran. His comments, not surprisingly, are suffused with current stereotypes.

Teheran, 29 June 1908

[. . .]

Mr. Loria. Young, ardent, lively, exuberant, and full of life, Mr. Loria is the epitome of the true southerner. His parents are of Italian extraction and his grandfather was a rabbi in Nice prior to its annexation. His features are expressive, open, and honest; he is the kind of person with whom one feels instinctively at ease from the moment of encounter. He has a sharp and penetrating mind, and he grasps and absorbs ideas with surprising quickness and precision. In addition, he has a sense of humor, and a good one. In short, he is the very picture of his father—minus the faults. He is as polite and well-mannered as his father is brusque and aggressive. His students adore him, and the community holds him in high esteem.

His pedagogical aptitudes are manifest. He expresses himself with ease and so is able to reach his audience and to charm and captivate it with his lively delivery, his striking imagery, and his highly original wit. His teaching is rich and full of life. The best illustration of this is the contrast between the same group of students from one course to another. The same students who, five minutes before, were falling asleep at their desks under the indifferent gaze of the Persian or Hebrew teacher awake with a start when Mr. Loria enters the room. As if a magic wand had passed over them, they are transformed. They become all eyes and ears, attentive to the lesson, eager to catch their teacher's every word.

It is a pity, however, that Mr. Loria does not have enough authority over his assistants. You have sent him two young people who were his classmates in school and who, for that very reason, have much too familiar a manner with him. There should be certain degrees even in comradeship and a line should be drawn. Such lines are nonexistent in Teheran. The director and his assistants appear to be completely lacking in tact in this regard. Mr. Benbassat uses the familiar *tu* with his director, and Mr. Toledo not only uses *tu* but also calls him "Loria" in front of the students. Mr. Loria follows their lead. This is bad both for the director's prestige and for discipline in the school in general. I made a point of discussing this issue with Mr. Loria.

Similarly, I would have preferred to see him exercise a little more sternness with the native personnel . . . In short, I wish he would have a little less kid in his glove and a little more iron in his fist. This could only increase the discipline and order in the school. You asked me to see what I could find out about his plans. He wants to leave Persia. He has had enough. I think he may have just written to you about a new position. But I have every reason to believe that if you increased his material advantages slightly, he would be willing to stay in Teheran for two or three more years.
[. . .]

A. Confino

Archives of the AIU, Iran I.F.1.

Teheran, 30 August 1908

[. . .]
I already had occasion to draw a brief sketch of Mr. Hochberg's physiognomy in my last report from Hamadan. I must return to this now and give a closer analysis of the psychology of this somewhat enigmatic person. Physically, Mr. Hochberg does not make a very favorable impression with his hatchet face, his cold eyes, and his pale, sickly, and fretful appearance. He passes himself off as and is considered by his colleagues to be a dreamer, an ideologue, a socialist. I myself, however, have had the opportunity to get very close to him and to spend a month observing him in his private life. I have noted dozens of character traits which belie the opinion others have of him. This so-called socialist is the most selfish man I have ever met. The ideologue eats and drinks as if he were four people. The dreamer with his head in the clouds is perfectly capable of cold calculation when the occasion demands and exercises pronounced common sense where his own interests are concerned. In reality he is none of those things. If it is true that a Jew easily assimilates the customs and habits of the country which takes him in, Mr. Hochberg is essentially a Russian product. From head to toe he is imbued with Slavic attitudes, the Slavic character, and the Slavic mentality. And the Slav—as we all know—does not have the clear-thinking and the quick, discriminating eye which makes the Westerner, and especially the Latin, a man who . . . follows his impulses, who heads straight for his goal once . . . he has determined his plan of action . . . "Imagine a Latin and a Slav each with a telescope," said Mr. E. M. de Vogüé. "The former puts the instrument into focus. He will choose to shorten his field of vision and to see less so that he may see more clearly; the latter will use the full power of the lenses, widen the horizon, and

blur his vision so that he may see farther." The Slav has a good eye, but he lacks the ability to bring things into focus. It is in like manner that Mr. Hochberg seems to me to have somewhat lost sight of the purpose of his mission and his reason for being in Persia.

He came here to protect the Jews, and in order to do this he should be in constant contact with them. Instead, he has held them at a distance and has put off the best-intentioned among them with his free-thinking convictions and his disdain for religious practices. He believed it was enough to impress the Muslims with his aristocratic airs, by parading through the streets amid a flock of servants. He has succeeded only in extravagantly overspending without benefit to the community. His teaching has been limited to lessons on abstract ethics, deliberately eliminating prayer in the school. The most striking result of his teaching—or should I say the most destructive result— has been to turn his students into atheists. This is certainly not the role and these are certainly not the functions of a representative of the Alliance.

[. . .]

A. Confino

Archives of the AIU, Iran I.F.1.

Teheran, 4 September 1908

[. . .]

Mr. Saguès. It may be said of him that you made the right choice in giving him the appointment at Kermanshah. I did not know Mr. Saguès at all before my arrival in Persia. I was even predisposed against him as a result of the incident which nearly cost him his life. I knew that the Persians would never attack Europeans and that only an extraordinarily serious sequence of events could have led them to lay a hand on him. In short, I was convinced that it had to do with an affair related to morals in which the fault had to lie with Mr. Saguès. Once I had seen him at work, all my negative presuppositions fell away. He has a lively and penetrating intelligence, an open, friendly face; he is active, full of energy, industrious. He loves his work and it shows. It is true that Mr. Saguès had been advised of my imminent visit. I knew this when I arrived. But the hundred little details which do not lie, and which are for us precious indications of the true state of affairs, confirmed that there was nothing improvised, artificial, or out of the ordinary in all I saw. I was witnessing the regular and habitual train of events in the life of a conscientious and devoted teacher. The very incident in which Mr. Saguès came so near to death speaks highly of his honor. The version of the events which you were given by the French Legation is entirely erroneous. The investigation I carried out both in Teheran and in Kermanshah has left no doubt in my mind. You have perhaps been apprised of the facts. One of his servants got into a quarrel with a Muslim. The others came running to his aid. A few passersby began to intervene and a violent brawl soon developed. Mr. Saguès then made the unfortunate mistake of coming into the street to defend his servants. The Persians fell upon him with a vengeance and beat him up. But when they had realized the enormity of their action, instead of drawing back and running away, they went at him all the more fiercely and dragged him to the mosque, where, in order to justify their actions, they accused him of having hidden a Muslim woman in the school. This was a spontaneous, unreflective move on their part. There was never any woman involved. Such is the accurate account of the events.

Since then, this unfortunate man has been living in constant fear. His life in Kermanshah has become a nightmare for him. During my stay in that city, we both slept in the school courtyard at night. He would wake the servants ten times a night, thinking someone was trying to kill him. The wind rustling in the trees, a falling leaf, the slightest noise, would frighten him. One evening, we were walking back to the school at dusk and a suspicious looking Persian approached us. The poor boy was so overcome with fear he would have fallen over had I not caught him in my arms. His transfer from Kermanshah was an absolute necessity. In authorizing his departure, you have rendered him a great service.
[. . .]

A. Confino

Archives of the AIU, Iran I.F.1.

The Alliance, like most organizations, was not immune to some degree of friction, especially between the Central Committee in Paris and the teaching corps dispersed in various distant towns and cities. The Central Committee was paternalistic toward the teachers and, under the redoubtable secretary general Jacques Bigart (1892–1934), who ran the day-to-day activities of the organization, was rather autocratic in its overall stance. The Instructions générales pour les professeurs *makes this quite clear:*

In his correspondence with the Central Committee, an Alliance teacher must, in general, avoid the use of any terms which are not in keeping with a tone appropriate to administrative matters or which might signal a lack of respect for his superiors. If a teacher wishes to make an observation or submit a complaint, he will do so simply by indicating precisely the dates and the facts which concern him, without personal commentary, and especially without expressing his surprise.

The teacher should concentrate on the style of his letters and make every effort to convey in them the polite, urbane, educated tone which must be maintained in all administrative correspondence. He must seek a skillful handling of the French language and will arrive at a mastery of that language especially through the careful reading and rereading of a few authors who number among the great writers . . .

RULES OF RELIGIOUS, MORAL, AND INTELLECTUAL DISCIPLINE

The Central Committee does not at all wish to interfere in the private lives of its teachers. Teachers have only to realize the full extent of their social and professional duties in order for the need for dignity in their private lives to impress itself sufficiently on their consciences. This does not fall within the administrative domain. However, we deem it necessary to provide the teachers with certain directives which concern them in their roles as teachers and as representatives of the Alliance.

An Alliance teacher is placed in the midst of a community whose respect and goodwill he is expected to earn. He is responsible for the education of the children in that community and he is the representative of an organization which has entrusted him with the safekeeping of its traditions. It is essential that such a teacher scrupulously fulfill his religious duties and that he fully realize the gravity of his error in failing in any way to follow religious practices.

Directors and teachers must accordingly: 1. attend service at synagogue every Saturday and holy day; 2. observe religious practices concerning food, the Sabbath, and feast days and in no manner transgress any of the practices observed by the majority of the members of the community among whom they are living.

The Central Committee insists on a strict adherence to these instructions and will deal harshly with those who fail to conform to them. Directors should remember this when preparing their annual reports and, as concerns this matter, should serve as good examples to their assistants.

MARRIAGE OF TEACHERS

The Central Committee prefers to be consulted concerning the plans of those teachers who are considering marriage. By this the Committee in no way means to suggest that it would become involved in arrangements of a personal nature; it cannot condone, however—as has sometimes happened in the past—a young teacher whose salary barely suffices to support himself imprudently taking on the responsibility of a family.

The Committee believes that under these important circumstances its counsel may prove very helpful to our teachers. Teachers who choose to do without our counsel risk incurring our extreme displeasure.[24]

An unfavorable report by an inspector often caused conflict between the Central Committee and the individual concerned. Two different areas seem to have constituted the main sources of friction: requests for a change of teaching post and financial matters such as salaries or reimbursement for expenses. The following letter from A. Saguès offers an interesting illustration of the former:

Casablanca, 3 April 1909

Mr. President,

Please accept my apologies for not having responded sooner to your letter of 10 March regarding my request for a transfer. As I intended to respond at length, I thought it preferable to wait for the first few days of vacation, in order to write to you with a clear mind and without distraction.

I hope you will understand, first of all, that my decision was in no way motivated by any disillusionment with the work of the Alliance. It is true that my present state of mind prevents me from working with all the ardor and zeal dictated by the confidence with which you have honored me, but this is due neither to a lack of devotion nor to a weakening of my attachment to the organization I serve. I am fully aware of all that I owe that organization; it would be a sign of not knowing me to accuse me of ingratitude.

You inspire a great reverence in me, and I hold the Central Committee in profound respect and greatly admire the Alliance both for its direct undertakings and for the generous actions it has encouraged and inspired. All of this should have led me to bury my personal preferences inside myself and to consider only the beauty of the mission I was to fulfill wherever necessary, and especially under the most unfavorable conditions. Yet, in spite of my deep admiration and respect, I must confess that certain decisions you have made in my regard have not been in keeping with my hopes. Still feeling the effects of the blow this has dealt me, I was not always able to control the

24. AIU, *Instructions*, 13–17.

tone of some of my letters. I was racked with a tension which circumstances served only to aggravate, and I expressed this tension with a vehemence which I would certainly have faulted in another. I acknowledge my mistakes, and in order to prevent further misunderstanding, I respectfully submit that this present letter be withdrawn if there be but one sentence, one expression, one word which might be displeasing to you in nature.

If the ties between the Alliance and the members of its teaching corps were only those of an employer to its employees, my letter would be meaningless. In response to my constant complaints, you would have had the right to invite me to look elsewhere for suitable work if I were not satisfied with the position you were offering. In such a case, unless I had an ulterior motive, I would have refrained from writing to you at all. I would have made an effort to hide my feelings, and my personality would have become more and more bitter; I would have carried out my responsibilities in accordance with my conscience and habits, but grudgingly and without enthusiasm. As it is, this is exactly what I hope to avoid. I am repulsed by the practice of hypocrisy. I would like always to preserve the same enjoyment of teaching and the same passion for my modest participation in the work of the Alliance. This is why I have come to confide in you. I am afraid that by doing so, I am not respecting the reserve imposed by us on our official correspondence. The very fact that I am exposing my grievances to the person who holds my future in his hands, however, marks a step which must dispose you to be indulgent. This being said, I have come to the subject of my letter.

[. . .]

. . . Could anything be more harmful to the stability of the nervous system than the life of isolation, virtually a sequestration, that I have been living for the past five years? No one, even among my colleagues in Persia, has suffered as much as I have. Some find a compensation for the monotony of their lives here in the joys of family and are able to find a respite from their problems and their fatigues in the home; others find themselves in a less fanatical milieu or in a more clement climate; still others have the financial means to procure for themselves the distractions which I was obliged to forgo.

In spite of all I have suffered, the hope of a better future gave me enough strength and courage to take pleasure in carrying my task to completion. I did experience a few crises which nearly shattered my nerves. When Mr. Confino visited Kermanshah, he became aware of my state of mind and of the efforts in which I was engaged so as not to lose the benefit reaped from three years of conscientious work.

It is with utter sincerity that I reaffirm that I expected no reward and no advancement for this work; I saw it as strictly the fulfillment of my duty. The greatest favor for which I secretly dared hope was that I would be given a relatively unimportant directorship in a small community near Constantinople so that I might be able to briefly visit my family at least once a year. I considered such an appointment my due. It was only natural that I should hope to share again the warmth of family life and to enjoy a well-deserved respite close to my loved ones, especially as I had been so long deprived of this.

Friends had informed me that the Central Committee had considered me for the post in Gallipoli. I believed that my dream was to be realized until your letter of 12 October 1908 informed me of my appointment to Casablanca. You can imagine my bitter disappointment and frustration. No, this could not be. After I'd spent five years in Persia, it was just not fitting to entrust me with a directorship in Morocco, where both the customs and the language were totally foreign to me . . .

My hopes had been dashed; my natural affections and most tender sentiments thwarted. What then are the advantages of this appointment that might compensate for those it deprives me of? They are to be found neither in the kind of life I am leading nor in the living conditions imposed upon me.

My status as a bachelor does not allow me to form friendships among the Moroccans. As far as the Europeans are concerned, I must admit that those in Kermanshah, although most of them belonged to diplomatic circles, were much more approachable than those who are here. Cafés and cabarets provide the little distraction there is, and, frankly, I do not have much appreciation for this kind of entertainment. Yes, of course, once I have married and established a family, I will willingly go anywhere for I will be everywhere at home, whereas I now lead the life of an outsider. I am unable to take a real interest in my school or to joyfully carry out my duties unless I can see an encouraging hope shining in the distance; the hope of spending a few weeks of every year with my loved ones.

I am leading a bohemian life; I eat poorly and pay for it dearly. My two daily meals cost me one hundred francs per month, and what meager meals they are, my God! I live in my office because I cannot afford to rent even a single room with the two hundred francs you allot me and which, in any case, I put back into the school's account. The smallest of rooms costs at least thirty francs per month and I would need at least two rooms to live decently. My predecessors did not receive more than this sum, but for them it was pure profit because they roomed in either the boys' school or the girls' school. Like the jack-of-all-trades who was sometimes coachman, sometimes cook, sometimes butler, my office is, depending on the circumstances and the time of day, dining room, living room, or bedroom. I swear to you that I am embarrassed at having come to the point of conveying all these details, which could easily be judged petty. I am not doing so with the intention of asking for an increase in financial support. I am not asking anything of you. If I were to begin now to make such requests, I feel there would be no end to it. I am describing these circumstances only to ensure that my successor finds himself more fortunate than I.

[. . .]

At present my supreme ambition is to be given a small directorship, if at all possible, close to Constantinople. I would like to hope that you have sufficient interest in my future not to refuse me this legitimate request.

Please accept my thanks. Respectfully,

A. Saguès

Archives of the AIU, Maroc VIII.E.155.

Saguès never realized his dream of being sent by the Alliance to Constantinople. After a few years in Tunis as the Alliance director of the Hafsia district école populaire *following his stint at Casablanca, he was appointed in 1928 to head the Tangier school, where he finished his career.*

Even a teacher held in high regard, such as A. Confino, could have problems with the Central Committee over the issue of salary:

Teheran, 30 June 1908

[. . .]

You can imagine Mrs. Confino's torment upon reading in the papers about the violence that has broken out in Persia. I would have turned right around and come back had I not already paid for the trip—all the more so, as it is only with great apprehension that I am undertaking a journey against which everyone has advised me. I am responsible for lives; my first duty is for those of my family.

I will leave, then, and continue my tour of inspection on the condition that the Central Committee acknowledge my dedication and raise my salary to 4,000 francs per year beginning 1 January 1909, in addition to the bonus already promised me. If I am risking my life, the least you can do is to reward my dedication with something other than words. I have been sacrificed up until now; I must not be any

longer. I have noted, much to my chagrin, that after five years of
service Mr. Loria will be earning as much as I am after twenty. Or, if
you prefer, to better illustrate the inequality between Mr. Loria and
myself as far as salary is concerned, my stay in Persia gained me a
600-franc increase, whereas Loria's salary increased by 1,600 francs in
the same period of time, as he started at 1,400 francs. Did I provide
less service in Isphahan than did Mr. Loria in Teheran? I had established a solid and lasting foundation for the work of the Alliance
there. Is it my fault if unscrupulous and incompetent directors compromised this stability and caused its ruin? And the physical and psychological hardships that I am suffering at this very moment and will
continue to endure for an entire year, do they count for nothing to
you, Mr. President? To go without news of one's family for months at
a time; to be forced to travel in this torrid heat, which turns the brain
into jelly and a person into a limp, wet rag; along with that, to be
constantly alone with one's thoughts, not a soul with whom to speak
while crossing the scorching desert; to sleep in stables night after
night; to be covered with parasites and filthy insects, without the possibility of taking a bath when one arrives in a city; to be badly nourished, to eat bread that is made with more sand than flour (I'll bring
you back a few samples); to quench one's thirst with stagnant, nause-
ating water with the fear of contracting typhoid fever at any time; tell
me, Mr. President, are there many of your personnel who would be
capable of such dedication? Still, I accepted this, I ran to answer your
call never thinking to ask what you intended to do for me. I entrusted
myself to the generosity of the Central Committee. But now, the situation has changed. Serious, violent disturbances have erupted in Persia. My life is at risk, no more, no less. I need a solemn promise, I
must know with certainty that I will not be sacrificed. This would
provide me with the impetus to carry out my mission in complete
peace of mind, without hesitation and without fail.
[. . .]

A. Confino

Archives of the AIU, Iran I.F.1.

Algiers, 10 September 1912

Mr. President,
   I am writing in response to your letter of 5 September.
   Travel expenses. I fully deserve the letter which I received from the
Central Committee. I deserve it because I am an imbecile. No one
but I would ever have consented to undertake such a trip with a sick
wife and three young children. I did it only to please you; I didn't

want to have to telegraph a flat "no." But that the Dardanelles would be closed the very day before we were to leave, that we would be forced to make the crossing by land, that the train would derail upon arriving in Marseilles, which particularly aggravated Mrs. Confino's condition, these are events which we could not have predicted and for which we cannot be held accountable. If not for them, the costs would not have come to half of what they did.

Could my wife and children spend four days and nights on a train without a place to sleep? Could I allow my wife to go without medical attention in Marseilles? I have been so careful with Alliance funds in other circumstances that your reproach of my extravagance does not affect me. But I wanted to clear things up. If I told you, Mr. President, that the expenses for the trip actually exceeded this sum, you would find it hard to believe me. And if I told you that I had to sell for 1,000 francs new furniture for which I had paid 2,300 francs in Constantinople—with the insurance money—because you would not allow me a few extra days, you would find it more and more difficult to believe me. Yet, all of this was done with the full knowledge of my colleagues in Constantinople. If I told you that I chose to do this in order to spare you the considerable packing and shipping charges, you would shrug your shoulders and think me a fool and you would be right.

Sincerely yours,
A. Confino

Archives of the AIU, Algérie, I.F.1a.

However, ultimately what held the Alliance teachers at their posts, in spite of the fact that with their skills they could have easily found more lucrative positions, was a devotion to their jobs, an ideological and moral commitment to their work, that transcended momentary frictions with the Central Committee. The same Confino who had been deeply offended by the refusal of the salary increase he requested in 1908–9, penned the following letter to Secretary General Jacques Bigart in 1916:

Algiers, 26 February 1916

Dear Mr. Bigart,

[. . .]

Your letter of high praise for the speech I delivered has deeply moved me; I simply do not know what to say. I appreciate your words of praise all the more as they come from a superior who is, I know, not at all in the habit of spoiling his personnel with such kind words. In truth I was only following the dictates of my heart in speaking of

Mr. Leven[25] as I did. It was, for that matter, a sacred duty for all of the personnel and an even more solemn duty for one of the privileged few such as myself who had known Mr. Leven intimately and who had been witness to the riches which abounded in our dear president's heart. Even Mrs. Confino, in spite of her precarious health, put forth an effort requiring more strength than she had in order to attend the ceremony. And this is a woman who has not set foot in a public place, and with good reason, since the fire in Balat.[26] This may seem like an insignificant detail, yet it says much about the feelings of affection shared by the personnel for Mr. Leven, and it might point out more clearly than could any speech the place that our beloved president occupied in the heart of each and every one of the teachers.

You ask who could replace him in the role of ultimate judge and protector. Since you have asked the question, allow me to offer a response. Is there any reason why you yourself should not now fill this esteemed role? You do not have children; would it not be fitting for you to found a family within the great family of the Alliance? I can already hear your objections: that a special aptitude is required for such a position, that a certain kind of character, temperament, and vocation is involved. In short you will object that you do not feel you have the makings of a Leven . . . All right, then, let me tell you a story:

It is May 1885. A big, young boy who is a little rough around the edges, or, to put it plainly, barely civilized, arrives in Paris with only the shirt on his back and an avid desire to learn. He shows up unannounced at Mr. Loeb's[27] door and asks to be admitted to the *Ecole Orientale*. The late S. Kann[28] was present at the interview. It was immediately decided that the candidate would be admitted to the Springer school.[29] An employee of the Secretariat was asked to accompany the boy to the school in question. It did not take long for the employee to recognize the material . . . distress of the young stranger, who had not eaten in twenty-four hours. Without a moment's hesitation, he reached in his pocket, pulled out a coin, and said: "Here is enough to buy yourself dinner tonight. The school will take care of everything after you start tomorrow." Make note of the fact that the employee in question was just beginning his career at that time and

25. The president of the Alliance, who had recently died.
26. The fire had destroyed the Alliance schools in the Balat quarter of Constantinople.
27. Isidore Loeb was a noted scholar and secretary general of the Alliance.
28. S. Kann was one of the members of the Central Committee.
29. A Jewish boarding school in Paris that was sometimes used to house and train future Alliance teachers.

that his salary could not have amounted to much. Yet, the whole
thing was done so simply and naturally that the boy was moved to the
very fibers of his being, and from that moment he felt a gratitude
toward that employee which has remained unchanged ever since.

The big boy was none other than myself, and the employee's name
was Jacques Bigart. I cannot imagine that he does not have more than
a few such actions to his credit; actions all the more estimable as they
are hidden. It has been thirty years since this story took place; you
see, that certainly does not make either one of us feel any younger.
You may tell me that many things have happened in those thirty
years. You are currently at the head of the Secretariat; the Central
Committee has placed unlimited trust in you; you could not divorce
yourself from certain of your duties. I understand that. The teachers,
and especially the older teachers, those who have already gone a little
gray, fully recognize the delicate nature of your functions and are conscious of the responsibilities which they entail. We completely accept
the fact that there are times when you must show yourself to be severe, even inflexible. But kindness does not mean weakness. Was Mr.
Leven, who was kindness incarnate, ever accused of weakness? Remember that everyone—by that I mean all of the personnel of the
Alliance—is able to judge the true tenor of your most personal feelings. We know with what gentle care you saw your blessed mother
through her old age, and it is generally felt that a man who showed
such devotion for his mother and who so faithfully carried out his
filial duties could not have a hard heart. In essence, what we ask of
you is that you listen to our grievances with some benevolence and
that you examine them in a spirit of fairness. If you then find yourself
obliged to refuse a request, we only ask that this refusal not be put in
cold, biting terms but rather expressed in gentle terms of regret which
might assuage any bitterness. In short, the Easterners are big children, who are best handled through an appeal to the emotions. Given
to an excessive sensitivity, they respond to the slightest word of comfort and encouragement. Good intentions, even should they not be
carried out, act powerfully upon them. They could achieve anything
were they guided with kind words. It would cost you nothing to try. It
would be that much easier for you in that you would not have to fight
your most personal feelings. You would have only to open up the core
of natural kindness that is in you. Do not deny that it is there. If I
needed any more proof than I have already given, I would find it in
the letter you have written to me. If it were only to thank me for the
ceremony, you would have sent me a banal, typewritten note. I would
have found that perfectly natural. What emotion did you follow in

writing two long pages in your personal hand? I can answer that my-self. It was the affection that you had for our dear president. While he was alive, you did not analyze your emotions; you simply did not question them. It was not until his death that you began to feel the intensity of your feelings for him and the emptiness that has grown around you. Seeing someone who was sincere in the expression of his sorrow and who had in some way reflected your own thoughts, you were touched and you told him so. Is that not a mark of kindness? Because I am opening my heart to you now, I will tell you that I had harbored some bitterness as a result of a very painful episode which took place in 1909.[30] All of that has been swept away now, carried off by the inspiring tone of your kind letter. There remains only the glow-ing memory of the story from thirty years ago.

What you have done for me, do for others. You should know that I am acting as spokesperson for no one. I have spoken with you hon-estly and frankly, and have revealed my innermost thoughts. What-ever you might think of my letter, I do not regret having written it.

Very sincerely yours,
A. Confino

Archives of the AIU, Algérie I.F.lb.

This is a unique document, as it throws a very rare human light on the withdrawn and cold personality of Bigart and underscores the close and deep ties of affection that could exist, despite conflict, between the leader-ship of the Alliance and the teachers it had formed out of the youths plucked from distant lands and cultures. Although Confino uses his "East-ern" origin to render softer the touch of his "Western" superior, the letter is a perfect illustration of a voice developed among certain key teachers establishing a certain equality with the members of the Paris Central Com-mittee. For most teachers, the idealism for the cause that they had ab-sorbed at the ENIO was determinant. The following highly romantic letter by a young teacher at his first post represents the state of mind and soul of the personnel who served the organization faithfully:

15 February 1929

Mr. Navon,
Director of the *Ecole Normale Israélite Orientale,* Paris.
[. . .]

The first days I spent here, when all my thoughts were still turned back to the school I had just left, seemed to reveal the immense abyss

30. The salary dispute referred to in the letters of Confino quoted above.

which was about to separate, in such a short period of time, two very different styles of life. I was sad and often allowed myself to evoke the four years of my existence which had passed so swiftly under your wing. We like, sometimes, to be carried off by our dreams in order to escape reality. When I would awake from these vivid hallucinations, I would come hard upon a reality that, alas, promised to be quite grim. Suddenly expelled from that small corner of Auteuil, where there seemed to be gathered all things propitious for the gentle opening of young minds, I found myself at the foot of the dismal Atlas Mountains. It was painful for me. The people here were as foreign to me as the land. Everything reeked of ignorance. The town, with its row upon row of dark houses under low, flat roofs, made me nostalgic for the sun-drenched park I had just left behind. Everything was in contrast to the vivid images held in my memory. The air was oppressive and dusty in the streets, which teemed with throngs of Arabs in their white burnouses and Jews in their black skullcaps. A more serene spirit than mine would no doubt have been moved by such a unique spectacle.

I resented the injustice of a fate which had tossed me into the midst of this crowd to which I would never belong. And I felt the bitter loss of each day spent in your school.

And then, later, I encountered other obstacles in my path, and I formed the conviction that this beginning in adult life had been so difficult only because it had really been a beginning. I sought out the source of the discontent I was feeling so strongly and I saw that it came from the habits I had formed during the sweeter period of my life. So many had surrounded me with great affection, had purified my life of all pain, and had not for an instant let me foresee what my existence was later to become.

Now that the calm has returned after the storm, during which I sometimes went so far as to rebel, I see that in reality life is really more constant and coherent than I had thought. What was, in fact, the purpose of that happy existence I had just led in your school if not the accomplishment of an objective which I knew so well? I was suffering because I had lost sight of this. And then I understood that I would never have known the school at all were I not also destined, upon leaving it, to know the goal for which it was preparing me. This goal, this mission, seems completely natural to me now when considered in the light of resignation. Your educating me was only a means, for you, of educating a thousand other souls. I finally understood the beauty of that and the darkness around me dissipated.

Since then I have penetrated this mass of backward Jews, my brothers in blood and in spirit, from whom my first reaction had been to withdraw. I have seen in their dull, lifeless eyes the humiliated acceptance of their inferiority and of their wretchedness. From their hollowed chests I have heard a song of hope that tomorrow their children will not be as wretched as they are. From out of these downcast figures, from out of the weariness enveloping them, I have felt rise a moving and tragic call for the help of their emancipated brothers and for a final liberation, through learning, from the chains of ignorance. I have come to know them and I have become convinced that it is impossible except through direct contact with this utter misery to gain a real understanding of the work of the Alliance, and to love it.

My first days in class were equally difficult. The first day, I found myself in front of about forty very young, very dirty, and very poor students. The sight of them sickened me. Their faces seemed to disappear under a blackness: they were covered with flies. I needed to start by gaining their confidence but my language betrayed me as an outsider. The room was hot and uncomfortable. Beyond the window a formidable wall blocked my view, the Atlas, a dark giant that rose to the sky. It seemed to have been placed there on purpose, by the same hand that had brought me to this place. It was there to deprive me of the sky and of my view of the horizon.

And now, it is a real pleasure for me to stand in the same place, across from the same children with alert, laughing faces. They crowd each other like sparrows in a nest eager for their spiritual nourishment. What was yesterday my prison has become the one place in which life holds an interest for me. Of course, this life is not one of intoxicating beauty every day. But it is true that shining eyes, furrowed brows, little mouths twisted up to stutter a few timid, mispronounced words which hold the truth, like the gangue containing pure metal, all this brings joy and consolation.

Your former student,
Signed: Eskénazi

Archives of the AIU, France IV.E.4d.

PART II

THE DISCOURSE OF THE ALLIANCE TEACHERS AND THE "CIVILIZING" OF THE JEWISH COMMUNITIES OF THE LANDS OF ISLAM

4
The Moralizing Agenda

The discourse of the Alliance teachers, including their perceptions of the Sephardi and Eastern Jewish communities as illustrated by their correspondence to Paris, was a highly ideological one. The representational framework of these texts is the product of an almost total self-identification with the Jewish metropole by this first systematically westernizing Jewish elite. The raison d'être *of this elite was its mission to reproduce among the very societies from which it sprang the path toward the West that it had undertaken. For the teachers, the transformation of the East and the transformation of the self were one and the same. The Alliance Central Committee's discourse on the Eastern Jew did not entail the "mimicry" embedded in its colonial counterpart, which called for the natives to become imitation Europeans, only to problematize and ultimately reject the end product.[1] It demanded total identity between the Eastern and Western Jew without bringing to the project the ambivalence, doubts, and restraints of the colonial system of domination. Hence, the teacher, the first product of the Alliance civilizing mission, became the Western Jew in terms of self-representation and self-identity.*

However, there remained always the nagging suspicion that the process had not gone far enough, that the truly westernized self remained always at a remove, and could not be totally captured. The hierarchical relationship with the Central Committee in Paris, the very role of service that held the teacher in his or her place, reinforced the sense of inferiority fed by his or her Eastern derivation. The highly corrosive critique of all aspects of Eastern societies that is omnipresent in these texts is inevitably linked with the desire for confirmation of the successful transcendence of origins.

The letters reproduced the standard European triumphalist discourse of the time with its West/East binary oppositions which pitted the Western "good" against the Eastern "bad." Every aspect of life as depicted in these texts became fixed according to these categories. Each thematic genre that constituted the discourse echoed this juxtaposition already imbibed by the

1. See the discussion in Homi Bhabha, "Of Mimicry and Man: The Ambivalence of Colonial Discourse," *October* 28 (1984): 125–33.

teacher when he or she was a student at an Alliance school and at the ENIO, and which was further underscored by the circulars sent from Paris over the years.

The central aim of the Alliance was nothing less than the transformation of the Middle Eastern and North African Jewish communities through schooling. The "civilizing" mission of the teacher was to spread the values of Western civilization as interpreted by the emancipation ideology of Western European Jewry. The Jew, westernized and civilized, would become a moral, upright citizen of the country in which he or she lived. The model was that of the emancipated modern Jew of Western Europe.

But in the era of Western domination of North Africa and the Middle East, the paradigm of "citizenship" was distorted in the direction of association and indeed eventual fusion with the West, which became the ultimate good. "Citizenship" and its moral benefits applied in practice to Europe only. The East had to become like the West before it could be considered "civilized" enough for the operation of Western models.

The task for the teacher was not just instruction but an education that had at its core a "moral" component. The centrality given to the reforming of the manners and morals of the population is illustrated by the Instructions générales pour les professeurs *of 1903:*

The true goal of the primary schools, especially in the East, is not so much instruction as education. Education includes both intellectual and moral education.

Moral education is provided in part through religious teaching and through the family, but it must be reinforced and developed by the Alliance teachers. Our teaching, on the whole, must be a moral teaching. Through hidden routes and a constant but invisible action, it must strive to elevate the soul and the mind of the student. It must develop a moral attitude within him which will support him and uplift him. One of the principal tasks of the teachers will be to combat the bad habits which are more or less prevalent among Eastern populations: selfishness, pride, exaggerated egotism, lack of original thinking, blind respect for wealth and power, and violent, petty passions. The virtues that one must try to inspire in the children are love of country, love of all men, love and respect for parents, love of truth, honesty, loyalty, dignity of character, uprightness, love of the public good, a spirit of solidarity, a sense of devotion and a spirit of sacrifice for the common good, application and consistency of thought, and the love of work.

Intellectual education, which cannot be separated from moral education, calls for equal attention on the part of the teachers. The principal goal of our teaching must be to have students learn to observe and to reason clearly. The sum total of the knowledge imparted by any teacher will always be extremely limited. The child will forget much of it once he has left the school. He will never lose the sound intellectual habits he will have formed in school: the art of observation, reflection, reasoning, the ability to control impulsive actions and to see through the chimeras of the imagination which are so powerful in the East. To these skills, the teacher will add a corpus of basic and general concepts about the world, about nature, and about human society. Nowhere are such concepts more necessary than in the East. The child must develop the power to break out of the narrow, limited, sometimes impoverished milieu in which he lives. He must acquire an accurate and lasting knowledge of the world, of nature, and of the long development of human civilization.[2]

The Orient was the repository of many evils, which had to be uprooted. The Alliance, true to its time, had no doubts about the superiority of the West in all aspects of life. Westernization was the path of progress, the only means for the "regeneration" of the "degenerate" Eastern Jew:

What was, what is, the goal of the Alliance in providing the Eastern and African communities with primary schools? First, the goal is to bring a ray of Western civilization into communities which have degenerated as the result of centuries of oppression and ignorance. Second, the goal is to give the children the rudiments of an elementary and reasoned instruction, to help them find a way to make a more dependable and less disparaged living than they would through peddling. Finally, the goal is to open their minds to Western ideas and to destroy certain prejudices and antiquated superstitions which have been paralyzing the activity and growth of these communities. But the action of the Alliance also, and primarily, seeks to give to young Jews, and through them to the entire Jewish population, a moral education, which is more important than the strictly technical instruction. The Alliance is less concerned with producing half-learned men than in forming good and tolerant men who feel an attachment to their duties as citizens and as Jews, who are dedicated to the public good and to their brothers, and, finally, who know how to reconcile the demands of modern life with a respect for ancient traditions.[3]

2. AIU, *Instructions*, 28–29.
3. Ibid., 94–95.

The teachers echoed these sentiments:

The Moralizing Mission: Casablanca, 1898

Casablanca, 18 October 1898

[. . .]

Moral education. The art of shaping the heart and enlightening the conscience of children is a delicate art for any teacher in whatever country he may find himself. This art becomes exceptionally complicated when dealing with peoples who have degenerated through a history of persecution. Where does one turn for support? To religion? But as it is conceived here, religion is the very source feeding a reigning hypocrisy; it is the ever-present arm against all reason and understanding. Should one look for support in conscience and human dignity? One would be hard-pressed to translate these noble terms into the common parlance. To an understanding of the intrinsic value of right action? One would have to be very naive to think that this could be comprehended in a country where lies and violence dominate from the top to the bottom of the social ladder. Fortunately, we do not engage in pessimism. If it is true that evil will always find supporters, it is equally true that good also has a penetrating force. Loss of hope is not permitted in those who, especially because they are working for the children, must more than any others remember that no seed is ever completely lost in the domain of morality.

Naturally, this is a long-term undertaking. The lifetime of a single educator is not sufficient; advances are marked more with passing generations than with certain individuals. However, there have been some signs to show us that our initial efforts have not been unfruitful. The ABC's of education have been carried out along with the ABC's of instruction. When the school first opened, our students did not have the slightest notion of the existence of such a thing as good manners. A laborious initiation was required even to get them to exchange greetings appropriately, to sit in a decent manner, to talk without gesticulating, to ask questions politely, and to answer questions without vulgar interjections. All of the rough edges had to be smoothed over; the external casement of their moral being was sanded and polished; the inner composition of that being began to take form. An energetic effort was employed to inculcate the love of truth in our little savages. We used every means available to us through the school to implant in their young heads the idea that it was useless to try to win us over until they had given up their sly little ways . . . To our great satisfaction we can affirm that, in the eyes of our students, the Alliance school is a respectable place from which lying is banned, in which fairness alone dictates punishment and praise, and in which the right to pardon is gained through frankness and honesty. At the same time, we are trying to open up their hearts and to make them sensitive to the condition of their friends in poverty. Here some very palpable results have been obtained. Some of the more fortunate students, and even some of only mediocre means, have been assisting regularly in our charitable works and have become an important component in sustaining these undertakings. [. . .]

M. Nahon

Archives of the AIU, France XIV.F.25.

The School as an Agent of Social Reform: Tangier, 1903

Tangier, 3 December 1903

[. . .]

The eradication of alcoholism is an elusive goal, for in places where attempts have been made with various methods to put a stop to this tendency, no success has been recorded. The results of all these attempts have been conclusive, and simple reason also tells us why: for there to be no alcoholism, there must first be no alcohol. One could, however, arrive at a restricted consumption of gin. But this could be achieved only through centralized control of the sale of liquor or the imposition of a tax. This method, then, could only come from the government; consequently, the school has no role to play in it. For various reasons, it is impossible for us to try to limit this tendency by holding lectures and conferences, which would be the only method open to us. Even if this method were practicable, it would yield no results.

But if the school has no responsibility to act in response to this problem, our responsibility in two other areas is evident: dissipation and, especially, gambling. This is not a question concerning only the uneducated; it is our own former students who are involved. And if the latter have a tendency to abandon the behaviors learned at school, and in so doing bring harm to themselves, it is due to a certain lack of depth in their character. They act on impulse. If they take up gambling in their moments of leisure and if they frequent the cafés, it is because they have nothing else to do.

However, if the school would organize evening lectures, these two tendencies would be held somewhat in check. A young man who is occupied with ideas that engage not his senses but his mind would tend to follow the fixed principles that come from a habit of reasoning; he would be less likely to follow his impulses. If he were busy with lectures and conferences and the small projects he would be assigned, he would no longer have the time to frequent the cafés. These measures would not only put a halt to dissipation and gambling but would also be advantageous in another important way. During these evening lectures we could train this young man to give short speeches on subjects of interest to himself and to his audience . . . And this would be a significant advantage, for once the youth has left the school benches, he is no longer concerned with the development of knowledge, because youth tends to think that instruction is of no importance if it does not have an immediate, practical application . . .

Y. Cohen

Archives of the AIU, Tunisie I.D.1.

The new power relationship between West and East as reflected in the semiotics of dress is one of the subjects of the following letter:

Westernization through Schooling: Damascus, 1905

Damascus, December 1905

[. . .]

Our students, on the whole, make a generally favorable impression. You are familiar with the frightful dress of the Syrians: a long robe of garish cloth, over it a short jacket in the summer and a longer coat in the winter. Their feet are bare in flat clogs. The children's robes are made of calico or a local cotton fabric. When these robes are dirty or torn, which, as you can imagine, is often the case, the boys have the repulsive look of beggars. We insist that our students wear European dress: jacket and trousers. They look better in them and feel more self-respect when dressed this way. This might seem paradoxical. It is true, however, that in their robes the children are more casual and less well behaved than in their European clothing. It would seem that garbed in their *imbaz* [the local dress], they feel more "Arab" and, as a result, more like all the other boys who have never been to school, who know nothing about politeness, good manners, or respect for themselves and others. Moreover, the effect is the same on the adults as on the children and is more or less a general phenomenon. A Syrian in European dress has an air of superiority toward his fellow Syrians in robes, and he is more aware of his own conduct than when he is in his *imbaz*. Therefore, our students in their European dress look more neat and clean, especially as we see to it that their clothes are always in good condition, with no gaping holes revealing their undergarments and no shirts hanging out. Every day, we insist that their hair be washed and cut and that the filth be washed from their faces and hands. I will not tell you that all of this is easy; cleanliness is not a dominant habit among the Arab populations. But with perseverance we manage all the same to achieve relatively satisfactory results.

[. . .]

You are also aware that the Syrian, and especially the Damascene, although not lacking in intelligence, is very apathetic and lazy. I think that there are few people who enjoy idleness more than he. It is quite an undertaking to require of him sustained work and constant activity. He always seems to be thinking: "Why should I put myself through so much trouble?" And so, he does not. All of the teachers who have worked here know how unusual it is to come upon a student who really applies himself or who takes it upon himself to study with zeal and does not need to be taken by the hand. In general, the students approach their work with casualness and boredom. They do the work assigned because they are afraid of being punished, but their hearts are not in it, and much of their activity is simply automatic. The few exceptions appearing from time to time serve only to better prove the rule. Because of this, the teacher's task is a difficult and thankless one. To be at the head of a group of students who follow you with pleasure and make every effort not to fall behind is a joy. But there is nothing so discouraging as to take the lead, even when advancing with the smallest of steps, and to sense that the flock for whom you are opening the way is not behind you.

At the same time, the students have good attendance. Those who run from school to go hang about the streets or the fields instead of coming to class are very few in number. Is this high attendance the result of the combined efforts of the teachers and the family? I believe this is the case. This leads me to think that if the parents were to exercise tighter control over their child's schoolwork, the student would apply himself more. Neither the father nor the mother takes any interest in his studies. As a result, there is nothing to hinder the development of the natural laziness of the young Damascene.

[. . .]

A. Alchalel

Archives of the AIU, France XIII.F.23–24.

Alongside the severe critique of "Eastern" vices can also be seen an occasional romanticized image of the "upright" Muslim, the noble native/ savage:

The Goal of Moral and Material Regeneration: Tunis, 1908

Tunis, 6 February 1908

[. . .]

. . . After a third of a century of constant effort, although ignorance and superstition have begun to be replaced with some rays of enlightenment, there has been only a superficial change in the sentiments, emotions, customs, and habits of our fellow Jews.

Their intelligence is manifest and their industriousness is widely acknowledged, but for what other qualities would they be admired by the non-Jews, the French, and the Arabs? I need not remind you of their servility in poverty, the small respect for their persons, the ostentation and haughtiness of their opulence, the vulgarity of their manners, their tendencies toward intemperance, their ways of thinking and acting, which are rarely trustworthy and almost always marked with calculation and ruse, and their distaste for the burden of hard labor, which is the lot of most of mankind.

These faults are not insuperable and we believe that there is reason to undertake and to vigorously carry out, first, the task of physical and moral education and then that of professional education.

In the young Jew of the *Hara,* whose ancestors have left him as inheritance only the precious ability to endure suffering and privation with fortitude, must be instilled all the dictates of the innermost conscience of a free man, born of free parents.

The first virtue which a rational education should afford him is a fervent love of cleanliness. One can never do enough to combat the negligence with which the human body has been treated. The human plant has not fared well in the shadows of the *Hara;* its body is thick and fleshy, its back is bent, its constitution arthritic or neurasthenic. It is time for regeneration. Therefore, a good amount of well-directed physical exercise will render our students more fit for the demanding labors of industry and farming.

Love of physical cleanliness along with constant attention to keeping the vigor and agility of the body intact will engender moderation and temperance in the habits of our students, and they will develop an appreciation of their personal dignity. These are qualities which prepare the ground for moral purity and such qualities as uprightness, frankness, benevolence, initiative, courage, and *sang-froid.*

Along these lines, our students have much to learn if they are to resemble the Arab or the Frenchman. The native nobility of the Muslim, his moderation, his grave and sober manner, the simplicity of his tastes, all these are precious qualities that our fellow Jews must acquire. The refinement of manners, the generosity of heart, the enthusiasm for noble causes, the artistic sentiment, everything that makes up the appealing charm of the Frenchman, should be given as example. Conceived in these terms, our task is difficult but not impossible. What is needed is time, perseverance, determination, and the support of personnel who show dedication and resolve in the face of this task and who are conscious not only of its necessity but also of its beauty.

[. . .]

L. Guéron

Archives of the AIU, Tunisie II.C.5.

Moral Education: Iran, 1910

Shiraz, 3 August 1910

[. . .]

. . . If it is relatively easy to put the different parts of our program into practice . . . , it seems that it is much more difficult to modify the moral character of our students. We are dealing with little amoral beings to whom lying, deception, denunciation, and dishonesty are qualities as natural as their opposites are to young Westerners. They have inherited these defects. In order to wipe them out, we must undertake slow, methodical, persevering, constant, unflagging action. This action must entail a constant struggle and must find its parallel in similar action toward the parents if it is not to be doomed to certain failure . . . And what profound moral satisfaction, what cause for legitimate pride it would be for our teachers to succeed finally in eradicating from the school population all the base tendencies we are given to deplore: envy, selfishness, immoderate love of money, absence of self-respect. These would be replaced by the opposing virtues: tolerance, compassion, a spirit of solidarity, selflessness, and personal dignity. When the day comes that we have obtained this result and have achieved this wondrous metamorphosis, we will have saved Persian Judaism from the profound degeneration whose pitiful image we now have before us.

[. . .]

E. Nataf

Archives of the AIU, France XII.F.22.

5
The Emancipation
and Reformation of Women

An essential aspect of "regeneration" lay in the transformation of the Eastern Jewish woman. The work of the Alliance was to prove quite revolutionary in this respect. Jewish women in the lands of Islam, like their traditional Ashkenazi counterparts, did not normally receive a formal education. The instruction in Alliance schools was an entirely new departure. The reports by the teachers stress repeatedly that the girls made particularly keen students and were better than boys in assimilating new ways. The custom in many communities was to send the boys for a few years to the traditional Jewish schools, the Talmudei-Torah, *before they attended the Alliance schools. The preservation of the literate tradition was an exclusively male domain and, even in the face of the onslaught of a new civilization, retained for a long time its own validity and specificity.*

The female domain was that of the home and of the folk culture. The receiving of Western education by women was hence seen as less problematic for the perpetuation of tradition. It was perceived as beneficial for the acquisition of new manners and ways that would add polish and hence facilitate marriage in societies that had come to culturally value the outer accoutrements of Western mores. Thus, by the end of the nineteenth century, many Jewish women in Eastern lands began to receive instruction in Western schools, which constituted the only type of formal education to which they were exposed. As a result, the place of gender in the transmission of tradition in these societies became an increasingly ambiguous one. There were many counterparts in the Muslim world of women who, like their sisters in Central Europe, maintained tradition and folk culture in the home.[1] However, as in many instances in Eastern Europe, Sephardi and Eastern Jewish women sometimes also became vectors of the most radical forms of westernization, bringing the latter into the home and

---

1. For a European case study, see Marion A. Kaplan, *The Making of the Jewish Middle Class: Women, Family and Identity in Imperial Germany* (New York: Oxford University Press, 1991). See also the articles in Judith Baskin, ed., *Jewish Women in Historical Perspective* (Detroit: Wayne State University Press, 1991).

*influencing the next generation. Westernization appeared to many women
as even more positive than it did to the men. Within the constraints of
deeply patriarchal societies, it worked to improve their status within the
home and within the larger society by creating a new value system which
offered a new, bourgeois sensibility that could be aspired to even by the
poorer classes. Though the new Western model still fixed women in profoundly unequal gender roles, for the educated Jewish women in Muslim
lands these roles were preferable to the traditional female domain left
behind.[2]*

*For the teachers, the status of women in the Jewish communities in
Muslim lands had to be transformed. The woman was to become equal to
the man in status, his equal companion in life. The "servile" state in which
most of these women were held was anathema to the teachers, especially
the female teachers, who themselves had escaped similarly stifling conditions.[3] Hence, the schools for girls were seen as crucial for the improve-
ment of the position of the Jewish women of Muslim lands.*

*The education of girls was also deemed essential by the Alliance be-
cause of its potential impact on future generations. It was the woman as
mother who transmitted the most important values to the children. If the
Alliance wanted to reach future generations, it had above all to educate, to
"civilize," the female segment of the Jewish population. This aim was
stated quite clearly in the* Instructions *of 1903:*

There are certain qualities that we hope to develop in all of our
children: uprightness, love of truth and of the good, kindness, and
devotion to others. In addition to these, there are certain special qualities that must be instilled in the young girls: gentleness, modesty, simplicity of dress, the desire to shine through something other than a
ridiculous display of jewelry and trinkets, the sentiment of equality
between rich and poor, etc. What is lacking in the character and in
the upbringing of women in the East and in Africa springs from a
social status much too old to be changed from one day to the next.
But woman is endowed with such a marvelous gift of assimilation and
responds so quickly to the slightest modification that relatively little
time will be required to achieve good results. We cannot recommend
too strongly that you give your attention to this moral side of your

2. For the impact of social, economic, and political changes, including Western influence, on the status of women, see Rachel Simon, *Change within Tradition among Jewish
Women in Libya* (Seattle: University of Washington Press, 1992).

3. So far, there has been only one study devoted to the female teachers of the Alliance.
See Annie Benveniste, "Le rôle des institutrices de l'Alliance Israélite à Salonique,"
Combat pour la Diaspora 8 (1982): 13–26.

task. We know that, in general, education of this nature plays a larger part in the girls' schools than in the boys' schools, and these few words are written only to encourage you to continue to follow this path.[4]

Although the aim of the teachers, like that of the Central Committee, was to elevate the Jewish woman to a position equal to that of her male counterpart, they rarely went beyond what was acceptable to the bourgeoisie of the time in Europe. The poorer women could be taught a few trades, such as tailoring, if necessary, but this was seen as ancillary to the central goal, that of educating the girls to become good mothers. It was the civilized bourgeois mère-educatrice *who would break the vicious cycle of the reproduction of all the Eastern vices which had created "degenerate" societies.[5]*

The letters of the Alliance teachers are themselves gendered texts. Male teachers wrote on a wide variety of topics, from the internal conditions of the Jewish communities they were observing to the current political situation. The epistolary universe of the female teachers was much more restricted. Very few letters from the women teachers refer to political and communal matters. They wrote mostly on purely pedagogical issues concerning the schools. However, depicting the condition of women emerged as a genre which became their very own. Letter after letter painted a very sombre picture in which the liberation of local women would be realized only through the Alliance. The female teachers constituted the first cohort of educated Jewish women of Middle Eastern and North African origin and were the first professional Jewish women in the region. The westernizing zeal in their discourse, like that of their male counterparts, was deeply rooted in the legitimization and validation of their own trajectories.

A "Feminist" Look at the Women of Fez, 1900

Fez, 25 November 1900

[. . .]

A year ago, when I accepted the post at Fez, I knew I was taking responsibility for a very difficult mission. My purpose was already becoming clear and I admit that the undertaking frightened me. Nevertheless, I was firm in my resolve and I answered the words of discouragement which were addressed to me with a staunch hope of success.

4. AIU, *Instructions*, 99.
5. For a detailed study of an Alliance school for girls, see Esther Benbassa, "L'éducation féminine en Orient: L'école de filles de l'Alliance Israélite Universelle à Galata, Istanbul (1879–1912)," *Histoire, Economie et Société* 4 (1991): 529–59.

My goal became suddenly more serious. I was to restore dignity to the women of Fez, to give them a place in society, to develop their hearts and minds. Such seemed to me to be the duties I was to fulfill. [. . .]

A few words on the women of Fez. You are no doubt aware of the degrading condition of complete servitude which afflicts the feminine sex here in Fez. The man is master here, and his despotism assumes the most cruel of forms in what concerns the woman. A woman is a slave who owes passive obedience to her lord and master. If you entered any home in Fez you would have trouble distinguishing the servant from her mistress. They both perform the same household tasks; they both eat in the kitchen. Only his sons are allowed to sit at the master's table. The daughters necessarily share their mother's lot. From the moment of her birth, a woman in Fez feels the weight of her inferiority. Whereas there are cries of joy and endless celebration upon the birth of a son, it is cries of mourning which welcome into the world the young girl, whose only sin is to have been born.

I must confess that as a woman and a feminist, these practices did not fail to revolt me, and I would like to have the power to reform this society, which is deficient in so many respects. Daughters are so loved by their father that as soon as they begin to walk and to talk, a husband is sought for them, a convenient way to get rid of them. This explains the deplorable practice of child marriages.

For a long time I have looked for the origin of this practice, and I can now state with certainty: daughters are married in their earliest childhood so that they may be all the sooner taken off the hands of the father. A daughter is a curse for her family, and the father believes he has more than fulfilled his duty toward her in giving her as slave to another tyrant, this time with the name of husband.

Was it, then, from this backward population that I was to seek out minds eager for learning and knowledge? Was it likely that a father whose daughter is the least of his concerns would take an interest in my school, trust his children's education to me, make the necessary sacrifices to pay for his daughter's schooling? Such were the questions I asked myself day after day, and ended up with disappointment and a headache.

Today, I can consider myself fortunate. The fears that I had have disappeared and I have the pleasure of affirming that these parents, who inspire so little confidence, can nevertheless be reached by means of the good and the useful.

There are a few whose minds are a little less closed than those of their compatriots and who have shown themselves to be eager for progress and, consequently, friends of the school. These are the ones who first brought their little girls to me. Others soon followed their good example and we have seen the number of our students progressively increase. We had twenty for the first few months after the school had opened. The enrollment is now nearing one hundred, which clearly attests to the success of our school. The Chief Rabbi, Mr. Raphaël Abensour, was shocked to see the school so full of students in such a short time. He thought I would have had a dozen students at most.

This does not mean I have satisfied my ambition, for quite a number of my little girls left to be married during the course of this past year. I can assure you, they left reluctantly. They would have preferred to delay indefinitely the marriage which was to deprive them of the pleasure of coming to school.

Several of these young wives implored me to admit them into the school but, as I think I have told you, I did not want to accept any married girls.

Some parents have already come to see me to tell me proudly that they have turned down several offers of marriage for their daughters so that these girls might continue to come to school. My ardent desire is to put a stop to these early marriages. This may not be an impossible goal, but it clearly cannot be realized at this time. Only a new generation will be capable of understanding the immorality of these customs; all we can do today is to ready their minds for such an urgently needed reform.

[. . .]

Miss N. Benchimol

Archives of the AIU, France XIV.F.25.

Religious Instruction for Girls, Algiers, 1901

Algiers, 27 September 1901

[. . .]

Religious education for boys may have been neglected or ill-conceived for a time; there has never been any for girls. From time immemorial the whole of education for girls in North Africa could be summed up by the old talmudic dictum forbidding the teaching of the Torah to women. At one time this practice did not have very serious repercussions; everyone was familiar with our beliefs and precepts, with the meaning of certain religious practices, and with the most important stories of our history. One spoke of nothing else in the family. Religious ideas came with mothers' milk, with the air we

breathed. But as European progress and the European way of life began to minimize and even dispel concern with religion in the home, the women no longer had access to a source of nourishment and support for their beliefs. They continued to follow the laws for preparation of food, and they continued to celebrate holy days and to attend certain ceremonies; but they no longer attached any meaning to their practices. They began to confuse local superstitions, images, and legends with Jewish dogma; and these local superstitions were coming more and more into conflict with their developing European culture. The idea of a religious and historical bond uniting all the sons of Israel had lost its most precious support: that of the mother, the sister, the wife. The danger became all the more serious as rival religions tried every kind of propaganda in their efforts to attract the more easily persuaded to leave Judaism. Especially among the young girls and the poor (although I even know of some cases among the wealthy), it is not unusual for the women to go hear what they call the word of God at Protestant meetings. Charitable organizations are set up to attract the consciences of those who have no defense; I need hardly mention the proselytizing obsession of the nuns in the hospitals. In some circles in the community there is nothing more natural than to discuss conversion; some even use it as a weapon when needed. How many times have I refused some request to a family only to be threatened that the family would then go talk with the "priests." All signs of moral degeneration are to be expected from an unfortunate population that has been too long abandoned and neglected by its religious leaders and too long tormented and frightened by persecution.
[. . .]

M. Nahon

Archives of the AIU, France VII.F.13.

A Sympathetic Account of the Condition of the Women of Marrakesh, 1902

Marrakesh, 13 August 1902

[. . .]
We have spoken on many occasions of the condition of women in the cities of the East and of Africa. Everywhere there is the same indifference to the wife on the part of the husband. Everywhere she remains in the background, happy enough if she is not being beaten or ill-treated. In Marrakesh one senses this unfortunate situation more so than anywhere else. Let us consider the case of an affluent

family, in which the wife is not obliged to work to gain a living. Her existence is not for that devoid of worry. She must not—and, in any case, does not—dare raise her voice to her husband. Her opinion, good or bad, is considered worthless, and the husband, a veritable tyrant, will do whatever he pleases concerning either his wife or his children. A mother must not even think of defending her children against the authoritative hand of their father. When the father thinks it is necessary to beat his child, the mother must stand immobile in her corner, even when her maternal instincts rebel at the sight of the unjust treatment to which her son, or more often her daughter, is being subjected.

It goes without saying that even in the affluent families the wife must never be seated at the same table as her husband and male children. On Saturdays and holidays a high table, surrounded with chairs and properly arranged, is set up in the main room. The husband, the male children, and the guests take their places around it.

In another room, a low table with only a simple cloth for ornament is set up for the women, the girls, and the female servants. Here the female servants are treated like children of the family and eat at the same table with their mistress. Naturally, the choicest dishes are served first at the men's table. What is left, if there is anything left, is considered sufficient to feed the women.

I have had the opportunity, on several occasions, to attend family celebrations such as weddings, Bar Mitzvahs, engagements. In each of these cases, the celebration extends over a period of several days and never in any case does a woman have the right to sit at the table of honor. It is true that in my case there was an exception to the rule, and the poor ladies looked on with wide eyes when I received the honor of being served first. This was a sign of deference with which they had never been treated and they could not have been more astonished.

Even in the most respectable families polygamy is permitted and it is not surprising to see the two wives living in the same house. Each one has her own floor of the house. And what is more, they often get along quite well with each other. I currently have in class two little girls who are children of the same father but different mothers. The other day I was telling the older girl that she should be nicer to her little sister and help her with her homework once in a while. What was her response? "But she's not my sister; my mother is not her mother." I have to say that little girls only see their fathers at rare intervals here; as far as they know, their only parent is their mother! It was perfectly natural that the two girls did not see themselves as related at all.

So even though she is not obliged to work or struggle, the woman whose husband is well-off is still exposed to the ill-treatment, the indifference, and even the disdain of her husband.

How must it be for the woman who is obliged to work in order to feed her children? In this case, which is more or less the rule for the majority of women, her condition is worthy of compassion. All of the work and all of the worries of the home fall to her. The husband, for lack of any other occupation, can go out and get drunk. When he comes home, dinner must be ready and there must be food in the house. He has no thought to the manner in which his wife procures the necessary money or how hard she works for it . . . Most of them do sewing; some have struggled to save enough money to buy a sewing machine. They are paid between four and five centimes per meter of work done on the machine.

The less fortunate of them head to a square in the Arab district early in the morning and there they squat on the ground, rain or shine, and wait for the Arab women, who bring them some item to mend. In this way they try to earn some forty centimes per day.

Others embroider shoes; they are no less unfortunate. When the Sultan was in Marrakesh with his retinue, there was plenty of work and they made a good living. Since His Majesty has left our city, these poor workers have known the blackest misery and the most unhappy of lives.

The water carriers are another category of women to be pitied. They can be seen at the crack of dawn, going back and forth from the public fountain to the homes of their clients with their jars on their shoulders; this goes on until nightfall. As payment for their work they receive only a piece of bread or a bowl of soup.

On many occasions I have admired the dedication and the strength of will of the women in Marrakesh. How many times has some poor woman come to beg on behalf of her husband? The husband has borrowed money from an Arab; when the loan has come to term he does not have the money to pay. The husband is charged and brought before the *Pasha,* who of course puts the Jew in jail, and here is the miserable wife trying to move heaven and earth to have her husband freed.

No matter how she is treated or how many times she is refused, she does not become discouraged. She spends the day in the excessive heat running from place to place and from person to person, dragging her children along behind her; she has no time to earn the money to feed them. With enough begging and pleading she finally manages to gather enough money to pay off part of her husband's debt. This money serves to hold off the creditor for a month or so, when the loan will again come due and the whole process will begin again. Such scenes are repeated time and time again in the poor families, always because the husband has gotten into debt.

And do you think that the wife is rewarded for such devotion? When the husband feels so inclined he can go to the rabbi and, for one or two pesetas, divorce his wife; she is left with full responsibility for the children. Other times the husband will go off to another town and never be heard from again. Then it is up to the wife to work and struggle to make enough money to feed her children. In light of these conditions our task was perfectly clear: to make of our young girls women who are different from their mothers. We think it essential that the lessons learned in school serve to help these women. Once they have developed better judgment and a keener intelligence, they will no longer be at the mercy of their husbands' whims. Their wishes and their decisions must count for something in the running of the home. They too must be allowed to voice an opinion on questions concerning their children. Once a woman has received some instruction and has begun to develop her intellect, it will not take long for her husband to recognize that in his wife he has a companion whose advice and opinions are worthy of consideration. In this way the wife will no longer be an object of indifference or disdain to her husband but a sensible companion who can advise and assist him.

Obviously we can achieve such results only over a period of time. For now we can make sure that the girls who have spent two or three years in our school will have fewer hardships than any who have not been with us. The counsel they are given on a daily basis, as well as their lessons, will, I hope, prove to be of valuable assistance in creating their future happiness. This is our goal, and all of our efforts are aimed at the accomplishment of this task.

Because of their work, the number of matters to which they must attend, and the ever-present worries of the women of Marrakesh, they scarcely have the time to take good care of their children. [. . .]

Education. What most surprises the parents of your girls is the cleanliness and the polite manners acquired by the children at the school.

All of our efforts in this direction have been crowned with success.

Prior to the foundation of our school the young girls one would see in the streets were dirty, unkempt, and barefoot; now they are unrecognizable, as they come to school every day perfectly presentable.

Even today, at the end of the school day, a good number of women stand in their doorways to watch the "girls from the school" pass by. There is whispering and chattering. "Look over there, So-and-so's daughter is wearing stockings and shoes; see that other one with the hat?" These little scenes are played out day after day.

At present our girls laugh about it and are amazed that, not long ago, they could have gone out of the house without stockings, sometimes even without shoes.

In my first letters to the Central Committee, I found many occasions to discuss the character of our girls: dishonest, sly, selfish. Those were the principal faults against which we had to fight. They would not hesitate an instant to accuse one of their friends, even their best friends, or to try and fool the teacher. Some progress has been made in this direction also. I am not saying that the girls are models of solidarity, cooperation, and kindness. But I have noted with satisfaction that there is no longer the same spirit of cunning and deceit among my students. Before, it was always a question of who could find the best ruse to get out of a difficult situation. There was joy on their faces when one of their classmates was being punished. Now they have stopped trying to trick their teacher, and when they have done something wrong, I am able to get at the truth of the matter, something that was impossible in the beginning.

[. . .]

Mrs. M. Coriat

Archives of the AIU, France XIV.F.25.

"The Backward Women of Fez": A Negative View, 1915

Fez, 22 September 1915

[. . .]

Here more than anywhere else the school must work toward the moral and intellectual development of the women, whose condition leaves much to be desired.

The women are by far inferior to the men in every respect.

Why is there this difference? Rare are the women who have been to school; those who have been stayed there such a short time that they were not able to truly assimilate everything they were taught. As a result, they barely remember a few words of French, and the education they received in the classroom has left hardly a mark on them.

Fortunately, those early marriages, which caused so many girls to leave the school when they were still very young, are becoming more and more rare. This is partly because the men have become more civilized and partly because of the women themselves.

All of the younger generations of men who have profitably spent a long time in school and who are either employed by Europeans or in constant contact with them through their trade lose through this contact the bad habits they had developed at home. In this way the moral and intellectual development, so fruitfully begun in the school, continues in these young men.

These youths, whose minds have already been opened and who are capable of assimilating many new ideas, want to marry women who understand them. They want companions who can share their ideas and work along with them, in every sense, in establishing homes, which they hope will be completely different from the homes in which they were raised.

As far as this is concerned, they are totally correct: the women here are, in general, quite backward. It goes without saying that I am not talking about the women from affluent families (alas, only too few in number) who have traveled and who have lived for a while in a more advanced culture, thereby adopting more or less Western ideas. I mean to speak about the women of Fez in general, those who come from the ordinary, simple families, in which life is lived one day at a time. These families are made up of basically good people, whose households are, because of the conditions imposed on them until now, mediocre at best.

These women have no discernment and no knack for the little touches by which a good housewife succeeds in making her home attractive and comfortable. In addition, these women are apathetic; they are ignorant of the most elementary rules of polite conduct and personal hygiene. They don't even know how to care for their children. As a result, the infant mortality rate is very high in the *Mellah* [Jewish quarter] of Fez.

Their treatment of children runs counter to all common sense; they regulate neither what nor when their children eat. This is true to such a degree that the doctor at the dispensary was obliged to pay for criers to make announcements so the mothers would know to feed their children every three hours.

As soon as a child is able to hold something in his hand, he is never without a crust of bread or a piece of unleavened biscuit.

After a mother has given birth to a baby, she does not give him her milk for three days; a neighbor or a relative who is breast-feeding feeds the newborn, even if her own baby is a year old or older. They do not know that if a newborn is given the milk to which a much older baby is accustomed, the milk will be too rich for his little stomach and too difficult to digest.

This also deprives the newborn of his mother's milk, which, in the first few days, is a purgative and cleanses the little one's intestines. As a result of this ignorance, from his very first days, the baby suffers from horrible colic and diarrhea, to which he is lost more often than not. "It was the evil eye that killed the baby," the mother will say.

Therefore you must be very careful not to compliment the mother when you see a beautiful infant; when the least little thing goes wrong as a result of her negligence or lack of hygiene, she will accuse you of having put a curse on him!

There is also too much negligence in dressing the child. As soon as he can move around on all fours, his little gown is rolled up and, as undergarments are not very common, he is left to crawl around almost all day with his little stomach bare on the cold, humid tiles of the floor. Once again, this produces the poor digestion and the diarrhea which quickly destroy the health of the children.

I could go on and on with examples proving how ignorant these women are. The school is the only thing that can remedy such a state of affairs.

The first thing we must do is to provide our girls with the practical knowledge they need to keep a house properly, to raise their children wisely, and to be conscientious in their duty as wives.

[. . .]

Mrs. F. Bénaroya

Archives of the AIU, France XIV.F.25.

The symbolism of Western dress is also a favorite topic in the letters on women:

"The Marriage of Regina": The Beginnings of Westernization and the Women of Baghdad, 1903

Baghdad, 4 February 1903

[. . .]

The whole city was talking about Regina's wedding. I should tell you first that Regina is one of our former students. People were saying, "Yes, Regina is *à la franca*" (the expression means "European-style"). "She is making her own trousseau with the help of a seamstress who comes from the West. She is sending for clothes from Europe, she won't accept jewelry from here, and her hair is all curled like a sheep."

The day of the ceremony people came from every part of town to see the young bride *à la franca*. As she was one of our students, I thought it important to go see her that day. The crowd was thick; with difficulty I was led through it to a room on the second floor. The young bride had just finished dressing. She looked beautiful but exhausted. "Why do you look so tired?" I asked her.

"It's because I've worked very hard, night and day, with only one person to help me." And tears began to well in her eyes.

There was a lady who was a friend of mine in the room; she came over to me and said, "Do you see how the poor thing has grown thin? Well! It's because she has had to fight; she has fought for every item in her trousseau. And it's not because her parents refused her anything, but because the things that were brought her were not to her taste. Her parents want her to buy a fabric which is too gaudy. She won't accept it. Or else it's an ankle bracelet they want her to wear. She refuses. Or else they want her to wear rouge and henna on her hands and to paint her nails black; she protests. Again today," my friend continued, "she sent for me to come to her aid. She wanted to wear her hair the way she's used to wearing it in school; they wouldn't let her do it. They were trying to force her to hang heavy gold rings on the ends of her braids. The poor girl isn't used to them; they would make her ill."

She started coming to school when she was still very young, so she has never worn them. "The poor little thing," I thought to myself. Finally the groom arrived. A rabbi gave the blessing. What a contrast there was between those two young people. In her white satin dress with a long flowing train, carrying orange blossoms, a net veil covering her face, she was altogether the European bride but for the few excessive adornments that it had been impossible not to wear.

He wore a *ziboun* (the local traditional costume) woven in gold thread, with a great cloak over his shoulders. He must not have attended the school and so had not had time to become a little civilized. But what difference does that make? Now his wife is seeing to that task. She has him wear European dress, she dines at the table with him and not in the kitchen, in contrast to all the other women in Baghdad, and against the wishes of everyone in the family, she dresses according to what she sees in the newspapers she receives.

She does not hide herself from visitors, even when they are gentlemen coming to see her husband. She has not forgotten the school, and, with the permission of her husband, she stops by from time to time to visit her former classmates. She takes as much care of her home as she does of her person. A short time after her wedding I visited her at home, and the house was clean and in good order. Even now she must often struggle to maintain what she has accomplished.

Sometimes her husband refuses all change; she is often mocked by her in-laws. From a distance, her husband's mother and sisters look upon her actions with apparent malevolence. They tell each other, "We'll see if she will be able to do this, if she really knows how to sew." They are biased against the girls from the school because the latter know how to read books, and in this place a *savante* [a learned person] (that is what people call the girls who have finished school) could never be a good housekeeper. But our former students are proving these people wrong. They have been successful in whatever changes they have undertaken in their homes, and now people are finding them sensible and capable.

Regina has a baby and she takes care of him well enough. The first few times she gave him his bath her mother-in-law ran out of the house saying that Regina was going to kill her child. But she does not run away anymore, for she sees that the baby looks healthy. She even takes pleasure in seeing him clean and nicely dressed.

This is a student who truly has succeeded, but how much she had to go through to do it! At the same time there are others who fail in spite of their great energy. The proverb says, "The goat cannot graze beyond the length of its tether." No doubt it tries to reach farther but resigns itself when it cannot.

In the end, these first students are victims, for it is hard to live in a house where everyone looks at you with an air of defiance. The struggle against so many people joining forces against them, against their ideas, against their actions, is very difficult for these young women to endure. Nevertheless, their efforts are not lost. What they have not been able to attain for themselves, they will leave for their children to do. A new generation will begin with them. It will be more enlightened, more aware, more capable of understanding the morality taught them in the schools. Here, as in all noncivilized countries, women are very ignorant. They do not accept innovations. They are like servants in the home but they always manage to get their husbands to do what they want. This power of influence is truly extraordinary. Because it is so, once this influence starts being exercised by the young women who have studied in our schools, it will serve to improve the conditions of family life.

[. . .]

Mrs. Dj. Douec

Archives of the AIU, Irak I.C.2.

6
The Transformation of the Social Structure of the Jewish Community

For the Alliance teachers, one of the causes of the "degeneration" of Eastern Jewry lay in the lopsided social structure of the Jewish communities and their heavy concentration in the occupations of petty commerce, peddling, and money-lending. The teachers, beginning with David Cazès in Volos (in present-day Greece) in 1872 and Samuel Hirsch in Tangier in 1873, all sounded the theme of "productivization," a constant in all the "enlightened" plans to reform Jewish society from the eighteenth century onward. Productivization would transform Jewish social structure through the promotion of manual trades and agriculture.[1] The return to "healthy" and "productive" trades and to the soil was considered essential to the program of "regeneration."

In 1870, Charles Netter, one of the leaders of the Alliance, founded the pioneering agricultural school Mikweh Israël *in Ottoman Palestine to train graduates of Alliance schools in agricultural work.[2] Many graduates were sent to this establishment and, later on, to similar institutions such as the agricultural school in Djedeida in Tunisia and* Or Yehuda *in western Asia Minor. They were taught the most up-to-date agricultural techniques in the hope that they would eventually become farmers.*

In addition to this system of agricultural education, artisanal training was considered indispensable by the Alliance. The project of Cazès and Hirsch of placing students with local master-artisans to teach them trades was quickly adopted by the Central Committee and made a standard feature of the school network. More advanced training was provided in the Ecole Professionnelle *founded by the organization in Jerusalem in 1882. This school, as well as the apprenticeship system as a whole, though not a resounding success, did introduce many new professions to the Sephardi and Eastern Jewish communities.[3] The concern for productivization remained of paramount importance to the teachers.*

1. On productivization, see the still useful work by Bernard Weinryb, *Jewish Vocational Education* (New York: Jewish Theological Seminary, 1948).
2. See Weill, "Charles Netter ou les oranges de Jaffa," 2–36.
3. The effects of the activities of the Alliance on the social structure of the Jewish

The Apprenticeship System in Smyrna, 1887

Smyrna, letter received in Paris on 20 February 1887

[. . .]

The number of boys placed as apprentices since the foundation of the program (July 1878) is 125.

Of this number, 57 have become skilled workers who earn a respectable living and 39 have not yet completed their professional training. The rest have discontinued, which is not at all surprising in the first years of the implementation of such a program.

The number of boys who have yet to be placed is 40.

Thanks to the renewed generosity of the Baron de Hirsch,[4] we will be able to increase from 39 to 80 the number of apprentice boys. This last figure corresponds well with the size of the population of the community of Smyrna and we hope thus to be able to gradually eliminate the state of extreme poverty prevalent here.

The number of apprentice girls is 45.

The workshops in which these young girls are trained, with the exception of the apprentice milliners, are located in the school itself and function under the immediate supervision of the headmistress. The trades for which the girls are trained are dressmaking, laundering, needlework, lacemaking, millinery, and pressing. This eminently productive program was founded in 1884. A few workers have already left our program and are now working on their own.

There is need to double the number of these apprentices by enrolling another 45 girls.

The maintenance of the workshops, including the monthly wage paid to the apprentices, currently costs 2,000 francs per year.

community of Salonica are described in Paul Dumont, "La structure sociale de la communauté juive de Salonique à la fin du dix-neuvième siècle," *Revue Historique* 263 (April–June 1980): 351–93. See also idem, "Jewish Communities in Turkey during the Last Decades of the Nineteenth Century in the Light of the Archives of the Alliance Israélite Universelle," in Benjamin Braude and Bernard Lewis, eds., *Christians and Jews in the Ottoman Empire,* 2 vols. (New York: Holmes and Meier, 1982), 1:209–42. The impact of the Alliance apprenticeship programs in Turkey is examined in Esther Benbassa and Aron Rodrigue, "L'artisanat juif en Turquie à la fin du XIXe siècle: L'Alliance Israélite Universelle et ses oeuvres d'apprentissage," *Turcica* 27 (1985): 113–26. For comments on the productivization efforts of the Alliance in Morocco and Palestine, see Michael Laskier, "The Alliance Israélite Universelle and the Social Conditions of the Jewish Communities in the Mediterranean Basin," in Simon Schwarzfuchs, ed., *L'"Alliance" dans les communautés du bassin méditerranéen à la fin du 19ème siécle et son influence sur la situation sociale et culturelle* (Jerusalem: Misgav Yerushalayim, 1987), lxxx–lxxxiii. See also in the same book the general overview by G. Weill, "L'Alliance Israélite Universelle et la condition sociale des communautés juives méditerranéenes à la fin du XIXe siécle (1860–1914)," vii–lii.

4. Baron Maurice de Hirsch was a famous banker and philanthropist who donated great sums of money to the Alliance.

The community of Smyrna gives no financial support to the apprenticeship program, due to lack of means.

This program is supported exclusively through the donations of the Baron de Hirsch, whose annual subsidy has increased, beginning in 1887, to 8,500 francs for the 80 apprentice boys. Half of these boys are still to be placed.

The trades practiced by our current apprentices are the following: typographer, coppersmith, bronzesmith, blacksmith, plumber, tinsmith, mechanic, locksmith, tailor, cabinetmaker, joiner, woodcarver, clogmaker, mattressmaker, painter, tanner.

Other trades for which training would be useful in Smyrna are marble worker, cooper, wheelwright, coachbuilder, saddler, watchmaker, stonemason, carpenter, goldsmith, engraver.

We are currently involved in trying to place some of our young people in training with the railroad. After a successful trial period, we now do everything possible to give preference to trades demanding both more physical and more intellectual effort. When we are not able to teach a trade of our choice here in Smyrna, we attempt to place the young men abroad. It was in this way that we were able to have three of our youths trained under coopers in Bordeaux. They have just returned and we will open a workshop for them. At this moment, we have three apprentices at the Jerusalem trades school and another at the *Ecole de Travail* in Paris . . .

Among the poor, the young men and women who have not learned a manual skill generally have the following occupations:

a) The boys become hawkers, peddlers, shop clerks, domestic servants.

b) The girls do day work in the fig and valonia warehouses or take positions as servants with Jewish families.

[. . .]

S. Parienté

Archives of the AIU, Turquie LXXXVI.E.

The Need to Turn the Jews toward Agriculture: Smyrna, 1898

Smyrna, 27 November 1898

[. . .]

. . . Instruction alone cannot feed our 2,500 students; skilled trades alone cannot improve our material condition . . . We have left to us no other means of remedying the horrible misery of our community but to channel a portion of our population to work in the fields. It is through a return to the healthy, honest, and fortifying labor of farming that we can restore our brothers to physical and moral health and, at the same time, guarantee their livelihood and the future of their children . . . we hope to be able to open an agricultural school near Smyrna in the near future. This will mark a new era for this community . . .

[. . .]

G. Arié

Archives of the AIU, Turquie LXXXV.E.

The Ideology of Agricultural Education: Mikweh Israël, *1900–1901*

[. . .]

Education. I understand this word to include both the theoretical education the students receive in classes and the actual physical work they are asked to perform. In a word, it includes all the theoretical and practical training they are given at the school. This training is carried out in a five-year period.

[. . .]

. . . Their bodies, their souls, and their minds must be molded and shaped in a manner to conform to the new life we would have them lead. In this struggle we must oppose the inclinations of our students and their parents, the demands of foreign advisors, and the fragility of the body. Their muscles must be developed; their bones, strengthened; we must combat the influence of nerves, which are, alas, too fragile among Jews. They must become hardened to fatigue so that they become adept at agricultural work. A complete physical and moral education must be undertaken along with the agricultural preparation. This can only be accomplished in the long term and must not be hurried. This transition must be carried out gradually and under close supervision. Five years is not too long to effect this slow metamorphosis.

[. . .]

In all honesty, it must be admitted that the school was not making any progress or establishing a solid foundation until the Russian Jews began immigrating to Palestine, settlements were created, and the idea of farming began to spread more and more among our fellow Jews.

A workforce was required in these settlements; help was needed in

the planting of the crops to be exploited. It was only natural that
people came to us for this help . . .
[. . .]
    The Jews do not readily embrace the idea of farming communities,
and the official administrative system has not yet produced impressive
results! . . .

J. Niégo

Bulletin Semestriel de l'Alliance Israélite Universelle, 1901, pp. 152–56.

Apprenticeship for Women: Marrakesh, 1902

Marrakesh, 13 August 1902
[. . .]
    As I mentioned in my last letter to you, I believe that we would
derive great benefit from a sewing workshop here in Marrakesh.
    Until only a few years ago the women and girls of Marrakesh wore
Jewish dress: a length of cloth wrapped around the waist which fell
into a kind of skirt; a sleeveless bolero cut low in the front which
served as a blouse. It was only a few years ago that women started
wearing dresses. There are very few seamstresses in the city, and
those few are not very good at their work. The more affluent families
have to send to another town to have their dresses made. Still, the
few seamstresses here in Marrakesh make quite a good living. All of
the families of moderate means come to them, and around the holidays they sometimes earn as much as five to seven francs each day,
which is quite a large sum in Marrakesh. Consequently, among the
poor families the mothers do everything they can to have their daughters apprenticed to one of these seamstresses. If we had machines and
a workshop here in Marrakesh, our apprentice girls from poor families would be making a reasonable living after two or three years of
training.
    We would accept in the workshop only those young girls who had
already been in school for two years and who knew how to read,
write, and figure. There are about twelve of them. As for the girls
from more affluent families, if they wished to enter the workshop,
they would have to pay five francs per month in addition to what they
pay for their schooling. I think that our workshop would be a source
of income for the institution.
[. . .]

Mrs. M. Coriat

Archives of the AIU, France XIV.F.25.

The Results of the Alliance Apprenticeship System in Salonica, 1880–1908

Davos, 13 January 1908

Trade	Master artisans trained by the Alliance	Skilled workmen trained by the Alliance	Skilled workmen who have left Salonica	Skilled workmen who have left their trade	Skilled workmen who work in Salonica	Apprentices in training
Brush makers	—	20	20	—	—	—
Chair makers	1	20	2	7	11	1
Cap makers	—	1	1	—	—	—
Box makers	2	19	2	3	14	4
Coppersmiths	—	1	1	—	—	—
Cobblers	4	16	5	3	8	4
Dentists	1	2	2	—	—	—
Picture-frame makers	—	5	—	4	1	—
Tinsmiths	—	5	5	—	—	—
Heating mechanics	2	21	5	3	13	—
Blacksmiths	1	55	21	12	22	1
Watchmakers	3	—	—	—	—	—
Lithographers	—	1	—	—	1	—
Marble masons		20	1	4	15	8
Joiners	10	107	13	29	65	21
Goldsmiths	5	7	5	1	1	1
Haberdashers	—	21	6	5	10	—
Pharmacists	—	3	—	1	2	—
Painters	—	2	1	—	1	—
Bookbinders	1	1	1	—	—	—
Woodcarvers	2	2	1	—	1	7
Saddlers	—	2	—	1	1	—
Tailors	7	10	7	1	2	—
Upholsterers	2	30	8	8	14	3
Coopers	2	4	—	2	2	1
Turners	—	1	1	—	—	—
Typographers	—	9	5	11	13	3
TOTAL	43	405	113	95	197	54

[sic, 385]

N.B. All the master artisans are currently practicing their trades.

G. Arié

Archives of the AIU, Suisse A.

The Professions of the Graduates of the Alliance
Ecole Professionnelle *in Jerusalem, 1914*

Jerusalem, 1 February 1914

[. . .]

. . . Please find below the statistics that pertain to our vocational school:

	a	b	c	d	e	f	g	Total
Blacksmiths/mechanics	107	85	66	34	24	88	4	408
Joiners	115	50	20	4	11	58	5	263
Sculptors	30	37	23	5	9	42	2	148
Coppersmiths	19	14	5	—	2	36	1	77
Machinists	40	7	2	—	—	—	—	49
Casters	10	10	10	—	5	14	—	49
Saddlers	6	1	2	—	1	3	1	14
Miscellaneous	11	—	4	—	3	6	—	24
TOTAL	338	204	132	43	55	247	13	1,032

a. Practicing in Palestine.
b. Practicing in the East.
c. Practicing in Europe or in America.
d. Location unknown.
e. Currently in school.
f. Have left the trade.
g. Deceased.

[. . .]

. . . the failure rate of scarcely 30 percent is not a discouraging statistic. Our students can be found working all over Palestine, Egypt, in Beirut as well as in Constantinople, in Paris as well as in Berlin, in New York as well as in Buenos Aires. They are in Rio de Janeiro and in Somalia . . . Almost all are practicing the trade they learned here with us; almost all are earning their own living.

[. . .]

Trades schools are necessary in all countries. In the East they are indispensable. The Alliance is pursuing regeneration through the instruction and the work of our fellow Jews, who have until now been condemned to peddling or petty commerce, either through lack of industry in their country or through the exclusivity of the artisan guilds. The trades school is absolutely essential for the training of intelligent workers, knowledgeable supervisors, and experienced employers. In a word, the school is the only possible establishment for the training of the leaders of a responsible and able-bodied proletariat. This trades school must accept only the best apprentice workers, hand-picked, and of proven potential. They will be made into workers and artisans in the most scientific and least common of the manual trades.

It was with these ideas and this goal in mind that our school was first envisaged. But is Jerusalem the place destined to bring these goals to fruition? In answer to this question my conscience as a private individual dictates silence. It is true that, as a technician, one opposes the industrial and commercial sterility that inhibits the capacity to form good workers at a reasonable cost in the Holy City. It is also true, however, that as a Palestinian, one cannot disregard the condition of the Jews in Jerusalem in 1882. The proof lies in the fact that Jerusalem gave Palestine its first vocational workshops and in so doing engendered the love of their trade in the hearts of those young people for whom the *halukah*[5] had been the end of the horizon. Still today, although one might tend to believe that the functioning of industrial factories in Constantinople, Cairo, or Tunis would allow for better, less costly, and less lengthy training, the reverence in which Jerusalem is held in the hearts of our fellow Jews is sufficient justification for the additional sacrifices which would be imposed if your only trades school were maintained in the Holy City . . .
[. . .]

Yes, in the Palestine of 1913 there are vibrant new forces unknown to the Jerusalem of 1882. But Palestine can be compared to a fertile field in which many laborers have sown a variety of the choicest seeds here and there, at random. It may be that the seeds will grow together in harmony and the crops appear healthy. Yet, where is the harvester who will be able to separate the good from the bad in this entanglement? Only an expert hand can succeed in putting each thing and each person in its proper place and in coordinating the organized division of labor. We must remain at our posts while evolving and changing according to the conditions of the particular moment and of our times . . .
[. . .]

A. Antébi

Archives of the AIU, France XI.F.20.

5. Donations from diaspora Jewry to support a religious Jewish presence in the Holy Land.

The Importance of Agricultural Training: Morocco, 1924

Tangier, 4 June 1924

[. . .]

Agriculture. I am taking the liberty of bringing this question to your attention again. You tell me that this kind of undertaking has no chance of success when run by your organization. For the present I have asked you only to accept the idea in principle; possible means of putting it into practice can be discussed later.

But is it true that you have had so little success in this direction? Until now I had been given to believe that the Zionists themselves had recognized the validity of your efforts. Certainly the results you achieved were not equal to what you had expected. Still, it would be equally unjust to consider them negligible. You have broken new ground. When it is the enormous moral progress of a collectivity which is envisioned, the extent of the material sacrifice required must not be an issue.

That is not the question. You have proven the necessity of a return to the soil for a certain number of our fellow Jews; what you have accomplished or encouraged for Russian and Middle Eastern Jews would be equally beneficial to the Jews of Morocco. Here all of our fellow Jews, all of the students in our schools, have their eyes turned toward commerce. This is all the more the case as in the last few years several men have amassed rapid, outrageous fortunes. Therein lies the danger for the future; the danger of disappointment, of misery for the masses, of jealousy directed against individual successes provoking antisemitism. It is an accepted fact among the Europeans that the Jewish community of Tangier is enormously wealthy. There are twenty families in high standing; they have automobiles, travel in luxury, and indulge in their pleasures with no thought for the costs. Two thousand families struggle to earn their meager subsistence; no one takes any notice of them. And whenever I mention that our kitchens distribute more than five hundred free meals daily to our indigent students, the response is surprise and incredulity. People are unaware that there is such misery in our midst . . . This is why I feel that our Jewish youth must be rescued from those uncertain occupations which perpetuate instability and distress in the families. I believe we must decrease the number of peddlers, porters, messengers, money changers, ironmongers, pack-saddle makers, cobblers, etc., and try to encourage our youth toward a healthy life in the open air of the country.

[. . .]

Y. D. Sémach

Archives of the AIU, Maroc I.C.1–2

An Overview of the Productivization Efforts
in Algeria, 1939

Algiers, January 1939

[. . .]

VOCATIONAL TRAINING

If the Jewish proletariat suffered so much during the 1898 crisis,[6] it is because it was not organized; it had earned recognition neither for its professional capacities nor for its cohesion.

For the boys as well as for the girls, the need for a program of economic regeneration had become urgent.

The Central Committee established such a program with benevolent resolve.

There was already in place in Algiers an organization, "*Le Travail*," which had been tending to vocational training for a long time and had even achieved some success.

Nothing is more in keeping with the spirit and the goals of the Alliance than to encourage private initiatives already being organized locally.

The Alliance hastened to grant a considerable subsidy to the organization, whose administrative council, a group of educated and open-minded men, could not have been more pleased to work in collaboration with us.

A series of measures was adopted that completely transformed the functioning of the organization.

It was understood that the local trades, which were overoccupied and not lucrative, were to be strictly banned from the program and that the youth in poverty would be persuaded to take up skilled trades, new for the Jews, especially those relating to wood, steel, mechanics, and electricity.

This program soon became so successful that it could easily forgo the pecuniary support of the Alliance.

It has trained a whole spectrum of honest, respectable, and capable workers, some of whom have had enviable financial success.

There are currently 21 apprentices in the program; they include 8 typographers, 4 mechanics, 2 engravers, 2 plumbers, 1 sheet metal worker, 1 coppersmith, 1 upholsterer, 1 electrician, 1 painter.

---

6. A reference to the antisemitic riots of 1898.

WORKSHOP FOR GIRLS

Parallel to the apprenticeship program for boys, the Alliance has founded a workshop for sewing, needlework, and pressing for the girls.

It was first directed by Mrs. Ruff, then by Mrs. Sol. It is currently being directed by a young lady who is herself a former apprentice. She performs her duties well and to the complete satisfaction of the directory, which is composed of some of the finest women of Jewish society in Algiers.

This program is funded through endowments and contributions. It is also subsidized by the Alliance, the Office of the Governor General of Algeria, and the Regional Council of Algiers.

[. . .]

A. Confino

Archives of the AIU Algérie II.F.1g.

7
The Critique of Traditional Judaism

The Judaism practiced by Sephardi and Eastern Jewry was believed to have "degenerated" because of persecution and ignorance. The whole program of "regeneration" was predicated upon a sometimes violent critique of traditional Jewish society and popular culture. The railing against the superstition of the local Jews and the fanaticism and obscurantism of the rabbis was a constant theme in the letters of the Alliance teacher. To some extent this was natural, since the raison d'être *of the teacher was to erect an alternative educational system to the one headed by the rabbinate. The dismantlement of the latter system was a corollary of the work of the Alliance. The rabbis and the teachers were rivals in the quest to mold the minds and souls of future generations, and the critique of local Jewish culture was part and parcel of the* kulturkampf *between essentially secular and religious value systems. It comes as no surprise that the teachers frequently referred to themselves as "missionnaires laïques."*

The radical critique of traditional Judaism reaffirmed the personal rejections by the teachers of Eastern civilization and their opting for the West. For a few of them, this rejection went as far as the abandonment of all Jewish religious practice, an action for which they were chastised by the Central Committee:

We must make a further observation here, one that has been made several times before and that is closely tied to the subject at hand: on more than one occasion we have received complaints about the personal and religious conduct of certain teachers. It is not permissible for teachers of our Jewish youth, representatives of the Alliance, to regularly offend the religious sensibilities of the people with whom they live through their marked indifference to the rules concerning food, the Sabbath, synagogue attendance, etc. Through our printed instructions, through our memoranda, we have again and again called upon our teachers to observe the fundamental practices of our religion. Nevertheless, we believe it appropriate to inform those who fail to respect these instructions that we will not give further warnings and that the Committee will not retain in their functions those teachers who do not conduct their private lives in conformance with the teachings they are giving our children.[1]

For the Alliance, as for the "enlightened" sectors of European Jewry in the nineteenth century that it represented, the ideal was a Judaism shorn of "superstition" and "fanaticism" and in complete harmony with "reason" and "civilization." This certainly did not mean a weakening of the commitment to Judaism. The Alliance has too often been criticized for having fostered "assimilation" to French culture in the Jewish communities of the Mediterranean basin. Although the charge is undoubtedly true, it misses the point that "assimilation" and devotion to Judaism were not seen as mutually antithetical stances by the Alliance leadership and personnel. The commitment both to European culture and civilization and to a Judaism perceived to be in complete consonance with that civilization was an integral part of the ideology of regeneration.

In practice, of course, westernization very often did lead to greater secularization and to the weakening of religion within the Jewish communities. The Alliance was not happy about this development. In response to evidence of growing religious laxity and disinterest among the communities of the Middle East and North Africa, the Alliance sent a circular in 1896 stressing the need to be vigilant in the imparting of the higher values of Judaism and Jewish civilization:

We would have cause to regret our work if its result was to snuff out faith in Jewish souls, to extinguish the source of inner happiness and fount of energy which have carried the Jews through centuries of persecution and oppression unequaled in all of history. The men who created the Alliance, like those who guide it at present, wanted rather to strengthen and purify religious sentiment in the Jewish populations of the East and of Africa, to give to our students, and through them to their parents, ideas of moral dignity, to bind them to all things noble and good, to deepen their attachment to Judaism, to its history, and to its traditions . . .

Our published instructions contain excellent counsel on this subject and we need only to refer to them. What we think is important to point out here is the obligation of our teachers never to lose sight of this aspect of their mission. To those who have failed to recognize this, we say: "You must provide instruction, but must always include moral instruction; you are preparing students who will know how to profit from the instruction received at school, but you must also pre-

1. AIU, *Instructions*, 98.

pare men for whom material well-being will not be the sole preoccupation and for whom self-interest will not be the sole motivation. Part of
your duty is to make war on prejudice and superstition, but your duty
also includes the cultivation and preservation of religious sentiment
and attachment to Judaism, to its doctrines, and to its practices. In
the esteem and confidence of the community, you will find the first
reward for your efforts toward making the children good Jews. In
them you will develop a nobility of heart, kindness, compassion for
the weak, the desire to be of help to their brothers, devotion to the
community. Selfishness and indifference to the general good are the
enemies against which you must fight. You could not fulfill your duty
with more dignity or give greater service to the Jewish population
than by combating these failings in the children whose moral future
rests in your hands."[2]

*Indeed, the Alliance began to be involved with Algerian Jewry at the
turn of the century precisely because it realized that the young people
there, attending only state schools, were no longer getting any Jewish
education at all. It had thought that in this country at least, now a "part"
of France since 1830, the task of regeneration could be left to the French
educational system. Growing signs of complete de-Judaization mobilized
the organization to create schools where children could learn Jewish
subjects after their day in the state schools was over. Only in Algeria did
the Alliance institutions teach exclusively religious subjects and Hebrew,
as a complement to public French instruction. A report written by the
Alliance director in Algiers in 1901 summarizes well the motivation of
the organization:*

Algiers, Annual Report, 1900–1901

Algiers, 27 September 1901

The work of the Alliance in Algeria owes its origins to the emotions aroused among world Jewry by the antisemitic outbreaks of
1898. Because its attentions had been focused in the East and in the
other countries of North Africa, the Alliance had not considered until
then that Algeria should be part of its sphere of activity. Was not that
country a French territory; had not our fellow Jews been, in 1870,
granted the honorable status of citizens of the Republic? They could
not wish for a more certain guarantee for their security, for a more
fruitful incentive to regeneration. It was thought that time should run

2. Ibid, 95–97.

its course and the civilizing contagion would do its work; thus, protected by laws and spurred on by French culture and institutions, a rejuvenated and emancipated Algerian Jewry would soon begin its life of freedom, its head held high. The antisemitic crisis of 1884 and the moral disorder that began to spread through the colony were already reason to give some pause and to temper the optimism. However, it was not until the terrible outbreak of 1898 that the true state of things was made clear. It then appeared that Algeria was the last country in which the Jews could aspire to a normal evolution. The Jews were stripped *de facto* of almost all the prerogatives of citizenship and slandered; the cynicism with which they were unrelentingly humiliated was like none ever seen before. They were excluded from society, in some cases hunted down and beaten like animals. A spineless magistrature sometimes defended them half-heartedly, sometimes harassed them further. In the end, the question became one of concern for their very right to work, their right to existence. These Jews, who had achieved so much for the economic development of the colony, saw themselves being trampled by a multitude of schemers anxious to do away with all competitors in their race toward fortune. They had been given their first glimpse of the French spirit, gentle and generous, in the schools. The liberal inroads which had been made at the time of the Revolution and during the nineteenth century had stirred among them the enthusiasm of neophytes. And so, their pain and suffering were compounded with bitterness and disappointment as they saw their ideal slain in its infancy. They were suddenly faced with a brutal alternative: either denounce civilization, at least strip it of all moral content, or denounce the vigor of the Jewish race, curse the religion and the very name "Jewish," which were the cause of all their troubles. It seemed as if this state of confusion had been intentionally prepared over the course of the preceding several years. Religious instruction had been discontinued, education had not been protected from any of the dangers specific to the new environment being created. The mission of enlightening the Jews had been carried out with the methods and institutions which were appropriate and successful for Europeans but of no value in addressing a race held back by history. Snobbery had driven our religious faith, leaving behind only a skeleton of superstition and rote practices. The spirit of solidarity, although not totally extinguished, worked only by fits and starts, like a flickering candle, and was no longer able to create any strong and lasting organization. And so when the fateful day arrived, the people found themselves with no support whatsoever, no anchoring point between their old society now in a shambles and the new French society, which was suddenly closed to them. The situation called for a vigorous effort; if rapid action were not taken, all hope of success would be lost. For those who had been emancipated and who energetically embraced the modern ideal, in spite of the contradictions modern civilization had demonstrated, there was a need for support. They also had to be shown that their moral being would not be whole until they also looked to the past and to their heritage. For those who had found confirmation for the old superstitions in the acts of crime and violence directed against them, there was a need to make clear that there can be no Jewish faith outside the realm of reason and progress. For those who had abandoned all in their desperation, renouncing both the hope of faith and the promise of science, there was a need to cry out that man cannot live unless he clings to something eternal and immutable. For all there was a need for hope in economic recovery through labor, so that the burdens of some and the poverty of others could be alleviated. Finally, and this was the essential point, there was the need for the creation of a place for peace and labor, a center for solidarity in which all differences would be ignored and from which unity would burn bright. Hence the work of the Alliance was established.

[. . .]

Religious instruction. Religious instruction had formerly been highly valued in the community; in fact most children received no other kind of instruction. The pedagogical techniques of the *midrashim,*[3] organized according to traditional Muslim methods, consisted only of rote repetition and group chanting punctuated by the crack of the whip, but the tirelessness and frequency of the work, the energetic support of the families, and the intensity of religious life in the home and in the community all compensated for the lack of method. There were very appreciable results. Most of the elderly and adult men of today have clear ideas of biblical history and of their faith, they can read and understand the prayers, and they are familiar with and can even quote sacred texts accurately. As the number of French schools grew and as secular education became more necessary, conditions began to change. The program of general studies gained prominence and religious studies were relegated to moments of leisure. At one time a kind of compromise was reached: religious courses were organized in the public schools themselves, taught after the day's classes were finished. This stopped in 1880. When primary education became secularized, a place for the rabbis was set aside in the synagogues. Their

3. In this context, religious elementary schools.

purpose was less to give the students religious instruction than to keep them out of the sun and off the dangerous streets. It occurred to no one to make an effort to protect Jewish traditions; the more wealthy families provided their children with some hurried instruction when it was time for their Bar Mitzvah; the poor were left to themselves. This situation finally stirred a few concerned men to action in 1894; through the leadership of Mr. Morali, a group called the Society of the *Talmud-Torah* was founded. They obtained funding from the consistory and started a school for religious instruction under the name *Talmud-Torah Etz-Haim*. With 6 teachers, 500 pupils, and a deeply pious and dedicated director such as Mr. Morali, this institution was already a great step forward. The people took interest in it, and half of the budget of between 8,000 and 10,000 francs came from membership dues and donations. The Chief Rabbi, A. Bloch, understood the advantages to be derived from this initial effort. At his request, the support from the consistory was increased to 8,000 francs. There was even a worthwhile attempt to reform teaching methods. But the regular guidance and leadership of a professional were lacking. In spite of his good intentions and efforts, Mr. Morali was unable to provide close supervision, and all of his devotion could not take the place of the pedagogical experience he simply did not have. Several incompetent staff members were kept at their posts because they were protected by certain members; the selection of students to be admitted was haphazard and followed no rules; no effort was made to attract students who could pay tuition or to develop a spirit of brotherhood among students from different social classes. The school was housed in an old Moorish building that was poorly lighted and poorly ventilated. This served to minimize the attractiveness of the organization. The need for a radical reorganization had become pressing. It was the Alliance that undertook this reorganization.
[. . .]

M. Nahon

Archives of the AIU, France VII.F.13.

The Alliance introduced postbiblical Jewish history into its schools' curriculum in 1892–93 to strengthen the Jewish identity of the students. The teachers had to use as guides the works of European Jewish historians such as Heinrich Graetz, Salomon Munk, and Theodore Reinach. By 1897, all history had to focus on events that had affected the Jews directly. Of course, this history was to illustrate the emancipation ideology of the Alliance:

It is our hope that . . . the teachers devote all their application and zeal to the teaching of Jewish history. The need has perhaps never been so great for the Jews to learn about their past, the long and painful martyrology of their ancestors, and the eventual settlement in their various adopted countries, which took place only after enormous difficulties and recurring periods of sometimes bloody violence had been faced. You know how instructive, uplifting, sound, and engaging this history is, and you also know what eagerness the children bring to it. Although our history demonstrates that the same prejudices have always been harbored, the same bias maintained, and the same abuses practiced against the Jews, it also shows that, in the end, human reason and the ideas of tolerance and love will overcome hatred and superstition. In our history we can read that always and everywhere the Jews must strive, while remaining faithful to the memories of their glorious past and loyal to their faith, to surpass their fellow citizens in loyalty, courage, honesty, and patriotism. Here lies the moral lesson of Jewish history such as you must teach it to your pupils, such as it must emerge from your lessons.[4]

In spite of the Alliance's concern, when it came to Jewish matters, the teachers remained deeply equivocal. Attempting to straddle many worlds, those of the West and the East, of reason and tradition, of secular, modern culture and Judaism, the teacher ultimately found himself or herself incapable of understanding or appreciating the civilization that he or she had abandoned. The very dynamic of the radical westernizing discourse did not allow for empathy. In the end, the rupture dividing the westernizer and contemporary traditional Judaism led to the latter's representation in the letters as devoid of any substance or content.

Religious Opposition to an Alliance School in Palestine: Safed, 1898

Safed, 22 December 1898

[. . .]

Safed had a boys' school for ten years, thanks to the munificence of a wealthy philanthropist. After having excommunicated this institution for a long time, the rabbinate finally came to accept it, for it knew where to turn in times of trouble.

The Alliance also tried to found a school here eighteen or twenty

---

4. Leven, *Cinquante ans*, 2:34.

years ago. A letter to this effect sent from the Central Committee to the community leaders of Safed bears witness to this initiative. This document was once proudly shown to foreigners as proof of the offers made by the Alliance to the community, which the conservative Safedians had courageously refused. Today, however, when an outsider comes by chance to Safed, his host is proud to take him to visit our school, in the same way guests in other places would be taken to visit a museum or some other interesting site. How times have changed, and how far we have come since those difficult early days!

When I first undertook the founding of our school, the people here were unanimous in looking upon the Alliance as an intruder who must be refused admission. The Ashkenazi rabbis did not wait for my arrival to resolve this problem. As soon as they heard that the Alliance had taken over the school, they pronounced a right and proper excommunication (*herem*) which forbade any father to allow his children on our premises under penalty of losing his part of the *halukah*. This document was kept in the archives of the rabbinate until the day when, like a bolt of lightning, it was to be hurled at the crowd.

The motive behind all this was one of financial interest, not religion. The administrators of each of these settlements (Russian, Romanian, Hungarian, etc.) take advantage of any opportunity to deprive their fellow countrymen of the *halukah* so they may keep a greater share for themselves.

The Sephardi rabbis were also motivated by self-interest, but they were more open about it. On the very day I first arrived, the leaders of this rabbinate paid me a visit and told me in no uncertain terms that I was to undertake nothing without their authorization . . .

. . . Ashkenazim and Sephardim, so divided on all issues, were united in a common explosion of fanaticism. And the same day, the same Saturday, at the same time, during the morning service, our school was excommunicated in every one of the thirty-seven synagogues of our city.

After that they believed they had crushed the Alliance, the school, and my humble self. Of our 150 students, there remained only 40. There was only one thing to do: it was a question of keeping heart, perseverance, and endurance. And we have endured. Now our school has come to be accepted by the rabbinate as a not too pleasant neighbor, but one whom it is easier to tolerate than to fight.
[. . .]

M. Franco

Archives of the AIU, France XI.F.20.

The Population of Fez Resists the Work of the Alliance, 1903

Fez, 1 September 1903

[. . .]

. . . We are held in esteem because people know that above us is the Alliance, which for them is a charitable organization and nothing more. But to join us in running the school, to help us in overcoming the thousand problems we face here every day, to contribute with us in the work of the Alliance, to show enthusiasm for the presence of these schools, from which they are the first to benefit and which put them at an intellectual level equal to that of the other communities in the cities along the coast and in Turkey: these things they would never deign to do . . .

[. . .]

For these good people, schools are a superfluous luxury. Only the poor, and not all of them, and some families who have traveled or who benefit from European protection send us their children. The others, the vast majority of the Jews, stubbornly continue to send their children to vile little *Talmudei-Torah* to learn the Talmud and the Torah.

So many times I have been stunned to hear people who are considered intelligent say that the schools are totally useless in Fez, that what children need to be taught first and foremost is Hebrew and nothing else, that these children will never need to know a European language. Several of our fellow Jews still consider our schools profane and impious places.

I was given manifest proof of this attitude on the part of the Jews of Fez, and manifest proof of their fanaticism, during the *maamad* [meeting of the community council] we held to discuss whether a new school or a new *Talmud-Torah* should be founded. All the important people of Fez attended the meeting. After I had read them the letter from the Alliance and stressed the advantages which would result for the community of Fez if a new, larger school were founded to replace the thousand filthy hovels where Hebrew is so poorly taught, they responded in one voice that they would have nothing to do with such an institution. Since I know that they do not like any interference from a foreigner in their affairs, I told them that the *Talmud-Torah* would be administered entirely by them and that our only responsibility would be to direct and guide the teachers. They replied that they considered it a great sin to bring 1,000 Jewish children together. To

guard against the evil eye, they told me, it is better to have smaller, unattractive, and pitiful-looking *Talmudei-Torah* of 50 to 100 children, where the evil eye would be powerless, than a large *Talmud-Torah* with 1,000 children, which would inevitably bring the worst calamities upon the Jewish community. For these good people, hygiene and good education are not important, they are afraid of the evil eye . . .
[. . .]

This obstinacy on the part of our fellow Jews in refusing to send their children to school can be traced to several sources. Fez is a city inhabited only by Muslims and Jews, all equally fanatic, all animated by hostile feelings toward foreigners, and enemies of any innovation. The sanctity of this place and the fierce fanaticism of its inhabitants have until now kept away all Europeans, the only representatives of progress. Furthermore, the difficulty of communication with the outside and the dangerous conditions of the roads have prevented our fellow Jews from traveling. They have not seen much of the world and are therefore not very appreciative of the benefits of education. To this must be added the persecutions to which the Jews have always been subjected. This is why the customs and ways of our fellow Jews in Fez have changed so little until now, and why fanaticism is still so prevalent here. And it does not look like there will soon be a change in these customs, which are so faithfully handed down from generation to generation and with which the Jews here are so comfortable and content.
[. . .]

                                                                J. Valadji

Archives of the AIU, France XIV.F.25.

Religion and Education among the Jews of Tangier, 1903

Tangier, 3 December 1903

[. . .]

The Law. It would be of interest, first, to discuss the religious situation in this community. In part, dogma has not been destroyed here, and it can almost be said that the Jewish faith has been preserved intact. What has served to conserve this faith, and this is understandable, is the relatively adequate number of synagogues. Each synagogue is named for the street on which it is found. And it must be said that these synagogues are able to maintain the profound faith of the people and for the most part the prestige of the religion. Here things are not as they are in Tunis, for example, in a state of decadence beyond remedy. For upon entering any synagogue in Tunis, with a single exception, one can scarcely believe he is standing in a Jewish temple, the room seems so much like a prison and the state of cleanliness is so pitiful. In Tangier there is nothing of the sort, for these houses of worship were built by private individuals who took care to see that the rooms were spacious and who keep them in surprisingly clean condition. Almost all of these individuals also built *azarot* in the synagogues; these are grilled balconies big enough to hold the women, who may then also attend religious ceremonies. Because of this prosperity, the faithful here are not overcome with a feeling of depression and are not forced to breath putrid and unhealthy air.

[. . .]

Teaching. The schools for the Jewish population of the city are private schools. There are schools or classrooms run by private individuals of all religious beliefs and all nationalities, except among the Arab population. A little bit of everything is taught in these schools, including singing, drawing, and needlework. For the small children there are classrooms or schools for both boys and girls. The Alliance Française[5] also has an educational institution here, but it is only for Arabs. Children are taught Hebrew in the home if their parents are rich or prosperous. When the parents are very poor and the children are not attending your schools, they are sent to the *Talmudei-Torah*. You have already been given descriptions of these small establishments on many occasions. There is always the same swarm of students, often dirty and sometimes barefoot or dressed in rags. They run and jump around an indifferent rabbi, who is less concerned with his own lack of authority than with the possibility of losing students if he demonstrates the slightest severity. However, it must be acknowledged that in all the *Talmudei-Torah* of Tangier there is much less confusion and filth than can be seen in those of the cities in the interior. They are far from resembling, for example, the extreme filth or poverty of the *Talmudei-Torah* of Tunis. There are not the same shouts and screams as the children leave, nor that indescribable racket raised around a child who has fallen and been trampled by the others.

In general, the rabbis are in the habit of walking home with the children or seeing that they are accompanied. They do this to avoid being held responsible for any harm that might come to the children and that would prove detrimental to their interests.

---

5. An organization subsidized by the French government to propagate the knowledge of French. It offered language classes in many cities throughout the world.

All of the institutions mentioned above, in general, serve both boys and girls and offer elementary or middle school teaching.

For higher education there is only *el Estudio*. *El Estudio* (the place of study) is, in a manner of speaking, the school of theology in Tangier; it is also the school of law.

It is a small room into which the light pours from two windows in the ceiling. In the middle of the room there is a table with a few benches. Next to this table there are a few cupboards which hold copies of the Talmud. That is the extent of the furnishings. Two or three times each week the Chief Rabbi comes to *el Estudio* to present commentary on the Talmud to the other rabbis and to administer justice. It is, in fact, in *el Estudio* that cases are argued and decided. Out of deference, the rabbis rarely give their opinions. But if the rabbis intervene only rarely, the *mursheh* intervenes quite often. The *mursheh* can be considered the bailiff of *el Estudio* for he is in charge of what could be called the summonses, but he also pleads the case of one of the two parties. As he is sometimes versed in the laws of the Talmud, he will intervene in the discussion and can in that way influence the verdict; he does this when promised a certain sum of money. There are generally two *mursheh*s, but these are not men who are preparing to become Chief Rabbis, for they are not included in the group of twelve rabbis who engage in profound study of the Talmud.

[. . .]

Y. Cohen

Archives of the AIU, Tunisie I.D.1.

Traditional Schools in Constantinople, 1906

Constantinople, letter received 27 April 1906

[. . .]

Any private individual who is without work and knows his prayers passably can bring twenty, thirty, or forty children into the small room which serves as his home, teach them the most basic elements of reading Hebrew, and, lo and behold, a small *Talmudei-Torah* has come into being . . .

The children spend one or two years learning the Hebrew alphabet, and as many in approaching the mysteries of vowel points; it takes no less time to learn to chant verses of the Bible . . . in a few of these schools, translation is also taught, a mechanical, word-for-word translation into an archaic, immutable Judeo-Spanish, which is often as little understood by the teacher as by the student. The translation is sung in the same melody as the Hebrew text.

In the larger *Talmudei-Torah* the teachers are better versed in the Hebrew language, but the methods of teaching are the same and have not changed in centuries . . .

[. . .]

The text and its translation are there to be chanted in singsong, to be whined, not to be understood. There is nothing more strange and more ridiculous than to hear recited in this manner the most vehement prophecies of Isaiah or Ezekiel, the delicious idyll of Ruth, or the fiery pages from the Song of Songs.

[. . .]

I visited three of the large *Talmudei-Torah* of the Haskeuy[6] . . .

Each time one enters one of these places, one's heart sinks, and one is filled with pity and disgust.

In a small room of between eight and ten square meters, on a dirty and greasy floor, there are seated from thirty to forty unclean children. With his stick in his hand, the *hakham*[7] squats upon a foul and grimy pallet in his corner. The children cry out the verses in high, shrill tones, each trying to outdo the other. They are accompanied at intervals by the loud, whining voice of their teacher.

Each of these establishments has four or five of these rooms.

On the day of my visit the weather was beautiful and the sun shone in all its splendor; a true spring day. Nonetheless, all doors and windows were shut tight. You can imagine how foul the air was in this building, where the children spend the whole day, from early morning until after sunset. I am certain that the windows are not opened from the end of one summer to the beginning of the next. I was unable to remain more than a few minutes in that oppressive atmosphere, which was rendered all the more fetid by odors coming from poorly maintained toilets . . . How happy are those little tramps I have seen idly wandering through the streets or running through nearby fields; they are fortunate their parents did not have what little money was asked to place them in these wretched schools.

[. . .]

M. Fresco

Archives of the AIU, Turquie LIV.E.

6. A predominantly Jewish quarter of Constantinople.
7. A name given to rabbis in the Middle East; also the name for the teachers in the traditional schools.

Representing Traditional Judaism in Algeria: Constantine, 1907

Constantine, 27 January 1907

[. . .]

The families of some means continue to send their children to rabbis who give private religious courses. These families are incapable of appreciating the benefits of a reasoned method of teaching or of a building with a healthy atmosphere which conforms to the rules of hygiene. It is only in routine and habit that they see the conservation of their faith, a faith built on routine and formalism.

There is nothing more saddening than to see the manner in which a religion of idealism and life-giving spirit has been transformed here. It is as if frozen into an inert mass of gestures and external expressions, which answer none of the needs of the soul, which resolve none of the problems facing our consciences at each step in our lives. Such is the product of the efforts of the so-called rabbis of North Africa, with the exception of those from a few Spanish-speaking communities in Morocco. In Constantine nothing of what constitutes the very essence of Judaism remains. By that I mean the open discussion and invitation to understanding of those things considered most sacred. For it is in this that Judaism is superior to all dogmatic and authoritarian beliefs, before which spirit and reason are supposed to defer.

Rites, words, gestures, customs, habits: this is the religion of our brothers in Constantine.

[. . .]

When the Jewish communities of North Africa find themselves swept up in the swirling current of ideas and pressing needs that is driving the modern world, they will be able neither to fight this current nor to follow it. Their state of inferiority, which is already so manifest, will only become worse. Inert and unspirited, they will be tossed about by the rising tide of progress, which, if it does not destroy them, will drag them along in its wake like hapless flotsam and jetsam.

[. . .]

I need not add that for our part we make every effort to respond to the legitimate concerns and fears of the parents by keeping our teaching strictly within the limits of pure orthodoxy. While we enrich our teaching with fruitful lessons in morality, history, and language, we fully respect the core of local educational traditions and conform to them completely. To make too many innovations in these subjects too quickly would prove more damaging and ineffective than to move too slowly. To try to reconstruct an archaic system from top to bottom, rather than patiently and progressively restoring it, would be to risk shaking it to its very foundation and witnessing its collapse. Evolution not revolution: this has been the direction we have taken since our arrival here.

[. . .]

Our school is divided into five classes, and teaching is spread over a period of years. The *petite classe* is for the beginners. Students who have finished are able to read adequately and can recite the most common prayers. They become more adept at these skills in the next class, the fourth class. In the third class they learn to read the Bible with the proper stresses; they are also taught certain notions of language and biblical history. It is not until they reach the second class that they begin to translate into Judeo-Arabic. In that class they learn about elements of grammar, declensions of nouns and conjugations of verbs, elements of language and writing, and, finally, principles of biblical history until the time of Joshua. For the first class, the program is as follows: reading and translation of the Bible into Judeo-Arabic and into French; reading and translation of prayers; Hebrew language; moral and religious instruction; all of biblical history and concise notions of Jewish history. One hour is devoted to the Rashi,[8] during the vacation, as well as to the Talmud. This is in answer to the demands of the population.

[. . .]

                                                              A. H. Navon

Archives of the AIU, France VII.F.13.

The Need to Create a Religious Leadership among Persian Jewry, 1910

Shiraz, 3 August 1910

[. . .]

VII. CREATION OF A RABBINICAL SCHOOL

Among the diverse institutions with which you may endow Persian Jewry, there is none for which there is a more urgent need than that of a rabbinical school.

In the communities of Persia, more than in any other communities in the East, the study of our sacred language has been neglected, the moral principles of our religion have been misconstrued, and supersti-

---

8. The commentaries of Rashi, the great sage of medieval Judaism.

tious practices have taken the place of religious beliefs. Of all the sound laws and admirable precepts which constitute the very essence and strength of Judaism, the only ones that have been preserved by our fellow Jews here are those that can be most easily reconciled with the satisfaction of their baser instincts. All that hinders and limits an individual's animal drives, all that forces some constraint on indulging the most ignoble desires of the senses, all this has been rejected, forgotten, banished. This profound ignorance of the spirit of our religion has led to a complete loss of faith. The absolute lack of religious restraint has had the most devastating effect on the morality and the mentality of the Persian Jews.

Another fact worthy of remark is that, contrary to what has occurred with consistency in all other places, persecutions have succeeded in weakening, breaking, and destroying the faith of the Jews in Iran rather than making it stronger. It is distressing to see with what remarkable ease, and under no duress at all, the Jews of Iran abandon the religion of their ancestors and convert to Islam. The first instinct of a Jew who has been pestered by his creditors, a woman who is unhappy with her husband and cannot procure a divorce, a son who is tired of submitting to his father's authority, or a young woman who has had enough of her parents' supervision is to go to a *mushtehed* (high priest) and ask to be accepted into the Islamic religion. There is no need to add that the eagerness with which such a request is welcomed is quite touching and that the postulant is certainly not left the time to change his mind.

Although conversion may not provide the convert much spiritual satisfaction, he benefits from appreciable material advantages. Conversion rehabilitates him, cleanses him, washes away all previous sin in the eyes of the judiciary; he becomes as white as the cloak of the Prophet. He receives the most kindly attention from his new brothers in religion, who work hard, at least in the days following his conversion, to ensure that he does not regret his noble deed.

This lamentable state of affairs is due in large part to the fact that for a long time there have been no religious leaders directing the communities of Jews in Persia. There has been no spiritual guidance from men who through their knowledge, their piety, and the dignity of their lives have enough moral authority in the community to maintain respect for our laws and loyalty to our faith. And this fact itself is the result of the isolation of the Jews in Persia from the rest of Judaism. The great obstacles and difficulties in communication have in fact stopped the flow of all intellectual movements among the Jews in Palestine or in the West from reaching the Jews in Iran. In the eigh-

teenth century, during the reign of the great Shah Abbas, a few rabbis, poets, and chroniclers tried to revive Hebrew studies and to create a Jewish literature in Persia. But the terrible persecutions, ordered
by that same monarch, totally destroyed this attempted intellectual
renaissance. Since then Jewish life in Persia has crumbled and declined. You cannot imagine to what degree the religious leaders in
these communities today are ignorant and unworthy of their vocation.

By creating a rabbinical school in this country and by training rabbis who are educated, enlightened, conscious of their duties, and capable, through their moral strength, of spiritually guiding the communities with which you would entrust them, you will rescue Persian Jewry
from the total decay with which it is threatened.
[. . .]

E. Nataf

Archives of the AIU, France XII.F.22.

De-Judaization among the Jews of Tunisia and the Steps Needed to Fight It: Sousse, 1929

Sousse, 7 October 1929

[. . .]

After nearly half a century of French occupation, what have been
the consequences? They are manifest and can only fill us with anxiety
for the present and sorrowful concern for the future.

If I consider in particular the city of Sousse, whose community is
the second largest in population in the Regency, what observations
can be made?

Hebrew instruction for children, which was highly valued in the
time preceding the arrival of the Alliance, can be said to be nonexistent. The *Keter-Torah* [the traditional Jewish school], which had been
functioning there for about twenty years, is now completely deserted.
Although it is true that on Thursdays and Sundays, as well as during
the school holidays, a few children do wander in, they do nothing of
value there. This has been attested by the very notables and members
of the committee who belong to this society.

The children are ignorant of all that represents the beauty and
uniqueness of our doctrine; they have no notion of biblical history or
of Jewish history; they are totally unaware that a modern Jewish literature exists. How can these children love and practice their religion;
how can they form a bond with their past?

I have observed the youth of Sousse in the temples on *Kipur,* which
is the only day of the year on which they come to the temple in great

numbers. They come only through habit or superstitious fears. Indeed, during the other feast days, on Saturdays, and for good reason on weekdays, only a very few faithful can be seen in the temple; these are usually old men in turbans. What I saw, then, on *Kipur* greatly enlightened me.

These young people come into the house of God. Wrapped in their *talit*s [prayer shawls] they approach the tabernacle and, with devotion, kiss the cloth covering it. The father or grandfather who has seen his son or grandson gestures to him. The young man advances, takes the prayer book which is presented to him, and sitting, or most often remaining standing, he tries to follow the service . . . but as he cannot read as quickly as the officiant, and as he is not drawn to this fastidious reading, which speaks neither to his mind nor to his soul, he soon withdraws to the terrace adjoining the temple, where he finds other young people already gathered.

Finding the air in the room a little stifling, and also pushed by curiosity, I myself go out to the terrace for a moment. It is like entering a public meeting place. Everyone has closed his book, circles of people have formed, and there is chatting, yawning, jesting, laughing. In the evening, more than three-fifths of those attending services are gathered on the terrace. Those who remain in the place of prayer are elderly men. These men alone feel it their duty to follow the various services to their conclusion on this solemn day.

Let us consider the cafés on Saturdays. They are literally invaded by Jews. With few exceptions, all are smoking, gambling—often for large sums of money—at cards or at backgammon, or discussing business.

And let us consider a house in mourning where there is grief over the loss of a respected father or a beloved mother. We first hear a *drashah*,[9] delivered by a rabbi who tries to inspire us with an avalanche of citations from the Bible or from the Talmud; the logic with which he strings them together is not always clear. After this, we see the sons form a circle around the preacher as they try to read, or rather mouth the words to, the required *Kadish*.[10]

I could provide many more examples, but I have said enough to create a true picture of the situation.

[. . .]

In short, there is a desertion of the synagogues, an almost complete

9. A disquisition on the Holy Scriptures.
10. A traditional prayer to commemorate the dead.

ignorance of the religion and of the Jewish past, a lack of observance of religious practices, an extreme decline in sacred studies, a continual decrease in the number of doctors in the Law, and a decrease in the number of sacrificers and others who hold special functions in our faith.

Can we remain indifferent to these observations? Can we imagine the abyss into which our communities will have been swallowed twenty or thirty years from now if some superior strength is not to intervene energetically in reaction to those erring ways?

Already, mixed marriages are becoming common. The conversion to Protestantism of an entire family still living in Sousse has been registered (I shall not even mention those that have taken place elsewhere, especially in Tunis, Bizerte, and very recently in Sfax). Is it not to be feared that this detachment from old traditions and these apostasies will become ever stronger and ever more frequent, until one day we will see the collapse of that ancient edifice raised by the respectable ancestors of these lost Jews?

[. . .]

What these failing communities need above all and without delay is the establishment of Alliance schools (for boys, girls, and younger children, as was discussed above). In these schools, where the facilities would be perfectly adapted to their needs, the young Jewish children would receive both a general education, in all respects as good as what they are currently receiving in the public schools, and the moral and religious education of which they are currently almost totally deprived.

The initiative must be forcefully undertaken to restructure these communities and to charge their welfare agencies, which currently handle only administrative issues, with the responsibility for the direction of centers of Hebrew education.

There is a need for the founding of *yeshivot*[11] and for the encouragement of theological studies. To this effect, the seminary in Tunis should be reopened; if it is well organized and well directed, it will fill a crucial void in the community.

Finally, there is a need to create a rabbinical corps whose members, with an adequate modern education, would be seriously trained in the study of the Law so that they may become pastors whose voices are heard and respected.

This is a vast and complex program, but one of high moral aims. We must not be frightened by the extent and the diversity of

11. Academies of higher Jewish religious instruction.

the tasks to be undertaken. The very preservation of Tunisian Jewry, which now shows so many signs of degeneration, depends on this undertaking.

The tireless activity, constant involvement, and prodigious efforts of the Alliance have had a profound effect on the intellectual and moral development of the numerous generations it has educated and on the economic development of the principal communities of this country. It is the duty of the Alliance to lend its support in the accomplishment of this undertaking and in the restoration of Tunisian Jewry.

Only the Alliance has enough prestige to impose its views on those communities that are so lacking in organization and so often torn apart by internal struggles.

[. . .]

L. Loubaton

Archives of the AIU, France VII.F.14.

8
The War Of Languages

In spite of the Alliance's concern for a proper appreciation of Judaism in its schools, the teaching of Hebrew remained a problem. In order to blunt opposition, local rabbis were recruited to teach Hebrew and other Jewish subjects, such as religion. The Alliance teachers, though having a good command of Hebrew as a result of their studies in Paris, were not trained to teach the language and were too burdened by the teaching of other subjects to devote much time to Hebrew. On the other hand, the local teachers of Hebrew had not been exposed to modern methods of pedagogy, which the teachers of French and other subjects had studied during their stay at the ENIO. As a result, Hebrew does not appear to have been a favorite subject for the students. It was compared unfavorably to French, which was taught according to the latest methods. The coexistence of two alternative systems of education in the same school, with one receiving all the attention and the other relegated to the background, did not prove beneficial to the teaching of Hebrew, which was eclipsed by French.

From the turn of the century on, the Alliance was increasingly attacked by Zionists over its neglect of Hebrew. Several inspections confirmed that this subject could be better taught in the schools if the local rabbis were replaced by Hebrew teachers.[1] But the Alliance was afraid that these teachers, influenced by the movement to revive the old language, would become propagators of Zionism. A Hebrew teacher-training school for the organization was established only in 1952 in Morocco.[2]

Furthermore, other Jewish languages such as Yiddish, Judeo-Spanish, Judeo-Arabic, and Judeo-Persian were disparaged by the Alliance. Echoing the "enlightened" elements of European Jewry, the organization considered these languages mere "jargons." They were viewed as corrupt

---

1. See, e.g., the findings of the Lévi-Porgès inspection mission of 1908 in the *Bulletin Semestriel de l'Alliance Israélite Universelle* 33 (1908): 34–35. This mission has been studied by Lucien Lazare in his "L'Alliance Israélite Universelle en Palestine à l'époque de la révolution des 'Jeunes Turcs' et sa mission en Orient du 29 octobre 1908 au 19 janvier 1909," *Revue des Etudes Juives* 138 (July–December 1979): 307–35.

2. Michael M. Laskier, *The Alliance Israélite Universelle and the Jewish Communities of Morocco, 1862–1962* (Albany, N.Y.: SUNY Press, 1983), 241–47.

mixtures of several idioms and as hindering the cultural evolution of Jewish society, and thus had to be eradicated.

Indeed, a functional hierarchy can be seen in the linguistic education dispensed in the Alliance schools. Hebrew was taught to enable understanding of the Bible and the Jewish prayer book. It had a primarily religious function and was not meant to be learned as a living language for use outside the religious realm. Local languages such as Turkish or Persian were taught to facilitate the eventual integration of the Jews in their home countries and to prepare the ground for full emancipation as well as to increase career opportunities in the local bureaucracies. However, as in the case of Hebrew, the Alliance could not find qualified personnel to teach local languages and was not really prepared to devote enough time to them in the school curriculum to make the effort especially successful.

The major priority for the Alliance and its teachers was the teaching of French. Not only was French seen as an important lingua franca, *whose acquisition would constitute a considerable advantage in trade and commerce, but it also had a moral function. It was the language of civilization* par excellence, *and was the main conduit through which the students would come to appreciate Western culture and civilization. The whole task of regeneration was predicated on learning French, through which the loftier values of the superior culture could be imparted. Nothing was permitted to impinge upon the centrality enjoyed by French in the school curricula.*

French to Replace the Local "Jargon": Casablanca, 1898

Casablanca, 18 October 1898

[. . .]

We must not lose sight of the fact that there is nothing more difficult than the study of French for the children who speak popular Arabic; the very spirit of their maternal dialect is so distant from the European spirit! The sounds, the expressions, and the ideas of the two languages clash when they come into contact. If the idiom popularly spoken here [among the Jews] were even closer to Arabic, our task would be much easier! But it is a jargon, a jumble of expressions from Arabic, Chaldean, Spanish, even Berber, composed without logic, mixed together in a small number of molds so narrowly formed that it is impossible to pour a new idea into them. There is not room enough for thought to function, only a very limited stock of clichés, applied more or less aptly to the diverse circumstances of life. There is no base to work from: ideas, words, and constructions must be created whole. It is a constant struggle to counter the unfortunate deformations of the ear. To our students *shé, zé,* and *ssé* are the same sound; *é, i,* and *a* are interchangeable. As it is useless to ask them to listen to the difference in sound, we have to resort to the visual. We are forced to gesticulate, to exaggerate the movements of the mouth, sometimes to physically shape the student's mouth with our hands to get him to imitate the sounds. It is desperately tedious work and it takes up much of our precious time. Once they have learned to distinguish and reproduce sounds more or less accurately, it is time to begin teaching expressions. Here we keep strictly to French from the beginning. It is imperative that their jargon be completely discarded, that translation be forbidden, and that the French form be imposed in its direct relation to the object, the gesture, or the action to be expressed. The methods developed by Mr. Fresco[3] for the teaching of written and spoken French have been invaluable to us in this endeavor.

Our students from Tangier and Tetuan easily surpass their classmates in all subjects because they have a better ear, their articulatory organs are more supple, and their vocabulary is much richer and much closer to French.[4]

[. . .]

M. Nahon

Archives of the AIU, France XIV.F.25.

The Corrupted Language of the Jews of Tangier, 1903

Tangier, 3 December 1903

[. . .]

Language. The language spoken locally is a form of corrupted Spanish. It is a veritable amalgam, in which Spanish is predominant; but to this Judeo-Spanish tongue have been added Hispanicized Arabic words; verbs and expressions borrowed from Arabic and Hebrew complete the bizarre mixture. This language is even more corrupted among the immigrants from the interior, who have already begun to assimilate to their fellow Jews here. Their accent is deplorable and they pronounce certain letters differently. One could posit with a high degree of certainty that the Judeo-Hispanic-Arabic language is spoken by more than two-thirds of the entire community. Those who know a relatively pure Spanish use it naturally in conversation, resorting to

---

3. An Alliance teacher in Constantinople who wrote several manuals widely adopted as textbooks by the Alliance schools.
4. The mother tongue of most of the Jews of these two cities was Judeo-Spanish.

the other language when dealing with others who would not understand them were they to speak correctly.
[. . .]

Y. Cohen

Archives of the AIU, Tunisie I.D.1.

The Traditional Method of Teaching Hebrew
and the Improvements Made by the Alliance:
Constantine, 1907

Constantine, 27 January 1907

[. . .]

PROGRAM AND METHOD

First, we made it our duty to maintain in our teaching all that was
useful and intelligent in the traditional rabbinical method, for, in spite
of the antiquated and outmoded nature of certain aspects of this teaching, as a whole the pedagogical practices instituted by the rabbinical
method and propagated throughout the Jewish world constitute a system and process that must not necessarily be totally rejected, or even
ignored. Indeed, a close examination of this method left to us by
tradition reveals a certain logic . . . Let us consider the teaching of
reading, for example. We note that there is a certain order and structure to it. The instructor teaches the children to identify letters, first
teaching them to discriminate between letters which have a certain
morphological resemblance . . . After the letters, the vowel points
. . . , then comes instruction in the manner of joining the letter to its
vowel, in the spelling of syllables, in putting syllables together, and
finally in the pronunciation of words. This is how I learned to read
some thirty years ago in Adrianople; this is how students are still
being taught to read in Constantine in the year nineteen hundred and
seven.

The teaching of tonic stresses, so difficult to demonstrate, is done
in a very clever manner in Constantine, much more intelligently than
in the East . . . The teacher distributes little cards to his students that
he has prepared himself, and on each he has written, or rather drawn,
the tonic symbols below their names. The child must not only learn
them by heart but, as he recites them, form them with his fingers.
This continues for about two months. The children in this course are
said to be the *zarka* class, taking their name from the first tonic accent in the series. They go on next to the *petit taam,* in which they

learn to apply the *taam,* or tonic stress, to the word by singing first
the one then the other. It is very much like a music course. The student learns the scale, then adapts words to the notes. Finally the student reaches the third step, which is called the *taam kébir,* or *grand
taam.* When the student has spent two or three more months at that
stage, he is able to read and to give the proper intonation to his
reading. The different stages of elementary instruction in Hebrew
each have their own names, just as do stages of nonreligious
instruction . . .

Translation, too, is taught according to a certain system: word-for-
word translation—for about six months—and then translation of
verses. There is no question that all of this is very regimented and
routine and that much time is lost in following this method. But the
method is considered inviolable; by that I mean that any modification
of this system is tantamount to breaking the law; whoever does so is
considered an independent thinker, which, to conservative minds, is
the greatest of insults . . . Nevertheless, we are doing our best to introduce a few revisions to the method . . . Little by little we have
brought the rabbis at our school to understand the advantages that
would result and the time that would be saved if the phonetic method
were applied to the teaching of reading. Today our students are learning to read as they do in our schools.
[. . .]

I would like to mention another small reform that has produced
excellent results in our teaching. I am referring to the [archaic] translation of the Torah. Whether it be done in Spanish, as is the case in
Turkey, or in Arabic, as is the case in Algeria, this translation is in-
comprehensible to our students everywhere. Translation has been continued from generation to generation in an archaic language that is no
longer the language of our students. It is as if one attempted to translate the Bible in French into the French of Joinville. The result is that
one language foreign to the children is translated into another foreign
language.

I have explained to the rabbis the futility of their efforts and that
they were going against the spirit and the goal of those who first
made it our obligation to understand the Bible, and thus to translate
it into the spoken language of the country. I have explained to them
that therein lies the strength and unique character of Judaism, which
is a belief accessible to all. This sets Judaism apart from Roman Ca-
tholicism and Greek Orthodoxy, both of which reject, and especially
until recent times have consistently rejected, any reasoned translation
of the Old Testament into the common language of the people. And

while asking that [the rabbis] maintain and preserve the traditional translation, I have urged that they comment and explain in the same Arabic they speak on a daily basis.
[. . .]

A. H. Navon

Archives of the AIU, France VII.F.13.

Teaching Hebrew in the Alliance School of Safed, 1898

Safed, 22 December 1898
[. . .]
   At the beginning of the year, that is, since the beginning of the school year, we broke with long-established practice and began grouping Ashkenazi and Sephardi students together according to their level for the study of Hebrew, as is done for all other subjects. It required much courage, some say audacity, to undertake this fusion. In order to effect this useful reform, we had to bring in from quite a distance a teacher who was an Ashkenazi, who knew his Hebrew well, and who had a Sephardi pronunciation of Hebrew. Note that all three of these qualities had to be united in a single person if we were to satisfy the Sephardim, the Ashkenazim, and the interest of the school. Today our children write in both Ashkenazi and Sephardi cursive without difficulty and, what is more important, speak fluent Hebrew.
[. . .]

M. Franco

Archives of the AIU, France XI.F.20.

The Survival of Judeo-Spanish: Constantinople, 1908

Annual Report 1907–8
[. . .]
   . . . Judeo-Spanish is the preeminent language of the people, and it will remain so for quite some time whatever we might do. Everyone agrees that we should do away with Judeo-Spanish, that there is no reason to preserve the language of our former persecutors . . . and nevertheless, the lower classes, the bourgeoisie, and even the "aristocracy," as they are called here, everyone still speaks and reads Judeo-Spanish and will continue to do so. In committee meetings where all the members are well educated and everyone knows French, a discussion started in correct, even elegant, French will, often in an instant, inexplicably move into Judeo-Spanish jabbering. The most "select," dignified Jewish ladies when paying a call on a friend will be politely

chitchatting in French and suddenly break into jargon. Turkish is like a borrowed suit; French is gala dress; Judeo-Spanish is the worn dressing gown in which one is most at ease.
[. . .]

M. Fresco

Archives of the AIU, France XVII.F.28.

The Utility of the Languages Taught at School: Iran, 1910

Shiraz, 3 August 1910

[. . .]

What is the practical purpose of the knowledge of French for our students? Should it help them to assimilate Western ideas and culture, to learn that almost everywhere, except in Persia, all men are equal, can live how and where they want, dress as they wish, enter a profession that pleases them? Should they learn that most men are, in a word, independent, free in their actions, with full personal rights maintained by principles of justice, and then compare this with their own pitiful condition? Would this not be horribly demoralizing and painful for them?

The use of French by our people is somehow anomalous in these barbarous regions, and nothing touches me more deeply as I walk through the squalid *mehalla* [the quarter] than to hear a child's eager "Bonjour, monsieur," or bits and pieces of sentences learned at school, in the midst of such poverty, humiliation, and persecution. The French language so strongly evokes the image of liberty, independence, justice, well-being, and human dignity that one is almost uncomfortable hearing it spoken by a people so oppressed they do not have even the right to walk in the streets in bad weather lest they dirty the raindrops that might run down their poor miserable backs.
[. . .]

The lesson to be learned from the considerations addressed above is the following: we must, within our system of schools, hearken to one essential principle, which consists of carefully measuring the dosage of instruction and intellectual development administered to our students according to the degree of practical utility it will provide them and according to the greater or lesser social liberty which they enjoy. If there is no harm, and even an advantage, in dispensing a large dose of French culture to our students in, for example, Teheran and, although to a lesser extent, in Hamadan, the same is not the case in Shiraz, in Seneh, or even in Isphahan.

This proper dosage, which must vary according not only to place but also to the time and the circumstances, can only be determined by the directors themselves. They are in the best position to make an appropriate and timely decision.

[. . .]

The teaching of Hebrew. The teaching of Hebrew should be an important concern of all of your directors. It must be acknowledged that this task is rendered particularly difficult for them because of the poor assistance they receive from the rabbis, whom they are obliged to recruit locally, and whose knowledge is as limited as their minds are narrow and resistant to change. But this is not all. Any innovation, any hint of reform in the traditional empirical methods of teaching, which have always been esteemed in these backward communities, brings the risk of alarming the parents, fanatic because of their ignorance, who would see in such change an attack on the very principles of their religion. Your teachers can, nevertheless, if they work simultaneously toward opening the minds of the rabbis and parents, create a more rational approach to the teaching of Hebrew and one that is more in keeping with the spirit of our religion.

Above all, they must seek to ensure that the rabbis, guided of course by the teachers themselves, bring out in their teaching the moral precepts which constitute the foundation and the beauty of our sacred language. This is perhaps the most difficult task of all, yet it is one your directors will hold close to their hearts.

The teaching of Persian. This is the subject matter which must occupy the most prominent place in the curriculum in this country. It is hard to imagine both the difficulty our fellow Jews have in giving up their awful jargon to speak good Persian and the degree to which this lowers them in the eyes of the Muslims, who instinctively disdain them for it.

This language of convention was first created so that this eternally persecuted people might communicate among themselves, in critical moments, without being understood by the enemy. Little by little it has come into general usage; it is now the popular, everyday language and has completely replaced true Persian in all communication among Jews.

In Shiraz, and I presume that the same holds true in all the larger Jewish communities in Persia, I have noticed that in fact in the small villages where the Jews have been less persecuted, their language of preference is a very correct Persian. There are two varieties of jargon among the Jews: one is nothing but a corrupted Persian, in which it is still possible to recognize a few mangled Persian words, a few syllables from Arabic or *"farsi"*; the other, colorfully termed *"leturai,"* is composed of a mixture of atrophied Hebraic terms, horribly mutilated syllables from Persian, and some common words, the whole pro-nounced in the most inharmonious manner, unpleasant to the ear. The beautiful language of Saadi and Hafez loses all its charm, sonor-ity, and melody in this mixture, and it is no wonder that the Persians exhibit so much distaste and so much repulsion in speaking with a Jew.

By making our students familiar with correct Persian and forcing them out of the habit of speaking in their jargons, not only will we have taught them the only language that will be of real use to them and whose knowledge may later procure them considerable material advantage, but also we will have eliminated an important cause of the disdain and hostility with which the Muslims view them. This will pro-vide them the means to improve and extend their relations with the peoples around them.
[. . .]

E. Nataf

Archives of the AIU, France XII.F.22.

The Multiplicity of Languages
in an Alliance School in Constantinople, 1913

Galata, letter received 28 July 1913

[. . .]
Included in the curriculum are French, as foundation for other stud-ies, Turkish, Hebrew, and German. Here in the East, if we want to begin preparing a child for his future as soon as he begins school, instruction in several languages is absolutely necessary. Yet peda-gogues affirm that the study of multiple languages is detrimental to the normal development of the child's mental faculties. Hygienists add that such learning has harmful repercussions on the child's physi-cal faculties by putting too much strain on a frail body and inhibiting the regular growth of its organs.

I do not deny that either of these affirmations is true and certain observations can be cited in support of this thesis . . . Some even go so far as to claim that if so few exceptional and brilliant men are found among the Jews in Eastern countries, it is due to the fact that, having allowed our mental faculties to grow dull through the course of four hundred years in our *juderias* [Jewish quarters], where no seri-ous intellectual cultivation has been practiced since our exile from Spain, we are now putting the brains of our young children through intellectual gymnastics to which they are not at all accustomed after several centuries of absolute repose. As a consequence of this sudden, rather than gradual, intellectual development, we are producing young people who speak and write in many languages but who possess neither the maturity of mind nor the logic nor the level of abstraction required to carry out any undertaking of significance or to show any sign of the true intellectual vigor required in the making of men of science and of letters.

. . . [B]ut the unfortunate truth is that we cannot ignore the importance of two significant factors. The first is that we are Ottoman Jews and must therefore satisfy the parents of our students by teaching Hebrew as religion and as language. The second is that we have to fulfill our duty as citizens by teaching our boys, from the moment we can, to speak the official language of the country in which we live. This holds true all the more as our students will be asked later to perform their military service,[5] and a knowledge of Turkish becomes, thereby, absolutely indispensable.

Naturally, French remains the very core of our teaching. It is through French culture, eminently suited to the diffusion of liberal ideas, that we can raise our children up from the state of dejection imposed by centuries of oppression and moral stagnation. From a double perspective, French is the language *par excellence* for instruction and education. At the same time it is a powerful tool which permits our students to derive immediate and very lucrative profit from the knowledge acquired in our classrooms.

[. . .]

A. Benveniste

Archives of the AIU, France XVII.F.28.

5. Universal military service was instituted in Turkey in 1909.

9
A Portrait of the Communities

The description of local Jewish communities and disquisitions on their customs, mores, and folkways constituted a distinct genre in the correspondence of the Alliance teachers with the Central Committee in Paris. These descriptions formed the mainstay of their annual and semiannual reports. As a genre, these letters closely resemble the European travel literature of the time. They report events and developments that affected the Jews. But on the whole, they provide snapshots of the communities and maintain a synchronic, static quality in their depiction of an East frozen in time and to which change comes only from the outside. These texts also are responses to directives from Paris urging the gathering of information about the life, customs, and mores of local Jews. The Central Committee and the teachers were concerned to capture the "exotic" before it inevitably disappeared. Hence the texts are also ethnographic accounts presenting data in a quasi-scientific manner and attempting to construct "knowledge" about "distant" communities. In these texts, and herein lies their fascination, the teachers are both the ethnographers and the informants, mediating the information reaching Paris through an ambiguous and veiled dialogue between a "self" and "other" that were one and the same.

The Jewish Community of Smyrna, 1873

REPORT ON THE SCHOOLS AND INSTITUTIONS
OF THE JEWISH COMMUNITY OF SMYRNA

Population. The Jewish community of Smyrna is made up of about 3,500 families; that is, about 20,000 people.

Economic situation. There are approximately 100 families who are considered rich, and their fortune is valued at between 8,000 and 12,000 Turkish pounds (Fr 181,000–276,000); they form the upper class and make up a sort of aristocracy. The heads of these families are all involved in trade. The middle class, which numbers between 1,500 and 2,000 families, comprises brokers, merchants, skilled tradesmen, and porters—that is, people who live more or less comfortably from the fruits of their labors. There are, in addition, about 500 heads of families who carry the title of rabbi. Finally, there are 1,000 or so families who have no means of subsistence, who live on public charity, and who make of the Jewish quarter one of the most sad and unpleasant areas of Smyrna.

Material conditions. The Jews of Smyrna, with the exception of a very few, live like the Turks: they sleep on the ground; the whole family eats from the same plate and drinks from the same bowl. As for the rest, the houses are kept relatively clean, at least in the courtyard, which most often serves as the main room. The bedrooms, on the other hand, are much neglected, and in the summer people are obliged to sleep on the terrace or in the courtyard because of the vermin which infest their apartments. They change their clothes once a week; very few men ever wash or comb their hair.

Condition of the women. It is about the same as in the Turkish community and households.

Education of the children. The mother is responsible for bringing up the children; the father does not return home until late in the evening, when the children are already asleep. At the age of three, both boys and girls are sent to stay with a *maestra.* This is the name for a woman who takes about thirty children into her home, has them sit on the floor in a room or in the courtyard, and leaves them there from morning till night, sometimes out in the sun, while she attends to her affairs. Children become habituated to frugality from a very early age: their midday meal is a piece of bread with a little cheese; the evening meal is more or less the same. In many homes there is meat only on Saturday. Through the week the noon meal is not taken at table, and the men do not return to the house; the women eat, as they say, "on the run."

Schooling for girls. When the children reach the age of six, they are taken out of the home of the *maestra,* and the boys are placed in *meldar*s, Hebrew schools, whose condition leaves much to be desired in terms of teaching, here in Smyrna as everywhere else in Turkey. The girls are kept at home, where they help their mothers with the household chores. It is not unusual to see the young women of the most respectable Jewish families sweeping out the courtyard or washing the floors, helping their mothers do the wash or bake bread. On Saturday it is like a different world; everything stops, everyone is dressed nicely; everywhere there are men and women standing in doorways or at the windows, all eating melon seeds.

Occupations of the boys. At the age of twelve or fourteen, the boys leave the *meldar.* Those who have parents with a permanent occupation help them in their work and begin to learn the trade. Those whose fathers are without regular work are left to themselves; they live in the streets, or they shine shoes.

Marriage. Marriage comes between the ages of eighteen and twenty. One phenomenon which is, in large part, the source of the poverty of the Jews in Smyrna is that many more girls than boys are born to them. The result is that every young man, who quickly becomes obsessed by the prospect of a dowry, gets engaged and married as soon as he can; and there is then one more family doomed to poverty.

Occupations of the men. As was stated above, the wealthy Jews are businessmen; the middle class is made up of brokers, skilled tradesmen, clerks, porters, etc. The kinds of skilled trades practiced are limited to those of tailors, shoemakers, and tinsmiths. Other trades, such as those of the carpenter, the mason, the blacksmith, the metal caster, or the goldsmith, are left in the hands of the Greeks and the Catholics. The women do not work, most often because there is no work to be had. They are thereby reduced to living on charity.

General education. It is not hard to understand after what has just been stated that there is much to be done to improve the general education of the Jewish community of Smyrna; charity alone will not suffice.

Until now much has been done to relieve the suffering of this dense mass that is the poor of Smyrna; unfortunately, nothing has been done to try to improve their condition.

[. . .]

D. Cazès

Bulletin Semestriel de l'Alliance Israélite Universelle, 2ᵉ semestre 1873, pp. 141–47.

A Jewish Quarter of Constantinople at the Beginning of the Alliance's Activities, 1875

Constantinople, letter received 16 September 1875

[. . .]

Balat has a population of approximately 30,000, of which 3,000–4,000 are Jews. In Turkey the exact number of inhabitants of an area cannot be determined with precision, because births are not registered by the local authority.

. . . The principal professions of the Jews are commerce, brokerage, money changing, medicine (without credentials), pharmacy, and small trade. In general, the Jews of the East prefer employment which is lucrative and which can be practiced without difficulty and without capital. There have been several cases of peddlers and money changers who started in their commerce with only 200 francs and after two or three years have become bankers or highly successful merchants; but most do not save their money and so do not get very far, nor do they feel any shame when they can no longer pay their debts. There is not a single Jewish blacksmith or carpenter, but many sell fish, wine, lemonade, fruit, and vegetables. Many run errands on foot or in small rowboats and are secondhand dealers. They all earn very little and live from hand to mouth. One never sees a Jew working on the boats at the many docks of the city. I will tell you why. First, because the Jews refuse to work on Saturday, and second, because they do not like to start work for low wages and to have to wait to earn more over time. For these reasons, to which must be added their lack of education, very few Jews find employment at the Sublime Porte. All of the skilled trades and all of the arts are practiced by Christians and a few Muslims. In Balat there are only two architects, neither of whom has studied the trade, a few joiners, and a few tinsmiths. As for beggars, the place is thick with them, and often they are young, healthy men and women. This is why in Constantinople, more than anywhere else, vocational schools are indispensable if we hope to improve the condition of the Jews.

[. . .]

WAYS AND MANNERS OF THE JEWS

The Jews of Balat, especially those of the lower class, have a seedy appearance; they are very vocal; nowhere is there such a prodigious outpouring of blessings and curses. They are quick-tempered, loud, selfish, unscrupulous in their means of making money, opposed to all work, and accustomed to living from hand to mouth. They have many natural gifts, but their vices dull or deaden their intelligence, give a sharp edge to their character, and leave them only with ruse and cleverness. They have more superstition than religion and although they pray in the temple almost every day, they do not truly think about God until poverty or illness keeps them from thinking about their own interests or pleasures. It can be said that the Jewish people are the least well considered here and the most despised; the Jews are the dregs of society. The Jews are made to suffer injustice only from the Greeks (the blood libel); but everyone despises them. A people may be persecuted unjustly, but when they are looked upon with general disdain, it must be that to some extent they are deserving of it. As a result, there are many Jews who are ashamed to carry that name. In order to uplift the new generation, we must spread instruction and honest labor throughout the capital; we must open a school for boys,

a school for girls, and a trades school in each district of the city and
expand those already in place. The Armenians and Greeks understood this a long time ago. Priests and laymen, rich or poor, all have
agreed to give part of their money and part of their time to open
beautiful schools and select the best teachers and thus to attract the
greatest possible number of students. Thus they can be found working
in all the offices and practicing every profession while never ceasing
to help and support each other.
[. . .]

N. Béhar

Archives of the AIU, Turquie XXV.E.

A Turkish-Jewish Community in Asia Minor: Bursa, 1886

Bursa, 28 April 1886

[. . .]
The Jews, their district, their material conditions. There were 2,179
Jews in Bursa in 1883, when the last census was taken. Today there
are around 600 families, more than 2,800 individuals, of whom only
two-fifths are males. They all live in the same district; it is not less
well located than the others, but it leaves much to be desired in terms
of cleanliness; with very few exceptions, the homes are old and dilapi-
dated with cracking walls. There is great poverty among them; they
earn very little and they eat next to nothing. Animals are not slaugh-
tered on a daily basis; vegetables and fish are the basic elements of
their diet. The midday meal, which most of our students bring to
school, consists of a small, round loaf of bread and a piece of cheese
or *halva* (a kind of nougat). But there is one curious thing, in spite of
the great poverty, there is no family, rich or poor, which does not
have its own home. Because they are free of the worry over lodgings,
which in other places creates so much anxiety among the poor, the
poor in Bursa have an easier life. They have very few needs and have
learned to endure privation.

As in all the cities of the East, Bursa has a bazaar in the business
district; this market is independent of the others. All of the merchants
meet there during the day. There too the Jews have their place apart,
even though they are allowed to set up shop wherever they wish.
Throughout the rest of the city you can find only bakeries, grocery
stores, cafés, and a few other shops selling various items. To make
any other purchase or to meet with anyone during the day, you must
go to the bazaar. I have visited the Jewish section of the bazaar many
times and closely observed it. They are involved with the silk trade,

like everyone else here, silk being the principal export of Bursa, but with this difference: The Jewish merchants do not have their own mills. They raise the silkworms, or pay to have them raised, and sell the cocoons to foreign mills. There are also Jewish money changers, haberdashers, cloth merchants, tinsmiths, peddlers, etc. The silk merchants and the money changers are the most comfortable; there are very few of them and their capital ranges from 500 to 1,000 francs; you can judge from that how affluent they are. The money changers add another string to their bow; they also lend money. But as they are too religious to deviate from the Law, they only accept interest from non-Jews. There are no Jewish landlords; each one has his own house and that is all. The Jews work only in commerce; they do not know how to do anything with their hands. Therefore, one has to go to the Greeks or the Armenians to find a cobbler, a tailor, a clock maker, or a goldsmith. Turkey is teeming with Polish Jews, as you know, especially in Constantinople; they also have their representatives in Bursa, three families. One family runs a hotel; it is there that I take my meals; the second are milliners; and the head of the third family builds and cleans heating stoves.

Moral and intellectual conditions. If their material conditions are uncertain, their intellectual state is even more appalling. The children, pressed by need, rarely stay long enough in the *Talmud-Torah* to acquire even the most elementary knowledge of Hebrew; they begin working very young and are earning their own living by the age of 16, 14, or even 12. Under such conditions, it is not surprising that there is much ignorance among them; they barely know how to pray. I have counted only eight heads of families and a few young men who have read the Talmud. There are no rabbis in Bursa except those at the school, the *hazanim* [cantors] at the synagogues, and a few *shohetim* [ritual slaughterers of animals]. The Chief Rabbi comes from Constantinople; he is the only one who reads as one trained in a *yeshiva*.

[. . .]

 . . . Needless to say, there is not a single Jew in Bursa who knows Turkish or French (as with Arabic in Morocco, everyone speaks Turkish but no one knows how to read or write it). There used to be a certain Behor Chilton, his Turkish was rather good and he worked in the office which kept the cadastre; he is currently in Cassaba.

In spite of this ignorance, or rather because of it, the Jews of Bursa are very orthodox. The temples overflow with people not only on Saturdays and feast days but on every day of the week. It follows that there is no liberal party in Bursa; we only have the orthodox and the

fanatics. The former, more influential, are in general in favor of progress and against the current rabbi, whom they have even tried to remove and replace with a more adept, more presentable rabbi who
would at least know Turkish. The fanatics who defended him at the
time are no longer constant in their dedication to him; they support
or abandon him according to whether he acts in keeping with their
preferences and their ideas and whether he leans more toward the
orthodox side or their own. Just recently, he was severely upbraided
right in the synagogue by a member of his own party, and this person
was not even one of the more influential members. The rabbi had
asked the community to offer Hebrew books to our students from
poor families, which was heresy in the eyes of the zealots, heresy
inasmuch as the school is leading us inevitably toward perdition. Another of the same group complained loudly one day because he had
seen a child with his head uncovered through the door to my classroom, which had been left ajar, and a few crumbs of bread on the
ground in the courtyard. These incidents describe more eloquently
than anything I could write the state of mind and the sentiments animating our fanatics; fortunately they are in a minority and make
more noise than cause harm. Add to all this a complete lack of unity
and an insubordination without equal. The rabbi and the notables
have minimal influence on the people; only those who live on charity
respect their superiors. The government does not recognize any judicial authority in the community; it will not inflict punishment on a
Jew at the simple request of the rabbi or the notables. The plaintiff,
should he be our spiritual leader himself, must appear before the tribunal and start proceedings according to the rule of the law, something which he avoids doing for fear of losing the case, as has already
happened to him once, apparently.

   The rabbi does have at his disposal one formidable weapon for
bringing the complainers and the recalcitrants to heel: the *herem* [ex-
communication]. He uses it very rarely, however. Timid by nature, of
weak character, of ordinary intelligence, and, above all, of questionable popularity, he does not dare excommunicate anyone without first
asking the opinion of the notables. Their opinion always prevails and
for one reason or another the punishment is most often reduced to an
indemnity to be used in the service of the poor. With more unity and
more submission on the part of its people, the community of Bursa,
in spite of its limited resources, would certainly be in a less critical
situation. Its budget, which is very modest but rarely runs a deficit
and which is balanced in difficult circumstances through the voluntary
imposition of a tax on the part of the notables, could show an excess

of revenue over expenses every year if the people in general would show more concern for the interest and the prosperity of the community.
[. . .]

J. Matalon

Archives of the AIU, Turquie I.C.1.

The Hispanic Heritage of Turkish Jewry: Adrianople, 1897

Adrianople, letter received in Paris on 30 January 1897

THE JEWS OF ADRIANOPLE

The Jewish community of Adrianople, which numbers approximately 18,000, is worthy in every regard of the interest which it holds for the Alliance. A truly curious phenomenon, on which all of the teachers who have had positions here agree, is that the average share of intelligence is much greater here than among other Jewish groups in the East. To what can this be attributed? I cannot say; I am simply stating the fact. In addition, this city has produced the majority of the good teachers in the Alliance, in particular those responsible for the teaching of agricultural methods in the institutions of this organization.

In a different vein, something remarkable to note is the vitality with which the memories of the history of the Jewish past are conserved here.

It is well known that this city already had a Jewish community in the time of the Byzantine emperors. The tombstones of the local Jewish cemetery—which date from before the Turkish conquest—bear ample witness to what I have said. History, too, teaches us that Sultan Murad I found a flourishing community when he came to this city in 1360. As vestiges of this community, there remains a synagogue called *K. K.* [*Kahal Kadosh*—Holy Community] *de los Gregos* or *Romania* and a few family names such as Pappo or Pappos, Mori (from the Morea), Sivricos, Canetti, etc.

Less than a century and a half after the Ottoman occupation, Adrianople served as refuge to the exiles from Spain (1492 and 1495), Portugal (1506), Italy (1534), etc.

While in the majority of the cities in the East the synagogues are given Hebrew names, here the faithful grouped together according to their city or province of origin and refer to their temples by those names. For curiosity's sake, here are the names of the major synagogues: synagogue of Portugal, of the Catalans, of Aragon, of Evora, of Toledo, of Major or Majorca, of Sicily, of the Italians, of the Pulia, of Budun (or Buda, in Hungary), etc.

A few family names recall cities in Italy: Pisa, Tarento, Mi-Trani (from Trana), Romano (from Rome).

Other names have been borrowed from Spain: Rodrigue, Menda(s), Toledo, Taragano, Espania, Zamero (from Zamora), Ghiron, (from Giron), Funès (a village in the Navarre), Dueñas, Bello, Rica, Présénté, Pava, etc.

Certain names clearly indicate a French origin: Carcashon (from Carcassone), Franka (term of endearment for a woman), Sarfati (a Hebrew word meaning "French").

Finally, the Barbary coast furnishes in turn a contingent of Arab-sounding names: Al-Saïd, Al-Cabès, Al-Fazza (from Fez), Saadi, Bordj(i), Bénaroya or Ben ha-rou'ia (the son of the dream), etc.

But what is stranger still are the memories of the Spanish Inquisition perpetuated among this population as if it were seeking to pursue the Jews even this far and to trouble their peace with retrospective nightmares. Here is a typical example of the sort of thing I have observed.

A short time ago, a distraught woman asked me to intercede for her with the person responsible so that her daughter, who comes to the girls' school, might be given a *zan-banetté*.

I pride myself on being rather well versed in the Judeo-Spanish jargon spoken in Turkey. Nevertheless, this mysterious word *zan-banetté* was completely unknown to me. To hide my ignorance and to avoid embarrassment, I promised the good woman her *zan-banetté*. This word kept haunting me for days. I had already given up hope of understanding the meaning of this strange term, when, as I was talking to my students about the Inquisition, I had occasion to mention the *san-bénito,* that coarse garment of sackcloth in which the victims of the Inquisition were made to dress. *San-bénito!* With this word every student's hand shot up as if on cue, as if a spring had been released. I let them talk and I learned, to my utter amazement, that the word for the smocks worn by their younger brothers and sisters, the *zan-banetté,* must be a corruption of *san-bénito.* And it was absolutely true! And that poor entreating mother had involuntarily taken me for a Torquemada, no more no less, in asking me to procure a *zan-banetté* for her daughter.

[. . .]

. . . Certain folkways and customs still observed in the Jewish community of Adrianople do not exist elsewhere, even in an agglomeration as large as that of Constantinople: for example, the making of bread by the women in their homes or the pâtés the Jewish women prepare, which have Castilian names such as *frojalda, tortas, fila-doña,* etc. The practice of covering the huts during the feast of *Sukot* with braided reeds woven into a cloth is no less unique and differs, for example, from the practice in Constantinople, where laurel branches are used.

Finally there is another custom here, as curious as it is moving. Nowhere in the East would any Jewish woman dare set foot in a cemetery. This is not the case in Adrianople. On the first two Sundays of the month the young Jewish widows, either alone or accompanied by their daughters, go in throngs to the cemetery, some in carriages, others on foot. There not only do they grieve at the tombs of their deceased husbands and give alms to the beggars and poor rabbis who are there, but they also confide touchingly and naively in their departed relatives. They share their domestic joys, talk about the hardships in their lives, tell them which religious feast days are approaching and how sad they feel to see an empty place at the family hearth; they mention the upcoming marriage of an orphaned girl or even the progress the orphaned children are making in school.
[. . .]

M. Franco

Archives of the AIU, Turquie VII.E.

The Dress and Customs of the Jews of Tangier

Tangier, 3 December 1903

[. . .]

Let us turn now to the homes and the inhabitants. The first thing that must be said is that there is no ghetto. Jews and Arabs can, and sometimes do, live side by side. Nevertheless, it is true that the Arabs generally seek out the isolated areas of the city where the streets are narrow and passers-by are rare. There are some Arabs living near each of the mosques, which are scattered throughout the city. There are others who have themselves formed a kind of ghetto; it is found in the vicinity of the *kasbah,* the square on which are located the government buildings and the local prison. In this district there are only Arabs. It suffices to see the closed doors to know that this is a Muslim district. Besides this, there are several characteristics setting it apart from the rest of the city. The streets of the entire city are paved in stone. The city has electric lighting and is relatively clean. The Arab district exhibits none of these characteristics. Because it is isolated, it is not paved; both lighting and cleanliness are lacking.

The houses located in the city are for the most part modern. The older constructions are disappearing; when a house is falling into ruin and must be torn down, the owner generally buys the neighboring land when possible to enlarge the construction. Three- or four-room houses built around a central courtyard used to be everywhere. From the red painted clay of the courtyard would rise a fig tree dense with leaves. These types of homes have almost completely disappeared.

And so the houses here are generally large houses of European construction, belonging to all three elements of the population. [. . .]

Population. The population can be classified in two ways, according to origin and according to dress. There are the Jewish immigrants from the coast and those from the interior. A great number of those from the coast dress in European style, as do virtually all of their fellow Jews from Tangier. The rest, and especially those from the interior, wear loose, flowing trousers with a *bedhia,* or Arab vest, the whole covered by the traditional *jokha,* or colored robe. The *jokha* is fitted around the waist with a red Spanish belt. To complete the wardrobe, a pair of clogs are worn off the heels so that they flap in the back, without stockings. Sometimes the clogs are dyed black, to lend an air of majesty. But this is the dress of the poor or that worn during the week. On Saturdays or feast days, the *yalak* is usually worn, a robe of heavy cloth with buttons that is again fitted at the waist with a bright colored belt, often blue. Over the *jokha* or over the *yalak* is worn the *capote* (capotet), a hooded coat; it is usually worn as a cape, the sleeves hanging loose. On the head there is always worn a *bonete,* a folded skullcap usually placed on the back of the head. The few Jews of an older generation who used to wear a spotted kerchief have almost completely disappeared; on the other hand, there are many who wear a *djilaba,* a garment that somewhat resembles the burnous in its cut. The children are dressed in one or the other style according to the family to which they belong.

Women. Women's dress can be divided into two categories: completely European and partly European. It is above all, as one would expect, those who form the modern element of the population who wear European dress; the rest wear the other style of dress, which is dying out. The only difference between the two manners of dress is that instead of a hat, a scarf is worn, knotted sometimes around the temples, sometimes over the forehead. Some women wear clogs instead of European shoes. In addition, when the women who have not adopted the European dress go out, they wear a kind of silk cloak that covers them from the head to the waist. The young girls of both sections of the population dress in the same way: if they belong to the modern element, they wear a hat; otherwise, they wear a ribbon wrapped round their braided hair.

[. . .]

Superstitions. There are superstitions in Tangier just as in any other city. But the tendency to have ideas of this sort has greatly diminished under the influence of the schools. Nonetheless, it must be remarked that in every class of the society certain superstitions remain. The merchant who has built a home, in spite of his European style of life and his contacts with the foreign, civilized element of the society, will not fail to hang a horseshoe over the door or sometimes a hammer and horseshoe together, sometimes also a fish. Needless to say, this practice is becoming less and less frequent. However, among the uneducated the tendency toward superstition is as profound as ever. The beliefs and practices dictated by superstition are precise and meticulous. This phenomenon is but the inevitable consequence of imitation and habit. As the members of each element of the population are in constant and exclusive contact with each other, their ideas or practices necessarily take on an aspect of permanence and a singular intensity. It has been said that volumes could be filled with material provided by this kind of superstitious thinking, and that is not an exaggeration . . .

[. . .]

. . . For example, if you have inadvertently spilled a little salt or forgotten to close a pair of scissors, woe unto you for the quarrels which will rage. On the other hand, if you have tossed away a match and by chance the flame has not gone out, that is a good omen: you will soon receive a sum of money. But do not be too hasty, for if the match has not burned up completely, your money may vanish; and so you remain in doubt. If again by chance your shoes fell one on top of the other when you took them off, you should be happy for you will soon be taking a trip. You can see, then, that time has not erased certain practices and crude beliefs, and I have only mentioned but a few which seemed characteristic to me.

[. . .]

Y. Cohen

Archives of the AIU, Tunisie I.D.1.

The Jews of Casablanca, 1909

[annual report, no date]

[. . .]

The Mellah. The *Mellah* is located in the southwestern part of Casablanca. Its population is much more dense than that of the other parts of the city. A shapeless mass of disparate constructions, arranged without the slightest regard to order or harmony; an impossible maze of narrow, twisting streets, gullied and rutted; a treacherous passage for the strangers who dare enter, especially on moonless nights; such is the Jewish district. This district is itself divided into two very distinct parts: the *Mellah* of the Jewish privileged class, which, although it too is dirty, at least has a number of spacious, though poorly maintained, dwellings; and the *Bhira,* which has the aspect of a *duar* [camp] temporarily set up on the outskirts of the city with its huts made of wood. The *Bhira* is teeming with a degenerate population of needy farmers whose entire fortune consists of one or two milk cows. There are no stables; the alleys disappear beneath a thick layer of putrifying manure. It is there in this miasma, in this atmosphere saturated with sickening odors, that hundreds of our fellow Jews are born, live in stagnation, and die.

The Jews are no longer obliged to live only in the *Mellah* since Commander Mangin [the leader of the French forces in the area] gave them the right to take up residence in any part of the city. A few families, the richer ones, of course, have taken full advantage of this authorization; but in spite of this emigration, the *Mellah* still remains home to the greater part of the Jewish population.

The Jewish community. . . . The term "community" itself is inappropriate as applied to the whole of the diverse agglomerations formed by the Jews in this city. They have divided themselves into several distinct groups, according to language or place of origin. The mutual feelings sustained by these various factions are not among the most cordial; they do not even associate with each other. These groups are the *Shylloks,* the *Rumis,* and the *Forasteros.*

The *Shylloks* are the descendants of the colonies of Jews who emigrated to Morocco long before the destruction of the Second Temple. They are the true natives. They live in the countryside and in *duar*s; they are mountain-dwelling tribes; their ways and their customs are identical to those of the Berber nomads. Those who settle in the city live most often in the *Bhira.*

The *Forastero*[1] is the indigenous Jew; his mother tongue is Arabic. The *Rumis*[2] are the foreign Jews; they generally speak Spanish.

---

1. Spanish for "stranger." This was the name given by the Sephardi exiles from the Iberian Peninsula to the native Jews of North Africa.

2. The term to denote Europeans used in many parts of the Muslim world. It dates back to the early contacts between the Arabs and the Byzantine Empire, "Eastern Rome."

There are no words to describe the scorn and disdain in the word "*Forastero*" when pronounced by a *Rumi*. Between these latter two groups there is no possible communication; they each despise the other more than either detests the Muslims or the Christians. [. . .]

A. Saguès

Archives of the AIU, France XIV.F.25.

The Professions of the Jews of Fez

Fez, 1 September 1903

[. . .]

Professions. There are Jews in almost every profession in Fez; but it is as goldsmiths and tailors that they excel and have, so to speak, a monopoly. All of the goldsmiths and all of the tailors in Fez are Jews. There are some true artists among them. The richest families in Fez, with the exception of those who made their fortune in usury, began as goldsmiths or tailors for the *Makhzan*.[3] Still today, the goldsmiths and the tailors of the *Makhzan* are all rich Jews. The goldsmith's trade has become so lucrative in Fez that all of the students who finished their training with us this year have become apprentice goldsmiths. These days there is something in the air; everyone wants to become a goldsmith.

The monopoly on *kif,* or snuff, is held by a powerful company whose members are Jews.

Moreover, here is a list of the professions that are practiced by our brothers in Fez. It should give you a fairly accurate idea of the activities of the Jews of Fez:

Goldsmiths, 154 with 77 apprentices; tailors, 158; moneylenders, 104; weavers, 56; makers of gold thread, 44; grocers, 57; cobblers, 26; metal engravers, 21; barbers, 10; innkeepers, 16; musicians, 20; carders, 11; butchers, 9; public criers, 19; tinsmiths, 28; money changers, 11; confectioners, 4; masons, 6; watchmaker, 1; coppersmiths, 9; well digger,1; doctors, 4; wood turner, 1; blacksmiths, 3; makers of amulets, 3; painters, 3; dyers, 6; wax maker, 1; soap makers, 2; rabbis, 39; *shohetim,* 7; *dayanim* [judges], 6; notaries, 9; flour merchants, 16; oil merchants, 11; silk merchants, 9; coal merchants, 5;

---

3. "Palace"; the term is also used to refer to the government of the Sultan of Morocco.

The school in Tunis, Tunisia, end of the nineteenth century

Prize day at the school for boys, Tangier, Morocco, 1928

Jewish refugees from the city of Settat in front of one of the Alliance schools
in Casablanca, Morocco, April 1904

A sewing class in Constantine, Algeria

A class at the school on Meschnaka Street, Tunis, Tunisia, 1886

A Jew of Bou-Saada, Tunisia

A Jewish woman of Tunis, Tunisia

Teachers and rabbis in Tunis, Tunisia, 1886–87

The personnel of the schools for boys and girls in Monastir (Bitola),
Ottoman Empire (Macedonia), 1912

Students of the school for boys, Monastir (Bitola),
Ottoman Empire (Macedonia), 1912

Students of the school for boys in Salonica, Ottoman Empire (Greece),
end of the nineteenth century

Students of the school for girls, Rustchuk (Ruse), Bulgaria, 1902

Students in the vocational program, Samacoff, Bulgaria, 1892

Orphans at the Alliance school in Tchorlu (Çorlu), Turkey, 1921

The personnel of the schools for boys and girls in Beirut, Lebanon, 1909

Advanced class, Beirut, Lebanon, 1909

Scouts from the Alliance schools in Damascus, Syria, 1933

The Jewish quarter in Damascus, Syria, 1920s

Students of the school for boys, Baghdad, Iraq, 1898

Students of the Laura Kadoorie school for girls, Baghdad, Iraq

Laura Kadoorie school for girls, Baghdad, Iraq

Students of the school for girls, Baghdad, Iraq, 1900

A girls' class, Laura Kadoorie school for girls, Baghdad, Iraq, 1925

School recess, Yezd, Iran, 1925

The first communal committee of the Alliance in Teheran, Iran, 1898

A boys' class, Isphahan, Iran, 1925–26

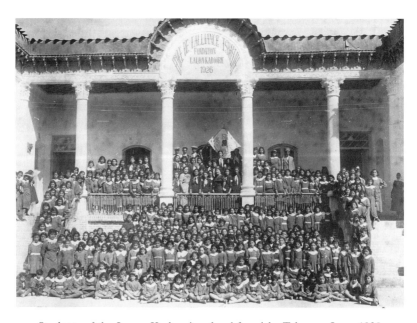

Students of the Laura Kadoorie school for girls, Teheran, Iran, 1938

vegetable, egg, and poultry merchants, 26; wholesalers, 21; brokers and agents, 10.
[. . .]

J. Valadji

Archives of the AIU, France XIV.F.25.

The Classic Mellah: *Fez, 1910*

Fez, letter received in Paris on 28 November 1910

[. . .]

The Mellah. The *Mellah,* located in the southwest part of Fez, belongs to a group of districts called *Fez el Djedid,* the new Fez. It is situated on a marshy plateau. It is encircled by high, crenellated walls, which isolate it from the Arab district on one side and protect it on another from incursions of the Kabyles [nomadic Berber tribes in northern Maghreb] who live in the neighboring countryside. From the *Mellah* there is only one exit to the outside, a massive gate guarded by a handful of armed soldiers; it is closed after sunset, shutting in the district's inhabitants. The *Mellah* happens to be in the same area as the *Dar al Makhzan* [palace in this context] and so is under the immediate protection of the sovereign. The palace of the Sultan, whose towering fortifications hold in check the insurrections of the rebellious population of the *Medina,*[4] has for three hundred years sheltered the timid and submissive community of the Jews of Fez in its protective shadow. The Jews are governed directly by a *Pasha,* invested with full powers; he in turn names the *Sheikh-al-yahud* [leader of the Jews], who represents the community in its dealings with public authority. It is to him that the *Pasha* speaks when he must exact a duty for the *Makhzan,* when he has a general order to communicate to the entire community, or when he wants to arrest an individual against whom charges have been brought. The *Sheikh* is also responsible for the general conduct of the inhabitants of the *Mellah;* it is he who enforces the law and maintains order. On important Muslim feast days or when a special event is celebrated, one of the Sultan's marriages or the birth of a prince, the *Sheikh* heads a Jewish delegation to carry congratulations and traditional gifts to the Sultan.

The exterior aspect of the *Mellah* is profoundly disquieting with its sordid throngs of men and women in rags and its narrow, stinking

---

4. The quarter of the city where the majority of the Arabs lived.

streets teeming with half-clothed children. The *Mellah* is an object of scorn and disgust for the rich Muslims as well as for the bourgeois of Fez, who never set foot there. The stranger who enters this district upon his first visit to Fez is overcome by a mixture of sorrow and repulsion at the sight before his eyes: narrow, vaulted streets where neither light nor air can penetrate; walls black with centuries of filth; heaps of rotting garbage at every corner of every street; a heavy, oppressive atmosphere laden with indefinable odors. The population which works and lives in this place, and which fills these streets with agitated movement, presents a no more comforting appearance. Their faces are sickly and pale, their frames are awkward and bent; the absolute lack of hygiene and excesses of all sorts debilitate these people, whose minds, however, remain quick and sharp. One wonders if Hercules and Alphea could ever clean these Augean stables; what miracle of civilization it would take to restore this population, to return it physically and morally to a more healthy way of life, to once again see men and women who bear themselves with pride and are conscious of their human dignity.

On Saturdays and feast days, the *Mellah* has a less repulsive air. The night before, some effort is given to cleaning. Dressed only in black throughout the week—black, the color of abjection: it had been a kind of mark of humiliation imposed by the Muslims and has become so much a custom that even today, in an age of freedom, our Jews refrain with an almost religious scruple from covering their heads with the red caps worn by the Muslims, red being the color most suited to the hot climate—our fellow Jews don clothing in a great range of delicate shades on Saturdays and feast days: woolen cloth or silk in pale green, yellow, pale blue, and salmon. Although the result is more pleasing to the eyes, the impression of effeminacy created by the color, cut, and style of these clothes is very disturbing. In every respect, the habits and customs of the Jews of Fez are deplorable. [. . .]

A. Elmaleh

Archives of the AIU, France XIV.F.25.

The Housing, Foodways, and Economic Activities of a Moroccan Jewish Community: Meknes, 1912

Meknes, 8 December 1912

[. . .]

Jewish homes. These are all constructed in the same style: an interior courtyard, the Spanish patio, around which are arranged the rooms, generally two or three rooms, and a sort of shed which serves as a kitchen. This last is shared by several families and also houses the toilet and the well, alas! all too often situated too close to each other.

The ground floor is, in most cases, built below street level. It is entered through a low door. The reason for this peculiarity of construction? Apparently, it is the result of a desire, during the period of Jewish persecution, to give a more miserable appearance to their dwellings. Add to this a total lack of windows and you will understand the unsanitary conditions of these lodgings, in which eight to ten people live packed into a single room.

The first floor, in the homes that have one, is already better disposed because of its elevation. The humidity is felt much less, or not at all, and there are sometimes windows. There is even one home, of very recent construction, it is true, which has a wide balcony running the length of the facade.

Mattresses comprise the principal furnishing. They take up one or two, sometimes three, sides of the room and function as chairs as well as beds. There are no wardrobes; I have never seen one here. Clothes, linen, valuables, etc., . . . are locked up in chests. Many families have copperware: platters, candlesticks, samovars, etc., . . . more or fewer pieces of better or lesser quality depending upon the degree of wealth of the proprietors. These objects, as well as the dishware, glassware, teacups, and knickknacks, are kept in the numerous cupboards or on the Moorish-style shelves which decorate the walls. In the homes of the more comfortable families, there are, in addition, clocks, fine carpets, and chairs. The last are reserved for European visitors.

Foodstuffs and diet. Meals are taken at small, low tables whose limited dimensions make them easy to move about. The table is carried in already set, and once the meal is over the whole table is removed, with everything still on it.

There are three meals per day: breakfast in the morning, tea and bread; the midday meal; and supper.

The midday meal is taken between 11:30 and 1:30. No one waits for the others; each person eats when he so desires.

Supper is rarely taken before 8:00 and is often as late as 9:00, 10:00, and sometimes even 11:00 at night.

Only on Friday evenings, Saturdays, and feast days can the entire family be found at table together.

The nourishment consists almost entirely of meat. This is the result of the limited variety of green vegetables produced in the country and the difficulty of transport, which inhibits the importation of vegetables from areas more than 20 kilometers distant from the city.

Cauliflower, spinach, green beans, peas, etc., cannot be found here. Europeans have recourse to canned food to vary their diet.

Potatoes are expensive, precisely because the production is so low in the area that they must be imported. For a long time we were paying 1 franc per kilo, and they have never gone lower than 55 centimes.

Dried vegetables are also rarely consumed. Rice and chickpeas are prepared on Saturdays; dried beans almost never, and lentils only on the eve of the Ninth of Ab.[5]

The needy, who do not have the means to serve meat regularly, make up for it by buying giblets, hearts, livers, etc., which are quite inexpensive. The meat itself is sold at only 1 franc to 1.25 francs per kilogram.

This diet, which is not very hygienic in such a hot climate, is made all the worse by the consumption of alcohol.

The bottle of *anisette* is the first thing that appears on the table of rich and poor alike. Wine is served only on Friday evenings, Saturdays, feast days, and for certain special ceremonies.

Nevertheless, there is one observation to note: there are no places for public drinking. Each individual distills his own *anisette* at the end of each summer and makes his own wine for the year.

[. . .]

Population. The Jewish population of Meknes numbers between five and six thousand. Although there are many births, this figure has remained relatively constant for a long time. This can be attributed to the feeble constitution common to the population, which has caused a decrease in the average age, and to a high rate of infant mortality.

Could it be otherwise in a place whose decay is accelerated by two destructive practices: alcoholism and early marriages? Either of these practices would alone be sufficient to provoke the degeneration of the race, without taking into account the ignorance of elementary rules of public and private hygiene and the unsanitary conditions of even the most respectable looking homes.

The physically destitute condition of the population has yet another source; it is materially destitute.

Means of existence. Meknes, although it bears the title of second capital of Morocco, had the look of a dead city in the days prior to

5. The day commemorating the destruction of the Temple.

French occupation. A population reduced to barely 25,000, spread throughout a city whose walls enclosed stretches of land vast enough to contain 200,000 easily, left the streets deserted and silent. Rent was minimal; property owners let their houses fall into ruin rather than sacrifice the slightest sums for even the most urgent repairs. To an outsider passing through, this served to strengthen the impression that he was visiting the ruins of an ancient city.

Commerce was virtually nonexistent, reduced to three main European imports: cloth, sugar, and tea.

A group of about twenty Jewish merchants dealt with the wholesale distribution of these imports; they could not participate in retail commerce as they did not have the right to rent shops in the Arab city.

The Jews thus turned to certain local trades; they worked as tinsmiths, goldsmiths, etc., trades that were not very lucrative and that barely supported a man. Many made their living lending money for farming. It was moneylending that afforded the Jews in this vast wasteland the possibility of a relatively comfortable life.

This important source of revenue abruptly disappeared between eighteen and twenty years ago with the death of Mulay El Hassan, father of the current Sultan, and the subsequent reduction of the authority and prestige of the *Makhzan.*

This was more than a simple halt to profitable commerce; it represented the sudden and complete bankruptcy of the population of the *Mellah,* for the Jews had placed all of their resources in the hands of now rebellious tribes.

The relative prosperity which they had enjoyed gave way to utter poverty.

[. . .]

A. Moyal

Archives of the AIU, France XIV.F.25.

A Tour of Some Western Algerian Communities, 1903

Algiers, 29 June 1903

ORAN

[. . .]

Jewish district. There is a Jewish district in Oran as in almost every city in Algeria. In spite of the abolition of the ghettos and the right which our fellow Jews now have to take up residence wherever they so choose, and many do exercise this right, a good number of them continue to group together, to show great solidarity, and to feel very close to one another, sharing a particular affinity with others of the same race and religion. Thus it happens that in Algiers two streets, the *rue Randon* and the *rue de la Lyre,* are inhabited exclusively by Jews. The same is true in Oran for the *rue d'Austerlitz,* the *rue de Vienne,* the *rue de la Révolution,* and the *boulevard National,* where there is currently under construction a temple which surely will be the most beautiful and the most vast in all of Algeria and which will have cost at least 900,000 francs.

MASCARA

The city itself offers nothing of interest from either an archeological or an architectural point of view. Squatting lazily in the sun, it is surrounded on all sides by immense plains.

The plains produce an abundance of cereals, wine, and fruit. The streets run ruler-straight, are bright with sunlight, and full of dust. There are one- and two-story houses, none bearing any stamp of originality. There are no monuments. There is nothing which recalls the Arab domination. The tourist who ventures as far as Mascara is shown around the old district of Bab-Ali, the local curiosity, which is not particularly original.

The Jewish community. It can be said of the Jews of Mascara that they do not live in a district apart here, for the simple reason that the community is of relatively recent origin. It is a very small community, for that matter, barely two thousand (exactly 1,976 persons). In spite of their small numbers, the Jews form one-tenth of the total population, which numbers 20,000 inhabitants. A good number of them are originally from Tetuan and speak Spanish. They are affable and friendly and live on very good terms with their fellow citizens of any and all persuasions. All professions are open to them. Bankers, merchants, government employees, artisans, even farmers—there are a few—they distinguish themselves in all areas of endeavor and contribute, through their intelligence and their business understanding, to the well-being and prosperity of the city. They are also respected by the authorities, with whom they maintain very good relations.

The Jews of Mascara are very charitable. The community budget reaches almost 25,000 francs, which is enormous when seen in terms of the relatively small population. Every day a great number of transient poor are given some relief through the care of the consistory. They come from Morocco, from Figuig, and from Tafilalet on their way to the harbors of Algeria. All of these poor are housed and fed during their stay in Mascara, and they each receive a certain sum of money to take with them on their journey.

The greatest part of the revenue of the community goes toward the maintenance of the synagogues and for articles used in worship. The synagogues, there are three of them, have nothing about them that would attract attention. In the biggest, the *Shebet-Ahim,* what is most striking to the visitor is the incalculable number of multicolored lamps, which bear witness to the piety and generosity of the faithful. The ceiling is literally covered with them.

[. . .]

TLEMCEN

Rarely have I been given the opportunity to visit a city which is so interesting in the historical recollections it evokes, as well as in the number and variety of its monuments, and especially in the beauty of its sites.

The present-day city is built on the site of the ancient Roman Pomaria (gardens). Occupied in turn by the dynasties of the Almoravids, the Almohades, the Beni Zeyan, the Merinids, by the Spanish, and by the Turks, the city had seen many vicissitudes up until the French conquest. But all of the kings who ruled in Tlemcen, to whatever dynasty they belonged, made it a point of honor to contribute to the beautification of the city through the construction of palaces and houses of prayer. The result is the great number of mosques, castles, *Meshuar*s (citadels), and mausoleums. It is true that most of these have fallen to ruin, but the ruins themselves still bear witness today to the former splendor of Tlemcen.

[. . .]

The city itself is attractive, with its public squares, its wide boulevards, its magnificent avenues lined with plane trees spreading their cool shade. It is surrounded by fortifications put in place by the military engineers. As soon as one has passed these fortifications, a marvelous spectacle unfolds. Everywhere there are gardens in bloom, orchards, fields of olive and orange trees, and as a background, green hills and plains stretching as far as the eye can see toward the coast. Running water flows to these gardens and orchards through an irrigation system which has been functioning since ancient times. Oranges, lemons, almonds, cherries, peaches, apples, and pears are grown in the orchards; the trees all bear excellent fruit. All of this greenery creates an incomparable setting, a wonderful adornment for the city.

Need I tell you that I do not regret the four days I spent in Tlemcen, and that if my time had not been strictly limited, and my loved ones had not been impatiently waiting for me to return to Algiers, I would gladly have stayed a week in Tlemcen to visit all of the monuments, which merit being seen.

The Jewish community. Just as the city has its own physical character that makes it so unique, the Jewish community of Tlemcen has its own particular style that sets it apart from the other communities in Algeria. Everything about it denotes an intense religious life, an ardent faith that eighty years of French occupation have not managed to weaken. The ways, the customs, and the religious practices of the community reveal a people of firm character, preeminently conservative, and nourished on traditions that have been piously transmitted from one generation to the next . . .

The Jewish district. The Jewish district, . . . located almost in the center of the city, just next to the city hall, . . . offers a striking contrast, with its archaic character, to the modern buildings surrounding it. The houses, generally one-story structures painted yellow or red on the exterior and blue or green inside, give the impression of a more comfortable, more hygienic *Mellah,* in which the town leaders have seen to it that there is enough penetration of air and light. The dwellings each have a central courtyard set at two or three meters beneath the level of the street, making them rather humid. Additionally, space is severely limited. It is, in fact, the poor and working-class people who live in this district. Many families have to share houses with other families, some of them having only a single room for themselves, which obliges them to live with a regrettable lack of privacy. The Jews who have more money live in other parts of the city, in much more comfortable homes.

The synagogues, seven in number, are all located in the Jewish district. One of them, the *Rab* synagogue, merits special attention. It is very old but has been restored and expanded several times. It is a long, rectangular hall divided lengthwise into three bays by two rows of stone pillars.

[. . .]

A. Confino

Archives of the AIU, Algérie I.F.1a.

The Administrative Problems
of the Jewish Communities of Tunis, 1892

Tunis, 31 October 1892

[. . .]

It has been quite a while since I spoke to you about the affairs of the community—or communities—in Tunis. This does not mean that everything is running smoothly. The administration of the Tunisian community goes along as best it can, receiving the funds we have procured for it, meeting only its most urgent needs, and putting off the resolution of difficult problems at the risk of seeing them grow. In a word, it is surviving, living from day to day without progress, without positive change, and without solutions to complicated issues, but surviving nonetheless. This is not the case with the Livornese[6] community, in spite of the fact that the best educated, the richest, and the most influential of the Jews of Tunis belong to it. The members of this group have always shown themselves to be fierce defenders of their own privileges. They were uncompromising and inflexible on the question of fusion between the two groups making up our Jewish world here. The Livornese wanted to have a separate cemetery, for which they were willing to make certain sacrifices. They demanded, even at the risk of causing tension between themselves and the central administration of the Tunisian government, that they have a separate accounting system and separate services. The government of the Protectorate is not very concerned with Jewish affairs; its policy is simply to avoid problems as much as possible. It allowed the Livornese to do as they pleased. As a result, the *Grana* currently form a separate state within a state in the Jewish community. They appointed a commission, which they called the Directory Committee, whose principal mission was to maintain the autonomy of the small community and administer its resources. To the head of this committee was appointed an older man who is very respectable and very charitable, but also of very weak character. The schemers and the most intransigent supporters of division easily persuaded him to support them.

But everything has its price and the *Grana* community is today reaping what it has sown. Discord has set in among the people in their camp, as close as they once had been, and there has been no direction to their affairs for some time now. The time seemed right to attempt to remedy this situation while working toward our desired goal, that is, the fusion of the two communities. Since the *Grana* rabbi was very old and sick, we proposed replacing him with a French rabbi. The mission of this rabbi, whom we would have the government recognize as the spiritual leader of Judaism in Tunisia, would be to smooth away the difficulties and to remove the obstacles which stand in the way of union . . .

Under these circumstances choosing the right person is very impor-

6. The community composed of Jews originating from the city of Livorno in Italy, also known as the *Grana*.

tant, but there are also other questions to be resolved. Such questions include the method of nomination of the rabbi; the definition of his authority; the definition of his relation to the communities, to the other rabbis, to the rabbinical court, and to the local authorities; the amount of and sources for his remuneration, etc. None of these questions appears insoluble. We will manage to resolve them if we succeed in choosing a rabbi who is capable, intelligent, skilful, and (if you will forgive my frankness) unselfish.

[. . .]

D. Cazès

Archives of the AIU, Tunisie I.C.4.

Comparisons between Tunisian Jewry and Other Groups in the Regency, 1908

Tunis, 6 February 1908

[. . .]

The status and conditions of the Tunisian Jews cannot be judged with precision except through comparison with the groups they live among . . .

[. . .]

. . . The Jewish population indigenous to the Regency numbers approximately 64,000. More than two-thirds of this number—that is, 43,000—are inhabitants of Tunis.

According to the most recent statistics (1906), there can be found in Tunis:

18,600	French
52,076	Italians
6,174	Maltese
1,643	diverse nationalities
43,000	Jews indigenous to Tunisia

(We propose to study the status of the Jewish population which is indigenous to Tunis. In addition to these 43,000 Tunisian Jews, there are also approximately 3,000–4,000 Italian Jews—called the Colony of Livorno—and another 500–700 French Jews. These are included in the figures given for the Italian and French populations respectively.)

Finally, assuming that the total population of Tunis is 200,000:

78,507	Muslims

The following figures concerning children (boys and girls) in school correspond to these populations:

2,875   French
7,470   Italians
        (The French and Italian Jewish population is again included in these figures. There are approximately 150 Jewish children in the French population and approximately 300 in the Italian population.)
  802   Maltese
  133   schoolchildren of diverse nationalities
3,218   Jews indigenous to Tunisia
2,228   Muslims

The school population thus represents a little more than one-sixth of the total French population, approximately one-seventh of the Italian population, one-thirteenth of the indigenous Jewish population, and one thirty-fifth of the Muslim population.

The first conclusion which must be drawn: in terms of the spreading of instruction [school attendance], the indigenous Jewish population cannot be compared to the French population; it is greatly surpassed by that of the Italian population; and it has an important lead on the Muslim population.

It must be noted, first of all, that the difference in the percentages of school populations between the indigenous Jews and the Muslims is greatly reduced if only the boys are taken into account. In fact, we have for a population of 43,000 Jews, 1,650 boys and 1,568 girls. For the Muslim population of 78,500, there are 2,097 boys and only 131 girls in the schools. Thus boys attending school represent 3.8 percent of the Jewish population and 2.7 percent of the Muslim population.

    . . . The percentage of the school population of the Jews is greatly inferior to that of the French and the Italians and will soon be matched by that of the Muslims.

[. . .]

The expatriate French do not ordinarily join the ranks of the elite. Far from it. They are, nevertheless, an educated group, living simply and frugally. The climate prohibits them from taking up tiring work. For the most part they are government employees. Protective of their own interests, they began by protecting themselves against any competition in the less demanding but more lucrative positions within the administration. The government employees of the Regency are French in the well-paying posts and Muslim in the others. There are only two Jews in respected government positions. They are General Valensi, Chief of Protocol; and Mr. Joseph Valensi, Director of Municipal Services in Tunis.

[. . .]

The Italians form the most hardworking component of the Regency. They are the respected and feared invaders of all fields of activity; their energy and perseverance prove victorious in spite of all the laws established to hamper their success.

The Italians show remarkable temperance and endurance; as workers they never shirk any task, working energetically and efficiently. Thus, they have become the most sought after work force and the only true and organized working class in Tunis.

On the economic front, the Italian working class represents not only a fearsome danger for the Jews but also the often victorious adversary of the French themselves . . . The Italians rank highest in agriculture, industry, commerce, construction companies, etc. . . . There are treaties which protect their interests, an active consulate supports their requests and demands, and in case of litigation, they deal only with the European courts. We are in the presence of an element of the society which, although supplanted in the official and political control of the country, continues to dominate economically and to struggle to protect its interests.

For many long years, the Muslims remained passive observers of the political and economic rivalries between the foreign populations living in their country. Sober, lethargic, and with a fatalistic apathy, they let things come as they may. They were satisfied with the rental income from a building in the city or rural property. Sometimes they lived only on what little they could produce in work requiring no effort. Those who took up trades formed guilds with strictly limited entry. As they were completely tied to routine and did not know about commercial deals and transactions, they spent their lives vegetating in tranquil indifference.

The rapid transformation of the conditions of existence in Tunisia, the influence and the example set by the schools, the considerable increase in food and housing costs, and finally simple necessity, all these things combined to set this inert mass in motion. A good number of young men trained in the French schools took up the task of waking their fellow Muslims from this morbid torpor and preparing for a new, educated, active generation aware of modern economic activities . . .

[. . .]

Whether it was to pursue its civilizing mission or to offset the influence of other strong elements in the society—Italians and Jews—the government supported this movement. The movement spread and has reached such a point that today almost the entire French population of the Regency is calling it a danger . . .

[. . .]

Adaptable, capable, industrious, and gifted with a precious instinct for business, the Jew served as indispensable intermediary for the native Muslim, procuring for him the basic necessities and making a relatively comfortable living through an easily maintained trade. This was before the dawning of modern production and methods in Tunisia. Confined to the *Hara,* his only concern was the running of his business; his favorite form of relaxation was a pleasant meal. It was not refinement he enjoyed in the dishes prepared, but richness and abundance. Greed and gluttony are faults still found in the Jews of Tunis; these faults have not been much affected by our thirty years of influence here.

After the occupation, as the progressive transformation of the country was creating the need for a population specially trained in intelligent and modern methods, the country found in the Jew a marvelous answer to its new needs. The Jews are the flexible element *par excellence* of this society, and they were aided by circumstances on this occasion, having received a sufficient primary school education thanks to the providentially opportune opening of our school. Banks, maritime agencies, commercial agencies, stores and shops of all kinds, everything was overrun by graduates from our school.

The rising need for these kinds of employees; the attraction of a salary higher than any their fathers had ever known; the ease of the work, for which they felt a natural aptitude; the success, which was the envy of their fellow Jews; the attraction, to which those who had been the persecuted were particularly sensitive, of becoming the representatives of the new masters; all these factors led to a veritable frenzy. All of the students finishing school now dreamed only of finding a position in a bank or of sitting behind a desk in an office.

Clumsily imitating their employers and supervisors, and not wishing to differ from them in any way, they abandon their traditional dress and put on European garb. They outdo the Europeans themselves in their concern for elegance and style. They become obsessed with luxury and slaves to the clock but, unfortunately, maintain the mentality and the morality of the Jew from the *Hara.* They remain vapid, cowardly, greedy, and vain.

The desire to be noticed and the rush to succeed fire their minds. They hurry to acquire a superficial instruction, they haphazardly assimilate a few notions of accounting, they learn the few formulas required for basic commercial correspondence, they find a job and . . . they strut about . . .

[. . .]

And while the Jewish youths get lost in this pursuit of desirable posts, the Italian and Arab members of the population take up solid positions in the manual professions the Jews have abandoned or scorned. The Jewish youths prefer to pounce on positions in the offices of lawyers, attorneys, bailiffs, and editors, and are happy if, after months of training, they are making thirty or forty francs per month.

The Jewish population of Tunis is going through a period of extreme crisis. There are no official statistics concerning the professions practiced by the Jewish population as there are for the French and Italian.

To have an idea of the kinds of activities performed by the larger Jewish population from which we recruit our schoolchildren, I have made up a list of the professions of the parents of our students . . . Of 1,562 heads of household we have counted 218 tailors, 164 clerks, 123 wholesalers, 108 cobblers, 75 jewelers, 69 brokers, 46 grocers, 41 café owners, 37 confectioners, 33 haberdashers, 31 tinsmiths, 31 peddlers, 29 barbers, 29 rabbis, 23 butchers, 23 painters, 21 fruit merchants, 21 messengers, 21 musicians, 20 salesmen, 18 dealers in secondhand clothing, 16 dealers in secondhand goods, 16 bakers, etc. The predominant professions are, as you can see, among the most miserable.

[. . .]

L. Guéron

Archives of the AIU, Tunisie II.C.5.

A Prosperous Community: Cairo, 1895

Cairo, 22 August 1895

[. . .]

The community of Cairo is certainly the largest in Egypt. It numbers, in all probability, between 20,000 and 25,000; the community of Alexandria is the second largest in number. As is the case for all of the cosmopolitan communities, the one in Cairo is composed of the most disparate elements: all nationalities and all languages are represented. But the indigenous element dominates, that is to say, the Arab element. It is this element which sets the tone of the community, so to speak. This is also the richest element and the oldest. It prides itself on having given birth to almost all of the illustrious Jews of Cairo. Regarding the rites, it is the Portuguese rite which predominates, but there are also 400 Karaite families, whose material situation is, it would seem, among the most prosperous. The German rite is represented by more than 400 families. It is the poorest, and also the most recent, element of the community but it is active and hardworking and will certainly manage to create its own place in the sun.

Until not long ago, the Sephardim and the Ashkenazim formed a single community having a common administration and the same spiritual leader. Unfortunately, a year or two ago, the Ashkenazim—for reasons which would be too long and perhaps too delicate to discuss here—broke off from the others and formed a distinct community. Thus they have separated their interests from those of their fellow Jews of the Portuguese rite.

[. . .]

I noted with true satisfaction that a great spirit of tolerance sustains the majority of our fellow Jews in Egypt, and it would be difficult to find a more liberal population or one more respectful of all religious beliefs. This openness of spirit does them great honor and perhaps has much to do with the esteem and kindness with which they are generally treated here. I can assert without fear of contradiction that the Jews of this country are liked by their fellow countrymen, both Muslim and Christian alike, and that at no moment in their common history have friendly relations ever ceased. This is a particularly consoling observation. One cannot help but make the comparison with other countries—and there still are many—in which members of diverse religions look upon each other with hostility, forming so many enemy camps, each ready to tear the others to pieces, and each harboring sentiments of hatred and scorn for the others. I might add that the Egyptian Jews render great service to their country; they are the principal factor in its prosperity. They have founded many new ventures—business establishments, banking and industrial institutions—from which Egypt has drawn great profit. Their presence has been invaluable, and it would be difficult to imagine a prosperous Egypt without this active, intelligent, and honest element of the population. Although more than half of our fellow Jews here are of foreign nationalities, they do not fail to establish loyal ties to their adopted country. They take advantage of every opportunity to demonstrate their affection and gratitude for the government of the Khedive, which has been so kind and paternal toward all the populations who live on the hospitable soil of Egypt.

If the Jews have contributed to the prosperity of the country, they have been generously compensated for it. They have in their turn built considerable fortunes, which permit them to live in great comfort and to do much good for those around them. The Egyptian communities are, without question, the richest of the East; the community of Cairo is perhaps the most prosperous of all. But great social inequality can be seen there: colossal fortunes contrast with unfathomable poverty and between those two extremes there is a rising middle class. The middle class is very large in number; its members live in honest comfort and are inspired by the finest spirit of charity and solidarity.

It would seem, however, that a certain division is prevalent in the community, whose president is Mr. Cattawi, the wealthy Jew whose reputation I am certain you know. In spite of its significant revenues, which are increased by considerable gifts and voluntary contributions, public assistance leaves much to be desired. One is unpleasantly surprised to see so many beggars in such a prosperous community. Complaints are made against the administration, which is said to lack vigilance in directing the finances under its control and to neglect public services. There is some demand for a more open administration which would regularly give an account of its management and publish a yearly report detailing revenue and expenditures. It seems that the requests of the contributors have never been answered on this point and this creates some irritation toward the notables—Mr. Cattawi among others—who hold the administration of the community in their hands.

[. . .]

S. Somekh

Archives of the AIU, Syrie I.C.4.

The Sephardim and Ashkenazim of Safed, 1898

Safed, 22 December 1898

[. . .]

. . . I believe it would be useful to begin with a few words about the population we propose to reform and renew.

The total population of Safed is 14,000; 6,000 of its inhabitants are Jews, of which 4,600 are Ashkenazim and 1,400 Sephardim.

The Ashkenazim come from Russia, Poland, Galicia, Austria, Hungary, Bucovina, Bessarabia, and Romania. Here they live away from the Christians and the Muslims in an isolated and sordid ghetto which could have been transplanted from Warsaw, Kiev, Vilnius, or Ekaterinoslav, the cities which they formerly inhabited. Their common language is a Hebreo-Russo-Germanic jargon. They have an instinctive scorn for the indigenous Jews, whom they treat as uncivilized brutes. In my opinion, this is due to the fact that the Jews native to Safed are more robust and of stronger constitution than the others and that their language is Arabic, a more guttural, more masculine language than the one spoken by the immigrants. The Ashkenazim are indeed puny and feeble; their strength is moral rather than physical. In school, as in daily life, the Ashkenazim are more apt to surpass the Sephardim in study and thinking than in any labor which demands great physical exertion. Nevertheless, the Ashkenazim of Safed do not have any *yeshivot,* or rabbinical schools, although such schools must exist in the spiritual centers of Poland or Galicia and do exist in Turkey, in Constantinople, in Adrianople, in Salonica, etc. They pray often and long: that is the sum of their wisdom and their piety. A very few of them, recent emigrants from Europe, practice certain trades. These few alone constitute the whole of the industrial class of the city. There are also several who are involved in trade. But all—or nearly all—without discrimination receive the *halukah,* which is sent to them from their places of origin listed above. The idea of the *halukah,* which is no more than alms in disguise, was praiseworthy in its conception, but in practice it has become deplorable. According to the accurate details I have been able to procure, the *halukah* received annually by the Ashkenazim of Safed totals 250,000 francs. There is even a case of one Russian Jew whose wealth is now estimated at 800,000 francs, a sum he received through an inheritance, who still continues to receive his portion each time the *halukah* is distributed.

As for the Sephardim, the degenerate offspring of a group known for its brilliance in the Hebraic literature of the sixteenth and seventeenth centuries, they too live today in an unthinkable state of ignorance and extreme poverty. There are four hundred of them who, in their capacity as heads of family or future rabbis, have no other means of subsistence than what they receive from the *halukah.* The Sephardim differ from the Ashkenazim in that the latter receive their pittance directly in the form of a check sent from Russia, Hungary, and elsewhere to the committees representing the Russian, Hungarian, etc., colonies respectively.

Regarding the Sephardim, to this day they continue to send their own representatives, their collectors (*shaliah*), to gather donations in such regions as European Turkey, Bulgaria, Asian Turkey, Yemen, Hindustan, Persia, Turkestan, Egypt, Tunisia, Morocco, and especially Algeria.

[. . .]

Among the Ashkenazim, in spite of certain abuses which would be too long to discuss here, there is a semblance of communal organization. Their Chief Rabbi (*dayan*)—although he is not officially recognized—commands an extraordinary respect from his flock. His will is followed blindly. He is by law the president of all the committees directing the *halukah*. In the eyes of all the pious Jews of Europe his participation sanctions all the decisions of these committees.

As for the Sephardim, from an administrative point of view they live in incredible chaos. They have neither committees nor administrators; just recently they have even relieved their official Chief Rabbi (*hakham-bashi*) of his duties. Among them everyone claims the title of chief; each man commands and no man obeys.

[. . .]

M. Franco

Archives of the AIU, France XI.F.20.

A Profile of the Various Jewish Communities Represented in the Alliance School of Jerusalem

Jerusalem, 26 August 1901

[. . .]

The 416 boys who attended our school this year are distributed according to their country of origin as follows:

22	Aleppo	7	Shiraz
7	Alexandria	5	Beirut
5	Cairo	13	Jaffa
3	Constantinople	7	Port Said
2	Smyrna	7	Salonica
24	Monastir	2	Aydin
4	Rhodes	6	Damascus
19	Morocco	1	Antioch
6	Bursa	3	Ayn-Teb
6	Tangier	9	Yemen
3	Tiflis	3	Gallipoli
1	Fez	4	Bukhara
4	Adrianople	1	Doubnitza
26	Sofia	1	Acre
4	Hebron	200	Jerusalem

The 200 boys from Jerusalem were born here, but most of the parents of these boys are from Russia or Turkey.

Thus, as you can judge from these instructive statistics, our student population comes from three parts of the world. It includes types, habits, practices, and languages each one very different from the others; it is a veritable Tower of Babel after the confusion of tongues . . .

Yemenites. The Yemenite has a pale and thin face. He has a thin but sturdy stature and bright, intelligent eyes. One senses that beneath this rough exterior there is an unhappy child who, in his distant country, had been made to suffer every kind of privation and who had endured moral and physical pain with calm and *sang-froid* . . . Almost all of the Yemenites speak Hebrew with relative ease and accuracy. This is an obvious proof that in the isolated cities of Yemen, far from any intellectual center, in the midst of fellow countrymen who brutalized them and treated them as slaves, these people sought refuge and supreme consolation for their ills in meditating on the Torah and the sacred books. They have a relatively good knowledge of the Bible rather than the Talmud. When they arrive in Jerusalem, they are already able to express themselves in Hebrew without difficulty. They are very industrious and have much stamina; they take up the most exhausting trades and give themselves to their work with an exemplary tenacity, as long as that work provides a living for themselves and for their families. The children share the qualities of the parents, but often these families, blessed by God, have many children, and the father's work alone is not enough to support the youngsters, who are left to run in the streets. This is why, in spite of our entreaties, the boys are taken from school at the age of ten or eleven and begin to help their fathers. Some work as laborers in construction; some begin to learn the stonecutters trade, at which they are past masters. No Yemenite student has yet reached the sixth class at school.

Persians. The Persian has a round, yellow face. His body is heavy and squat and his eyes are dull. His intelligence is totally asleep. There is nothing attractive or kindly about him. In these men from the country of Ahasuerus, everything denotes an oppressed, debased, and degenerate race even to the unintelligible Persian jargon that they mumble between their teeth. Apart from the mechanical reading of prayers and of the Bible, sacred study itself has probably been long neglected and forgotten in Persia. As a result the Persian students are the most lazy, the least advanced, and those from whom we expect the least progress. In spite of all the effort on the part of the teachers to reach all of their students indiscriminately, the intellectual development of the Persians proceeds with an appalling slowness. While the Yemenite who sits beside him at the same table is able to read a dozen pages of his French primer without difficulty, to stutter a few words in this language, and is taking an interest in basic arithmetic, his Persian classmate has not yet mastered the first two pages of his primer and rebels against abstract thinking. Thus the Persians in Jerusalem are called upon only for heavy work requiring many hands. They are employed as laborers in construction and in emptying cesspools, etc. Their daily pay rarely exceeds one franc, when there is work to be had. When they are without work they wander aimlessly through the streets; they have their own particular style of loafing about. The Persian children are all the more easily discouraged because it is impossible for their teachers to talk to them in their native language. They generally leave school abruptly.

Sephardim. The Sephardim come from cities in which instruction is already respected and valued by the poorest parents. These parents realize that in present times a young man cannot make his way in life if he has not spent his childhood years in a school and if he has not learned many things there. One touching example: Six months ago we had decided to create a German course in our school for a certain number of students, especially the Ashkenazim. One afternoon as I returned from school, I found an old woman, nearly seventy, waiting for me. She stood up to greet me; I offered her a seat and asked her what was the reason for her visit: "Monsieur," she said, "when I was a child there were no schools, but we understand that school is a useful institution for our children. I have come to ask you to have my son taught German too. If it is necessary I can pay a small sum; I will spend less on food for myself if need be, but I do not want my child to remain ignorant like his father. I have another son who finished his studies at the Alliance school in Adrianople. He is earning a living thanks to the instruction he received there. I want my second son to learn even more than my oldest."

A second example: In one class there was a disruptive student who was the despair of all his teachers. As a disciplinary action, I had sent him from school for a few days. No sooner had this been done than a very old grandmother came to beg pardon for her grandson. When I refused, she began to sob and she added: "His mother is recently deceased. Before dying his father's last request was that I not take him out of the Alliance school until he had finished his studies. He said that he did not want his child to suffer from ignorance as he himself had suffered." Naturally I hastened to take the child back. These are the consoling indications of an awakening in an entire population. Even the older members of the population, from whom we might have had to face opposition, recognize that there is no salvation without instruction. As a result, the Sephardim attend school more regularly and discontinue their instruction only in rare cases.

Ashkenazim. The Ashkenazim in Jerusalem form a kind of caste apart, so to speak, and have almost nothing in common with their fellow Jews of the Sephardi rite. Their community is entirely distinct from ours: they have their own revenues, their own tax on meat, their *shohetim,* their temples, and their schools. They are much more intransigent than the Sephardim for a good number of the latter buy their meat from Ashkenazi butchers, but an Ashkenazi would never buy meat from a Sephardi butcher; this meat is even considered *taref* [ritually unclean] according to the interpretation of the law of most Ashkenazi doctors. Concerning the question of instruction, they are absolutely inflexible. From the top to the bottom of the hierarchy, the teaching of any and all profane subjects is declared to be blasphemy against the Law of Moses. David said in one of his Psalms, "You will ponder the Law from morning to evening," and they hold strictly to the letter of the recommendation of the Poet King. Only, instead of the Bible, it is the Talmud that they scour and scrutinize in all of its parts; . . . their long hair falling at their temples, they are still, and for a long time to come, the outstanding representatives of the spirit of obscurantism and conservatism. They pose as the cherubim placed before the Sacred Ark, appointed as guardians of the true traditions of Judaism. Ah! if in fact they did preserve the pure, sound, and holy doctrine which flows from an enlightened and rational teaching of the Law, it would be easy to forgive them their characteristic aversion for the schools. But there is a shameful and nameless corruption among them. Recent scandals should have opened the eyes of the most unshakable pharisees and shown them that, beneath the exterior appearance of the holiness of their lives and beneath this feigned rigor, their religious leaders are hiding the most dissolute behaviors. In spite of all the measures taken by the Ashkenazi committees to prevent their children from contamination through contact with us, many of the more enlightened families have entrusted their children to us. The latter are so happy in the school that they have become disseminators of our liberal ideas. There is no doubt that the number of these children is imperceptibly increasing from year to year. This is in spite of the excommunications pronounced every year against all institutions which teach profane subjects, and in spite of the threats of withholding the *halukah.*

The study of the Talmud sharpens the mind in a general sense; it

develops and refines the mental faculties. For this reason the young
people who come to us after having spent several years in the *heder*
[the traditional school] are very bright. They do not take long in
reaching the head of their class. They have remarkable powers of
assimilation, they are models of perseverance, and they apply themselves well and exhibit exemplary conduct. Generally, they are a little
older when they begin in the school and do not leave until they have
finished their primary education . . . I must admit that I have taken a
special interest in the Ashkenazim, I favor them as much as I can, I
push them in their studies, and I use every possible means to draw
them to our school. This Great Wall of China which the Ashkenazim
have constructed between themselves and us will fall little by little. In
time the reconciliation will take place, and the young people who will
have been taught by us will be our best helpers in achieving this goal.
[. . .]

A. Benveniste

Archives of the AIU, France XI.F.20.

The Jews of Aleppo, 1931

Aleppo, 15 April 1931

[. . .]

JEWISH POPULATION OF SYRIA

A) Their number:

The Jewish population of northern Syria numbers more than 8,000.
All of these Jews belong to the Sephardi rite.

B) Their distribution according to principal regions and cities:

With the exception of a very small minority, all live in the city of
Aleppo itself. There are 20 Jewish families in Antioch, 10 families in
Alexandretta, 15 families in Tedef, and 50 families in Kamishli.

C) What are the trades and professions practiced by the Jews?

Of the 7,500 persons forming the Jewish community of Aleppo,
there are 3,000–3,500 who live in poverty. During the feast of Passover they receive unleavened bread through the generosity of their
fellow Jews in Aleppo. For the most part they work as shoemakers,
mattress makers, tinsmiths, bootblacks (this last is a very common
occupation in the East; there are many here who have their shoes
waxed and polished two or three times a day), porters, grocers, book-
binders, hawkers, and especially peddlers. In addition, among our fellow Jews in Aleppo there are a good number of small shop owners,
fabric merchants, about 30 brokers, 10 tailors, 4 druggists, 2 customs

agents, 4 forwarding agents, 15 jewelers, 7 or 8 powerful contractors, 20 wholesale merchants, each having between two and eight thousand pounds capital, and 5 or 6 bankers.

. . . JEWISH COMMUNITIES

A) In what cities are there Jewish communities?

There is in Aleppo a large Jewish community of approximately 7,500.

B) What are their powers and rights?

Because the Syrian constitution has not yet been promulgated,[7] the status of minorities and their powers and rights have not yet been clearly defined. However, the non-Muslim communities continue to enjoy the prerogatives granted by the Sublime Porte before the separation of Syria from the Ottoman Empire. Thus, each non-Muslim community in Aleppo has its own spiritual leader, its own communal council, its own religious tribunal, and its own charitable organizations.

C) How are they organized?

Our fellow Jews have as their representative to the Mandate and local authorities our Chief Rabbi. Differences of a religious nature, and sometimes of a strictly commercial nature, are decided by our *Beit-Dîn,* or rabbinical tribunal. The notables of the community entrust the communal council with the management of the internal affairs of the community. The communal council collects the necessary funds for payment to the Chief Rabbi, the *dayanim,* the *shohetim,* and others who serve the community. They are also responsible for the distribution of unleavened bread to the poor.

D) When were they created?

Certain inscriptions found on old stones in the main synagogue of Aleppo place its construction in the time of Alexander the Great. Our fellow Jews must have settled in northern Syria in most distant times. The Jews of Aleppo maintain that the citadel of Aleppo houses a great stone on which can be read the following inscription: "I, Joab ben Serouya, conquered this city for my lord, King David." I will mention in passing that I personally looked for this inscription with Professor Slousch when he was visiting Aleppo two years ago, but we did not find it.

Has this stone intentionally been removed for its reference to the former power of Israel; does the stone still exist? In the Psalms (chap-

7. Syria was still under the French Mandate at the time.

ter LX, Prayers and Lamentations of David, verse 2) King David makes an allusion to the combat of Joab against the Syria of Tsoba; and Aleppo is none other than "Aram Tsoba." This passage of the Psalms confirms the declaration of Joab mentioned above. Moreover, I will add that according to a very widespread legend among the Muslim and Jewish populations of Aleppo, the name Aleppo, or "Halab," was given to the city in memory of an encampment which Abraham had set up on one of the hills overlooking the city. He had his cow milked in this encampment and the word "Halab" means "to milk" in Arabic.

[. . .]

ECONOMIC CONDITIONS

On the economic situation in general in the country, and especially on salaries and the cost of living:

Before the building of the Suez Canal, the economy of Aleppo flourished. This city served as a commercial entrepôt between the West and the East. All merchandise shipped, especially from Europe to Persia and Iraq, had to pass through the city of Aleppo, from which it was sent on to its destination. Our fellow Jews, the majority of whom work in commerce and serve as intermediaries between the producers and the consumers, profited from the privileged situation of the city for many years, until 1869, when the Suez Canal was opened.

Since then, commercial activity in Aleppo has decreased considerably. Nevertheless, until 1918 our fellow Jews continued to profit, on a lesser scale, from the geographical situation of Aleppo by maintaining commercial relations with Cilicia, Kurdistan, Iraq, and Persia. Several recent treaties, most importantly the Treaty of Lausanne, have since created customs barriers between Cilicia and Syria and between Mesopotamia and Syria. The xenophobia of the Turks and the Iraqis hinders economic relations between Aleppo and its neighbors to the north and east.

Moreover, the new Damascus–Palmyra–Baghdad route has appreciably diminished the commercial role of the city of Aleppo. But it is nonetheless true that its importance has not been entirely extinguished. One day, the regeneration of its industry will certainly return it to its former prosperity.

[. . .]

E. Penso

Archives of the AIU, Syrie I.C.3.

The Kurdish Jews of Northern Iraq, 1934

Mossul, 26 June 1934

[. . .]

The Kurdish Jews who live in the villages that are far from police posts, especially those in the mountains, are at the mercy of their masters, or *agha*s. These *agha*s can dispose of the Jews and their belongings as they dispose of their own personal property. The few Jews whom I have seen had been sold by their masters to another *agha*.

Otherwise, the Kurdish Jew is apparently free. He works as weaver, dyer, small merchant, or farmer. Those attached to the household of the *agha* as slaves are rare. The Kurdish Jew can come and go from one village to another for his work. He does this not without some risk, but the *agha* is supposed to protect him, except in cases where the *agha* himself has one of his men rob the Jew as he makes his way. In exchange for this so-called protection, the *agha* can call upon the Jewish farmer to carry out certain farm labor on his property: transport of grain, cultivation of the fields, caring for the animals, etc., all this of course without remuneration. If the Jew comes to work for several days at the home of the *agha,* far from his own home, all he is given to eat is a little rye bread. The *agha* can also ask the Jewish farmer for a part of his grain or fruit harvest, for a few head of sheep, or for other products of his farm. He can ask the weaver to furnish him with handsome clothes. He comes to see the small Jewish manufacturer and leaves, without paying, with the finest cloth. It must be remembered that the Kurdish Jews, being also subjects of the king of Iraq, pay the tithe to the king's agents and all of the other taxes, like any other citizen of Iraq.

The Jew has no recourse to any authority against all these arbitrary actions. He would not be likely to complain anyway, for the vengeance of the *agha* would be terrible. He accepts the decisions of the *agha* without saying a word, happy enough that things went no worse for him.

These unfortunate people cannot leave their village to live somewhere else. If through great cunning one of them manages to leave the village never to return, his goods are immediately confiscated. He could not sell them before leaving, for the *agha* forbids the Jews to sell their belongings and the Muslims to buy them. The *agha* takes all these measures in order to keep the Jews from leaving his village, for in Kurdistan the Jews make up the most important economic element of the population. He also does not want them to leave because of the services they graciously render him.

The *agha* is also in charge of marriages, as a civil official would be, but he carries out this function in order to increase his revenues. According to Kurdish custom, the young man buys his fiancée from her parents. For this he gives them a certain sum, of which half goes to the *agha*. This exclusive power is a source of great abuse for, by means of money, the *agha* can force a young woman to marry a man whom she does not love. The pretty girls are not allowed to remain Jews. They are converted by force to Islam and made to marry Muslims.

Since the *agha* is the only authority in his village, he also appropriates the functions of judge. He does not punish according to the official civil code but rather according to his own inclinations. He is often cruel. He has the power to impose heavy fines, which he keeps for himself, and even capital punishment. Still, as the Jews are peaceful, submissive, and honest, none of them has ever been known to steal, betray, or kill. It is for this reason, too, that the *agha* likes them and has more trust in them than in his fellow Muslims.

The ignorance which reigns among the Kurdish Jews is incredible . . . All of our fellow Jews here are completely illiterate. This is due to the fact that the villages are widely dispersed and the inhabitants are few; thus there is never a sufficient number of students to hire a teacher. As they are also far from the religious centers, they are not familiar with even the most elementary notions of our religion. They are not completely isolated, however, and their ties to the religious centers are kept up through a rabbi who visits all the villages once or twice a month, weather permitting, to slaughter a few sheep or perform a circumcision.

The Kurdish Jews are not prohibited from observing the Sabbath. But in certain villages, where they are like slaves in the service of the *agha,* no distinction is made between Saturday and the other days of the week. The *agha* is often angered at the number and the duration of our feast days, and although the Iraqi government grants time off to all its Jewish employees for each feast day, the *agha* of his own personal volition orders his Jewish subjects to work.

We cannot say that all of the Jews are slaves. Jewish slaves are rare. But we can affirm that all the Kurdish Jews suffer from the completely arbitrary decisions and actions of their masters.

What can we do for these unhappy people who naively await the arrival of the Messiah to put an end to this slavery, which they call *galut* [exile]? Nothing, for whatever requests we made to try and improve their conditions would only serve to make them worse. A request for intervention on the part of the government would be fruitless, for the government would not be willing to create political complications in the country for the sake of a handful of Jews. The *agha*s, with their constantly armed men, are capable of stirring up bloody revolts, in which the Jews would be the first to suffer.

Suppose we could, with enough money, eventually buy them all back from their masters. In the city to which they would be moved, we would have to find them positions in which they could exercise their previous occupations. Let us not forget that they are all weavers and farmers (they weave a special cloth worn only by Kurds). What would they do in a big center like Mossul! True, they would be freer and protected, but they would die of hunger for they would not be able to work.

The best solution is . . . to move them gradually to Palestine, where they would constitute an excellent labor force. There again, we come upon the obstacle of the restrictions on immigration of Jews enacted by the Palestinian government.
[. . .]

Y. Franco

Archives of the AIU, Irak I.C.9.

Iranian Jewry Past and Present:
A Look at the Jewish Community of Teheran, 1904

Teheran, June 1904

MATERIAL AND MORAL CONDITIONS OF THE JEWS IN TEHERAN
[. . .]
One can conclude with certainty that these Jews have been totally severed from the rest of the Jewish world for as long as they have been in Persia. What other explanation could there be for their complete unawareness of the Jewish history of the Middle Ages? It would be inadmissible for any Jewish traveler arriving in Persia to fail to recount to his fellow Jews the heroism of the Jewish martyrs burned at the stake or the flowering of Hebrew literature or the lives of the greats. Left to themselves, what then became of these Jews in the movement [of change] which swept them up, and how did they survive this trial?

We must attest that, to their credit, they have proved able to maintain the faith of their fathers. Through centuries of oppression and vicissitudes, there was but one thing to cling to, one thing that saved their character and their dignity from destruction: their religion and its Law. But we must also add that their surroundings have had a profound effect on their lives. These Jews were hemmed in by Muslims on all sides, beleaguered by an intolerant and closed society, constrained by the demands of the indigenous ways of life, and made to abandon everything in their customs and practices that might prove offensive to Persian beliefs. They found themselves forced to jealously protect their rights, which were constantly violated by their persecutors. To this end, they began to use guile—the only weapon of the weak against the strong—to return lie for lie, and to answer greed with greed. Surrounded by the indolence, luxury, and extravagance of Persian glory—signs that announce the decadence of an old civilization—they began to lose their Jewish character and to adopt Persian customs and habits. They assimilated Persian ceremonies, customs, and superstitions. They even took from the Persians their way of thinking, of understanding life, their aspirations, their hopes for a better future—that is, everything which marks the unique character of a population. Finally there was nothing left of Jewry in them but the name. The Jews copied everything from the Persians. They borrowed everything, even to the lulling tone of their prayers, that familiar and almost patriarchal chant that has been repeated through the generations and preserved so that the children can remember the sweetness of prayer.

Those who understand the strength of the Jewish race and who know with what fierce energy it defends its traditions, its ways, and even its superstitions will realize what brutal force over a long period of time must have been imposed to have crushed to such an extent this wretched population. There is perhaps no other place in which Jews have been made to endure such misery. Let us consider them now at the moment when the Alliance first took them under its protection.

*   *   *

The material conditions in which the Jews live are still very precarious. This widespread poverty is the consequence of the persecutions, the exactions, and the restrictions which severely limit commerce and the struggle for life. When a person has constantly to protect an ever-threatened existence, he thinks very little about making his fortune. During a time when, through governmental negligence, the roads were not even safe for Muslims, and when bands of thieves would ransack an entire heavily populated section of a city without fear or hesitation, it is easy to understand that rich men, and especially wealthy Jews, became the target of Muslim greed. If we add to these

causes of poverty the rapacity of the governors, who imposed heavy
contributions on this fully exploitable people, and the stigma placed
upon these unclean beings by the superior order of the *mushteheds*
(high priests), so that their merchandise could not be sold, it is also
easy to understand how our fellow Jews have fallen into such complete destitution. Even today the Jews do not live on equal footing
with the Muslims. For example, they are not allowed to open shops in
the bazaars and are obliged to take refuge in closed caravansaries.

But even had they been wealthy, what would they have done with
their fortunes? The Jews did not have the right to build homes that
might have been judged luxuries by the *sayids* (Muslim priests). And
in the eyes of a *sayid,* any home that has any comfort at all is a
luxury for the unclean. The use of decorative patterns was rigorously
forbidden to the Jews . . . They were also forbidden to construct
dwellings of more than one story, to have a too spacious courtyard, to
build too many windows in the walls; simply put, they were denied
air, sun, and the right to be alive.

Because of these restrictions, the homes form one tight mass.
Whether as an effect of the directives which come from the clergy, as
a result of an essentially Persian indolence and negligence, or because
of ignorance of the laws of elementary hygiene, the ghetto of Teheran
is probably the most dense and compact district in Persia. In the cities
of the provinces, Hamadan, Seneh, Urmia, even in Isphahan, one can
find some buildings set apart and some homes without decoration but
with large rooms and spacious courtyards. In Teheran the search to
find a building that could be transformed into a school produced no
results. We were forced to use for this purpose two separate homes
that were joined by dark corridors.

Without exaggeration, the ghetto of Teheran can be called a city of
mud. Forming a tangled maze, the sometimes covered, sometimes
open streets are so narrow that you instinctively expect each one to
come to a dead end when walking through them. These twisting corridors border homes made of stones and brick or of clay baked in the
sun; they have never seen plaster. These homes appear to have become resigned to having the rain wash away their walls little by little
and to letting them fall in clumps on the heads of passersby. The
negligence of the property owners finally destroys the rest. They do
not know the English proverb "A tile in time saves nine." The rooms
are built around a narrow courtyard, which is hardly as wide as a
handkerchief, and they are stacked one upon the other, without openings, dark and bare. There are none of those little shaded gardens

which complement the homes in more hospitable regions. It is in these burrows that our fellow Jews have been living for centuries. [. . .]

L. Loria

Archives of the AIU, Iran II.C.6.

The Problem of Conversions: Hamadan, 1908

Teheran, 30 August 1908

[. . .]

Community. From the point of view of religious practices, the Jewish community of Hamadan is one of the least homogeneous of Persia. It is not unusual to find in the same family a mother who is a practicing Jew, a father who has become Muslim, the oldest son Bahai, and the rest converted to Protestantism. I am sure it will surprise you to hear that Orthodox Jewry is the least represented and that it is becoming more rare with each passing day. You may think this is paradoxical, but it is the pure and simple truth. This kind of report is not the place for exaggerating but for simply reporting the facts. I will ask Mr. Hochberg: "Who is this student?"—"The son of a Jew converted to Islam." "And that one over there?"—"Bahai." "And this other one?"—"Bahai." "And this one here?"—"The son of a Protestant Jew." "I see, so there are no practicing Jews in your school!"—"Very few."

It can be stated without exaggeration that nine-tenths of the Jewish population of Hamadan are affiliated with the Bahai sect, whose leader was forced to leave the country because of persecution and currently resides in Saint-Jean-d'Acre in Syria. The Bahai differ from the Muslims only in their more liberal interpretation of the text of the Koran. Like the Muslims, they recognize the authority of Mohammed and the divine mission with which he was invested. They are extremely tolerant . . . will not accept any differences in treatment of Muslims and non-Muslims, reject all directives concerning the *nedjes* (impurity attached to non-Muslims), and allow their wives to walk in the streets freely and without veils. They also reject polygamy. [. . .]

A. Confino

Archives of the AIU, Iran I.F.1.

10
The Impact of the West
and the Alliance Schools

The Alliance teachers were keen to report the changes and westernization taking place in the countries in which they taught. They gave the schools a lot of credit for initiating the transformation of the Jews in the lands of Islam. Their correspondence with Paris is marked by glowing accounts of the changes they believed their mission had effected, a mission they considered to be complemented by the growing Western presence in the Middle East and North Africa. This Western presence symbolized the wave of the future and was depicted with great self-congratulatory approbation.

The Challenge Posed by
the New French Presence in Tunisia, 1881

Tunis, 10 July 1881

Sirs,

The events that have just occurred in Tunisia are going to create an appreciable modification in the economic status of this country.[1] Agriculture and industry will soon undergo considerable development, and foreigners will pour in and considerably modify working and living conditions. In short, the inhabitants of the Regency will witness a radical transformation of the country in which they were born. Those among them who have the necessary education and intelligence to ride the rapids and follow the new current of events may profit from the change and improve their condition in proportion to their means. On the other hand, there will be those who stubbornly insist on living as they had in the past and who try to maintain their current state of apathy and inertia. Without fail, they will be outstripped by their competitors, who are better prepared for the struggle. As a result, they will be shut out of the general movement and will inevitably fall victim to poverty.

We have seen similar phenomena in our time, and we will again be

1. The reference is to the declaration of the French Protectorate over Tunisia in 1881.

witness to such events. Two peoples, equally persecuted and equally treated as outcasts, shared the monopoly on business and employment in Turkey: the Jews and the Armenians. These two people vied with each other for the best positions in commerce and for public and consular posts. The Jews have superior intelligence and so at first took the lead in the movement. But while they were resting on their laurels, the Armenians were preparing future generations for the struggle. They opened elementary and secondary schools for their sons and daughters. They began accepting adults into their courses. They founded libraries and chose to make enormous sacrifices to ensure a better future for their race. And success has crowned their efforts. Today we are witnessing what is a distressing spectacle for us, but from which we must learn and profit: while the Armenian communities are growing richer and prospering, the Jewish communities sink further with each passing day. The bigger stores are doing less and less business; the small shops are disappearing. The Jews are finding themselves, almost to a person, obliged to serve as brokers for those who have replaced them.

A similar situation is about to develop in Tunisia. An analogous future awaits our fellow Jews if we leave them to their own devices and do not profit from the lessons of experience acquired at our expense in other countries. We therefore have a duty to make certain sacrifices in order to prepare our Tunisian brothers, through the teaching of their youth, for improved physical and moral conditions. We must open schools for both boys and girls. We must accustom our young people to manual labor and especially to agricultural work. We must not allow the neglect of the cities of Tunisia: Sousse, Sfax, Gabès, Gerba, Bèja, etc. . . . .

[. . .]

We must without fail establish a group of schools in Tunisia . . . which have a unified organization, follow the same program, and are placed under the direction of the director of the school in Tunis.

Naturally, it will be quite expensive to open all of these institutions, but the communities are ready to contribute a major portion. In any case, we must recognize the inevitable. The French Protectorate over Tunisia will not be long in becoming an annexation of the country. This is only a question of time; the change will take place in the very near future. In light of this fact, we must consider that the current and future expenditures which the Alliance has chosen to make in Tunisia will naturally come to an end when the country becomes annexed . . .

Allow me to present a summary of what should be, in my opinion, the agenda for the work of the Alliance in this country.

1. An increase in the number of teachers in your boys' school in Tunis.

2. Study of French for all students in the school, Italian being reserved for the more advanced classes.

3. A reorganization of the facilities for small children modeled on similar institutions in Europe.

4. Adoption of a single and fixed program of study and a uniform teaching method for all teachers coming from the preparatory school.

5. Foundation of a good school for girls in Tunis.

6. Expansion of the apprenticeship system and the establishment of farming colonies that would work with French farming concerns operating in Tunisia.

7. Foundation of schools in Sousse, Sfax, Gabès, Gerba, and Bèja. [. . .]

D. Cazès

Archives of the AIU, Tunisie XXVIII.E.

An Overview of the Alliance's Work in Asia Minor: Smyrna, 1898

Smyrna, 27 November 1898

REPORT ON THE WORK OF THE ALLIANCE IN SMYRNA FROM 1873 TO 1898 [*address given on the occasion of the twenty-fifth anniversary of the foundation of the Alliance school in Smyrna*]

[. . .]

In 1873, the community of Smyrna had no school for boys or for girls. There were only a certain number of *heder*s for the boys . . . At the age of fourteen, when these children left the *heder,* the more fortunate ones went with their fathers to help them in their businesses. The others went God knows where, no one worried about them, and they simply did what they could. It is superfluous to add that no Jew practiced any trade but that of the tailor, the cobbler, and the tinsmith.

As for the girls, they received only the education that their mothers could give them. They had no instruction. They were asked only to know how to sweep, wash the clothes, and bake bread.

This state of affairs was deplorable. The persons who were then in charge of the affairs of the community realized that if they did not take steps to save the youth from their ignorance, our community would soon be hopelessly lost. The first Alliance committee was founded in 1871 with Mr. Behor David Hazan as its president. But

the committee that actually founded the school was that which succeeded the first in the following year . . .

In many of the communities where the Alliance has founded
schools, it has come up against obstacles raised either by the rabbinical body or by the community administrations. The community of
Smyrna will have the everlasting honor of having had for a leader at
that time such an enlightened and worthy pastor as was His Eminence
Chief Rabbi Abraham Palatche. He supported the new foundation
with all of his strength and thereby set an example for all rabbis and
for all the communal councils who have administrated our public affairs to this day. They have always given us their most sincere and
most devoted support . . .

The school in Smyrna, so fortunate in every respect, also had the
good fortune to receive Mr. David Cazès as its first director appointed by the Alliance. He was then and throughout the years of his
service in the Alliance the most distinguished and most accomplished
of teachers to share in our work. Under the guidance and impetus
given by Mr. Cazès, the school made progress each day . . .
[. . .]

To instruct boys and teach them a trade is an excellent thing. But
to transform the life of a people and to educate them require above
all the transformation of the internal life of the family. This is the role
of the woman. To accomplish such a delicate task, and to prepare the
women of our community to be wives worthy of young men filled
with modern ideas, the initiative of a virtuous, intelligent, and devoted woman was needed. Mrs. Dudu de Polako was this woman. It
was she who, with the cooperation of a few willing men, established
the organization called "Progress" and founded our school for girls in
1878. The school has 300 students today and the Alliance has just
sent us an excellent new headmistress to lead it . . .
[. . .]

. . . The *Talmud-Torah,* in existence for many years, was reorga-
nized eight years ago by an intelligent administrative committee which
turned to the Alliance to find a director capable of gradually improving the teaching. This undertaking, started by a very dedicated
teacher in 1890, is being continued today . . .

The last few years . . . have been devoted to perfecting the tasks
already under way and in trying to accustom our fellow Jews to working the land. In addition to the purchase of a small farm in Burnabat,
where several students were placed, considerable sums were devoted
to the support of Russian émigrés who have settled as farmers in the
province of Aydin. These monetary sacrifices were not unrewarded,

for they have given us the experience thanks to which we hope to repeat the undertaking in the near future . . .

[. . .]

Regarding instruction, our programs were further developed in Smyrna and in the provinces. Schools in Magnesia and in Chios had already been organized by Mr. Parienté. New Alliance schools were opened in Aydin, in Cassaba, in Pergamon, and in Tireh. In Smyrna a new school was opened in the Karatash district. A nursery school was opened to prepare the children for our schools and to develop in them, from a very early age, the habits and principles necessary for a good education. In our boys' school, an advanced business course was begun where our students who had completed the First Class were able to continue their studies . . .

[. . .]

G. Arié

Archives of the AIU, Turquie LXXV.E.

Social Reforms Initiated by an Alliance Director: Marrakesh, 1902

Marrakesh, 13 August 1902

[. . .]

There was a need for . . . someone to reach out to the many needy people confined to sickbeds who could no longer procure even the basic necessities. We saw that some modest institution had to be created to ease their suffering and that those who were living more comfortably had to be taught that charity is one of the most sacred duties we must all be willing to fulfill.

We took the initiative. Dr. Holzmann offered to take on the responsibility of medical services. He agreed to work without charge until such time as the organization we were founding felt it had enough funds to pay him a modest fee. Thus, the most important difficulty was solved. We needed some resources to set our project in motion. The notables of the community were called to a general meeting. There they demonstrated much goodwill and proved ready to help in the founding of a local charitable institution. A list of members was drawn up immediately. The dues of about one hundred members brought in around 150 francs in the first month; this first collection was increased to 250 francs by several generous donors, and this sum constituted our initial fund. Our organization, *Bikur Holim,*[2] was joy-

2. In Hebrew, literally, "visiting the sick."

ously welcomed by the poor. The indigent now had somewhere to turn when they fell sick; there would be someone to ease their suffering and to see that neither they nor their children would go hungry during the time they were confined to bed.

Our organization had barely been started when already there were one hundred sick to feed and care for, all from among the most destitute of our people. Dr. Holzmann gave consultations and distributed remedies without charge, and each of the sick received a daily allotment to cover the needs of his or her family.

[. . .]

With the help of Mr. Souessia, we formed a small choir with a few of the students at the school. It was very successful. At Passover people crowded into the new synagogue . . . Our choir attracted a good part of the more affluent faithful and they stayed with us. In the space of four months the synagogue deposited a net profit of 400 francs into the coffers of our organization. Next, the idea of a lottery was proposed; several more of the sick will receive care. In brief, thanks to the donated services of the doctor, our organization is building today on a fairly solid foundation. As for the assistance, both physical and moral, which the organization has given the community, it is much appreciated by our fellow Jews. And what is more, the indigent class, living in appalling filth, has made an effort to bring a little more cleanliness into their wretched homes. This was our most important task, and the families of the sick were assisted only on this condition. At the same time, the notables who were members of the organization realized that the best way to economize on the organization's funds was to do away with the piles of refuse standing in every street of the *Mellah*. That was the source of the problem. The streets were cleared of waste and refuse. Recently a letter from the Sultan arrived to second our efforts. By means of a new tax imposed on every animal raised for slaughter, a refuse service has been instituted in the *Medina* and in the *Mellah*.

Public criers announced to the inhabitants that a severe punishment would be inflicted on anyone who disobeyed His Majesty's order: no refuse was to be left in front of the doors or thrown out the windows (this is the route the refuse generally takes before landing in the middle of the street or on the heads of passersby).

A dozen or so persons have been given the responsibility of sweeping the *Mellah* every day and of taking the sweepings to be disposed of far from the city. An *amin* (head of a trade guild) is responsible for overseeing this service and for bringing to the attention of the appropriate authority the name of any person who does not conform to the

government order. The *zbale* itself, that hill of waste which lies at the gates of the *Mellah,* will be transported elsewhere. In its place new buildings will be constructed which will house the overflow of the indigent population. This excellent sanitary measure will save us from the epidemics which continue to appear in the Jewish district at regular intervals. It will also decrease the numbers of the sick and thereby increase the well-being of our families. The change in the state of mind of the people that our organization would like to effect is no less important than the change in their physical state. When the poor as well as the rich will have seen with their own eyes the good effects of the doctor's medications, they will little by little abandon their superstitious practices in treating the sick. In time they will cease to call upon magicians and spells to relieve suffering. They will refuse to pray through the night on the cold stone honoring some saint in the hope that the latter will decide to restore a crippled body to health. Eventually they will have more faith in the doctor's medicines than in the foul concoctions the old witch would have them take.
[. . .]

M. Lévy

Archives of the AIU, France XIV.F.25.

The Transformation of Casablanca

Casablanca, 28 November 1909

[. . .]
   Casablanca. Until a few short years ago, not many would have recognized the name Casablanca. The little lost port on the western coast of Morocco had no particularly original or striking features to draw the attention of foreigners. Except for the three summer months, when the exportation of grain created some signs of activity, each year slipped away in a wearisome and melancholy monotony. And the stormy harbor was as uninviting as the fanaticism of the Moors; it had almost become their unwitting accomplice.
[. . .]
   The peaceful penetration of the French into the region has not only changed its look but also greatly increased its commercial importance. The expansion the Europeans have helped to bring about is such that one can safely predict even now that Casablanca will have a tremendous future. Although Tangier remains the center for tourists and the diplomatic capital of Morocco, Casablanca has already become the capital of commerce. Casablanca is the gateway to one of the richest provinces in Morocco, which is better exploited and more fertile, so

to speak, since French arms have brought order and calm. [Casablanca] is a center of European immigration and of productivity. There is no doubt that this port is destined to become the horn of plenty that will fill the coffers of the Sharif's treasury.
[. . .]

Casablanca no longer bears its provincial and Moroccan stamp. It has undergone a complete metamorphosis, and many are saddened by this. The fever of trade has taken the place of tranquility and the charms of *far niente,* that sweet and poetic idleness. The melancholy of the autumn evenings is now gone. The noise of the trucks now masks the voice of the *muezzin* calling to prayer. The material has overcome the ideal; the needs of the body and the thirst for wealth have put an end to the aspirations of the human heart and soul. The people of Casablanca, fascinated by the golden calf, have forgotten God. European civilization has taken hold.
[. . .]

A. Saguès

Archives of the AIU, France XIV.F.25.

The Impact of the Schools on Salonican Jewry

Salonica, letter received 3 January 1909

[. . .]

The community of Salonica has been profoundly transformed by the work of the Alliance. If it is today one of the most advanced communities in the East, this is due to the institutions of the Alliance. The first school in Salonica dates from 1873. The Alliance founded that school. Six more have been founded since. More than 5,500 students—3,100 boys and 2,500 girls—have been educated in these schools. In addition, apprenticeship and vocational training organized by the Alliance has given more than 450 of our fellow Jews in this city the opportunity to learn a trade.

As it stands, approximately 12 percent of the Jewish population over the age of twenty has benefited from the action of the Alliance. Of the members of the Jewish community, almost all of those employed in commerce, the majority of our merchants, a good many of our responsible workers, and almost all of the doctors, lawyers, and engineers have attended schools maintained by the Alliance. What is more, under the influence of this legion of enlightened men, whose numbers are constantly increasing, other schools have been opened, and newspapers and numerous organizations have been founded. As a result, education has reached the common people; positive attitudes, pleasure in work, and the practice of solidarity have spread to the masses.

When the current state of the community is compared to that which existed prior to 1873, a happy metamorphosis can be observed. Before 1873, people who had received any kind of education were very rare. Today there are thousands. In a third of a century, the solicitude of the Alliance and the devotion of its agents have served to accomplish an important moral and intellectual regeneration.
[. . .]

M. Benghiat

Archives of the AIU, Grèce I.C.48.

Beginnings of Westernization and Reform in the Mellah: *Fez, 1913*

Fez, July 1913

[. . .]
. . . I would also like to mention that in the *Mellah,* European dress is becoming more and more common. It is the young people who first set the example. They have admitted to me that since they have had regular contact with the Europeans, they have begun to feel uncomfortable with the difference in dress, especially because their traditional dress sometimes causes them to be treated with a certain disdain. I can but encourage them in this direction. The adoption of European dress means more than just a superficial change. If only they could adopt the style of dress of the Europeans without also imitating them in certain habits and vices, to which our young men are only too inclined, I would be completely satisfied.
[. . .]
At the same time as they bring free and honest competition to the *Mellah,* the European population settling in this district is introducing new ways to the people here. The latter have much to gain from the presence of these respectable foreign merchants in their district.
[. . .]
Toward the end of 1912, the *Mellah* was given the right to form a municipal council, which was composed of six elected members and three appointed government employees. The first elections took place in September. The electoral college was composed of about fifty notables, those who had previously formed the *maamad* of the community. This restriction of the right to vote, conferred only on those who had until then been responsible for protecting the interests of the *Mellah,* was appropriate and reasonable. The six notables who were elected . . .

met with general approval. The population placed all of its hopes for a new system of order and justice in this municipal government.
[. . .]

To conclude this report I must now say a word about the future of the Jewish district of Fez, which I think I can predict with some accuracy. The *Mellah* is located on the outskirts of Fez, between Fez and the probable site of the European city which is to be created—we have this information from General Lyautey himself, who made a public statement to this effect in a meeting with the French community. The *Mellah* will naturally, then, serve as a link between the old city and the new. It will participate in the developing business, commercial, and industrial activities in Fez. The property values have already increased significantly in the *Mellah,* especially for property located on the main road, which we worked to widen and which serves as a main artery between the city of Fez and the camps.

I expect there will be a better future for our fellow Jews in Fez and I am doing everything in my power to bring it about. I hope that they will reach it more quickly through the instruction we offer them, through the inherent qualities of the Jewish race, which we try to awaken in them, and through a new moral strength.
[. . .]

A. Elmaleh

Archives of the AIU, France XIV.F.25.

The Revitalization of Baghdad Jewry, 1913

Baghdad, 26 October 1913

[. . .]

. . . The first service our schools fulfilled for the populations of the East was to lift them out of their material misery. In providing our students with an education that was both practical and suited to their environment, we rendered them capable of competing with non-Jews for the diverse careers open to youth but from which their ignorance had previously kept them. They were able to seek employment in government offices, in banks, in the consulates, and in large commercial ventures. A good number of them created both independent and lucrative situations for themselves in trade, finance, and industry. As Mr. Bigart has correctly pointed out, the general program outlined by the Alliance for its institutions was so well conceived that, with only slight modifications for each region, it has had the same success everywhere, and everywhere it has permitted the Jewish component of society to play an important role in the economic activity that began in Turkey in the second half of of the nineteenth century.

Placed at the intersection of the roads leading to Persia, to the Persian Gulf, and so to India, to Syria, and to Asia Minor, this capital has always been the meeting place of the great caravans, whether it was called Babylon, Ctesiphon, or Baghdad. Prior to 1869, Mossul attracted part of the merchandise headed to Iraq because of its close proximity to Aleppo. The Suez Canal struck that city a fatal blow and made of Baghdad the unique entrepôt of European products destined for all of Mesopotamia and western Persia. As it happened, the foundation of your first school in this city coincided almost exactly with the start of the digging of the canal; our fellow Jews thus had just time enough to prepare to take advantage of the fortunate effects that the work of Ferdinand de Lesseps was to have on the commerce of this region. Persia and Iraq import two major items from Europe: cotton cloth from Manchester and sugar from Marseilles or from Belgium. But it is essentially the cottons that pass in transit to Iran. It was, therefore, toward England that the efforts of our first students were to be aimed. You are aware of the influence the English have had in the Persian Gulf and in Baghdad. In the middle of the last century the English first began to seek a foothold in Mesopotamia. Today they have a major shipping line on the Tigris, they operate the best postal service between Baghdad, India, and Europe . . . Rich English companies have almost a monopoly on exportation (woolens, grains, liquorice, dates), from which the locals are shut out because of the risk and the large capital required . . . And once again, you had the foresight very early on to adapt the curriculum in Baghdad by adding the practical teaching of English to the general program followed in your schools.

Thanks to you, our youth in Baghdad were equipped with sufficient command of French, English, and Arabic to allow them to maintain relations with neighboring countries as well as with Europe. There was one gap in their knowledge, but their practical spirit did not take long in filling it. Accounting had been almost unknown among the merchants in Baghdad—at that time all Muslims. The keeping of a ledger with double entries had never been practiced. One of our first students, after having studied this science in depth, made it his duty to teach its basics to all the students who were preparing a career in business. He instituted a system of accounting in Judeo-Arabic, adapted for Baghdad, which has been learned by every generation for the past forty years. This teacher's name deserves to be mentioned; it

is Mr. Shalom Levy. Over a period of fifty years he has trained an
army of accountants for businesses in Iraq, Persia, and India; and it is
still he who is teaching our business course today.

[. . .]

With such good cards in their hands—education, honesty, and common sense, along with an innate spirit of economy and a marvelous
aptitude for business—you can imagine that our fellow Jews have far
surpassed their Muslim and Christian competitors. They have almost
monopolized the great import trade which once belonged to the Shiites. Their influence on the market is such that on Saturdays and Jewish feast days the *souk*s [markets] are deserted and the banks close.
There are several in the community whose fortunes are valued at over
a million francs; a few, more than three million. Many have between
100 and 500 thousand francs. Formerly, wealth was estimated in
piasters; today it is calculated in Turkish pounds. The upper class
grows every year, with the new members furnished by the new generations completing studies at our school . . .

If we turn from high commerce to the working class, there too we
can note the precious economic services rendered by our school. For
the marketplace of Baghdad we have trained several hundred clerks,
accountants, correspondence clerks, salesmen, etc., who earn their living thanks to the education we have given them. The great majority
of these employees have come from the lower class; we have therefore improved their condition. Some of them have created quite enviable positions for themselves. The sugar broker for the Ottoman
Bank, who is also a salesman for an Austrian company and an insurance agent for the Union, easily makes 40,000 francs per year. The
good accountants in the *souk* can earn up to 250 to 300 francs per
month; the clerks from 100 to 200. The students who have graduated
from our business course in these last two years have found positions
in which, without first being given a temporary status, they began
work with a starting pay of 100 francs per month. At the Ottoman
Bank we have a dozen former students. One is an assistant director
and earns 800 francs per month; the others between 150 and 250. One
English bank, the Eastern Bank, opened an office in Baghdad two
years ago. Almost all of its personnel were chosen from among our
former students. The head accountant, a young man of twenty-five, is
paid almost 400 francs per month; he also earns 250 francs as
dragoman [interpreter] at the Italian Consulate. His total monthly income is 650 francs. The dragomans at the German and Austrian Consulates are given between 250 and 300 francs per month.

The construction of the railroad and the expansion of the irrigation

system which is currently under way have brought economic activity
into the region. Our students have profited greatly from this activity.
Whether office workers or laborers, they have been hired in great
numbers with high salaries and wages. A single example among
many: we had a simple assistant instructor in our school in Hille
whom we paid 60 francs per month; he was hired to work for the
administration at the dam in Hindiya with a salary of 200 francs per
month. These are the positions which our school has procured for
your people who, without instruction, would have tried to make a
living either peddling or practicing the same demeaning occupations
that had miserably supported their parents. The people of Baghdad
are perfectly aware of the debt they owe you. Recently one of their
own was appointed Under-Secretary of State to the Minister of Commerce. This was the deputy Sasson Effendi, a former student of our
school. The people accorded all the honor and merit of this appointment to the Alliance, toward which they feel a profound gratitude.
They have given you proof of this on several occasions. Mr. Bigart
has cited the most striking proof: the wonderful Laura Kadoorie
School, whose expenses of 500 thousand francs were entirely paid by
Mr. Kadoorie, one of our former students who left Baghdad a pauper
and has now settled in China, where he is making millions. The case
of Mr. Kadoorie leads me to speak of another important factor in the
economic development of Baghdad Jewry. I am referring to the current of emigration, which has led some of the best of our former
students to Europe and the Far East. They have formed prosperous
colonies, disseminated throughout the four corners of the world.

   It is interesting to trace this current back to its source. We must go
back to the fifth century, when Jewish Mesopotamia was subjected to
a reign of terror and bloody persecutions under the last of the
Sassanid kings, incited by the fanaticism of the Guebres sect. To escape the fury of the people of this sect, the Babylonian Jews began to
emigrate to Arabia and India. A certain Joseph Rabban, accompanied
by a great number of families, went to settle on the coast of Malabar.
There he was received with great honors . . . The path toward emigration had been opened. From that moment on, India was always to be
looked upon by the Jews of Iraq as a place of refuge. It was precisely
in order to escape the vindictive rapacity of the *Pasha* of Baghdad
that, in the nineteenth century, David Sassoon fled to Bombay, where
he founded the commercial enterprise that still bears his name. This
company and its affiliates have drawn a great number of families from
Baghdad into their sphere of activity. This company was the origin of
those flourishing communities of Bombay and Calcutta, where the

Jews of Iraq, although adapting to their new milieu, faithfully preserved the language and customs of their native country. From India, the Jews of Baghdad extended their commerce to the Far East, spreading Judeo-Arab groups to every port, Rangoon, Hong Kong, and Shanghai.

At the same time, Baghdad's relations with Europe, and in particular with Manchester, Marseilles, and Vienna, drew a second current of emigration toward these commercial centers. The colony in Manchester is the most populous and the most wealthy; but all are flourishing. Our young people have also begun to set off for America and Australia in more recent times. Everywhere their aptitude for commerce permits them to overcome difficulties and to succeed. But in one way the emigrant from Baghdad differs from those who have left Morocco, especially Tetuan, who, after having made their fortune, want to return to their country: once he has settled abroad he remains there with no thought of returning . . .

It is appropriate to draw attention to the influence our school has had on this current of emigration, which draws some of our best students every year. If a survey were made in Bombay, Calcutta, Cairo, and, with all the more reason, in the cities of Europe which I have mentioned, it would be demonstrated that it is our former students who hold the most brilliant posts.

To complete my sketch of the economic evolution of the community of Baghdad under the influence of your educational programs, I must now speak about the considerable expansion we have effected in manual skills and trades. The word "expansion" is not quite accurate; creation would be more to the point. Before the Alliance came to Baghdad, there was only one trade practiced by the Jews: that of the goldsmith. This trade has always been practiced by the Jews in Arab countries. It was through our efforts that the first Jewish tailors, cobblers, carpenters, blacksmiths, and typographers were trained in this city. Today there are hundreds of tradesmen.

Our apprentices have done especially well in carpentry; there are 70 master carpenters and 300 workers. Among the master carpenters, I know a few who easily earn 250 francs per month. The good workers earn an average of 2.5 to 3 francs per day, which are very good wages for Baghdad. The Jewish cobblers and shoemakers are also among the best tradesmen in the city. There are about 400 of them. Our apprenticeship programs came up against the same obstacles in Iraq that they had encountered in the other cities of the East and that are inherent in the social, economic, and political conditions. Here, we had to combat the fanaticism of the Shiites, who held and protected all of the best occupations. In spite of all the difficulties, our efforts met with success. There is a very important and very large Jewish working class in Baghdad today; it is destined for rapid growth because the popularity of crafts and trades has spread among our fellow Jews.

    . . . Whoever would understand the results obtained through our efforts in this regard and would know what the customs of Baghdad Jewry were forty years ago would have only to travel through the interior of Kurdistan and Persia and visit the cities where the influence of the Alliance has not yet made itself felt. Among the men could be seen slovenly dress, filthy language, frequent drunkenness, lies and trickery in their dealings, and a total lack of dignity. Among the women, who at the time held a position in the family no better than that of a servant, could be seen early marriages, with all their damaging consequences, a youth faded before the age of twenty, and a life of confinement and physical deprivation spent in domestic slavery. The children were raised with complete disregard for the rules of hygiene and reason; they were given over to the demoralizing rule of the rabbi at a most tender age; they grew up with no respect for their parents, who set an example for many a base practice. Such was the common state of the Jewish family in Baghdad. Because the population was both ignorant and fanatical, and because its spirit was imbued with the most primitive superstitions, it was blindly submissive to the absolute authority of the rabbis, who managed the finances of the community through the arbitrary imposition of heavy taxes. There was not a single philanthropic organization in the community; there was no social unity. How different is the spectacle which the community now offers after a half-century of the regenerative efforts born in your school. And this spectacle is all the more comforting in the hope it implies for the future.

    The women are rising out of their slavery. The scourge of child marriages has almost disappeared. The young women who finish our classes bring precious gifts and abilities to the household, which earn them the esteem of their husbands. They have some education; they know how to sew and embroider; they have notions of hygiene and know how to run a proper home. Through their skills and their talents they manage to bring to their homes an air of cleanliness and charm that had formerly been unknown in Baghdad. They give care and attention to their personal dignity, and this elicits respect in those around them. They demonstrate an intelligent affection for their children and a more enlightened attachment to their husbands, whose companions and equals they have become. The Jewish homes, which

were formerly jealously closed harems, are slowly opening first to foreigners and then to the locals. The young girls in our school still
cover their faces when they go out, but the veil has changed gradually
so that it is now smaller and very transparent. This is a sign of the
times. The day is coming when this last vestige of feminine servitude
will disappear. That day will bring the definitive emancipation to
which the young generations fervently aspire.

Progress in customs and habits has been even more marked among
the men. Our former students, who are legion, can be easily recognized by their respectable appearance, their manners, and their civilized language. Many of them have been to Europe and this can be
detected in their ways of thinking and being. The contrast between
the former residents of Baghdad and the new is striking. In the same
measure as the Jew of old was humble, servile, and accustomed to
bowing before the Muslims, the young people today are conscious
and protective of their dignity as men and as citizens. The ratification
of the constitution has given them hope for a system of justice and
freedom, which they are anxious to see fulfilled.

The community is no longer under the supervision of the rabbis.
The management of finances has been taken away from them and
placed in the hands of an administrative council named by regular
elections. As superstitions and prejudices are falling away little by
little, the rabbinical corps, of a very backward mentality, has seen its
prestige and authority gradually decline. The young people who come
from our school join together to combat fanaticism and to spread
ideas of progress, cooperation, and solidarity among the masses. Lectures are given at the school or in the synagogue by the most educated of our former students. They are in the process of creating a
newspaper, which will be published in Judeo-Arabic. The goal of this
paper will be to develop public opinion and to create a more favorable spirit of reform in the community. A large group of them are
already asking that the *midrash* be given to the Alliance. There are
many signs to prove that this collectivity of 50,000 is in the process of
renewal. There are several indications of the moral and intellectual
awakening of the community: the *Taun* ("mutuality") school founded
by a group of young people, the "Meir Elias" hospital created four
years ago, the *Club Israélite,* the recently formed association of
former students, and the "Society" for the development of training in
skilled trades, which has recruited a thousand members within a few
months. The community is becoming more and more aware of the
true nature of its importance and its mission, for it knows that it has
received the inheritance of a glorious past. The community is, there-

fore, looking for a Chief Rabbi who will be an educated and enlightened spiritual leader, capable of his task, and worthy shepherd of a flock of 50,000 souls.

All of these changes and all of these new undertakings are the work of your former students, a continuation of your own work. You have given of your efforts and your money for fifty years in the capital of Iraq. Our representatives have struggled against all kinds of obstacles. They have faced the indifference of the populations, the opposition of the rabbis, the constraints of the authorities, the hostility of the climate, isolation, and exile. But they never allowed themselves to become discouraged. They moved ever forward, certain that the seeds they were sowing would take root and one day grow. The crops have grown high and it is almost time for the harvest. I feel honored to have been one of the humble workers in this long and demanding labor whose fruits are now brilliantly manifest. I had the pleasure of participating in the extraordinary development of your program of education in Baghdad and in its diffusion throughout Mesopotamia. The number of your institutions there has grown from four to sixteen in these past nine years; they were serving 1,500 and are now serving 4,500 students. It is with regret that I will leave this interesting community, so full of promise for the future. In a few years, as soon as the railroad linking Baghdad and Constantinople has been completed, civilization will make an explosive entry into Iraq. Our fellow Jews will be ready to welcome it. At that time, this community, so important for the size of its population and so brilliant in its economic prosperity, will advance boldly on the road to progress and will play the role for which it is destined in the Judaism of the East.

[. . .]

N. Albala

Archives of the AIU, France XII.F.21.

The Alliance Schools and the Jews of Palestine, 1914

Jerusalem, 1 February 1914

[. . .]

And as I was examining for the last time the archives which are about to change hands, memories flooded my mind, and I was overcome by reflections. 1882! Mr. Nissim sets out on his mission.[3] What confidence and resolve, full of hope in spite of the concern over the battle brewing within the great fortress of Orthodoxy . . . 1896! I in turn cross the

---

3. Nissim Béhar was the first director of the *Ecole Professionnelle*.

threshold of the Temple of Labor founded by Mr. Nissim. It was developing rapidly then but still receiving the periodic shocks inherent in the introduction of workshops in a city where only religious activities and commerce could flourish. 1913! Thirty years of activity and progress. The program is being examined. Has it already fulfilled its purpose, is its existence still justified? Can it survive amid the recent economic, political, and social upheaval in Jerusalem? Should the Trades School be maintained, reduced, developed, or modified?

Then and now! What a distance has been traveled! Then, Jerusalem had barely 20,000 Jewish inhabitants, packed into poorly lit dwellings in the interior of the city; each waiting for the *halukah* in exchange for readings from the Talmud and liturgical prayers recited for the prosperity of the generous donors in Europe; the children were being taught sacred Scripture in underground *heder*s. There were three schools just starting out: the *Laemel Schule,* the Blumenthal "*Doresh Zion*" school, and the Steinhart Montagu committee's center for young children. Each was multiplying its appeals to attract studious children to modern and scientific instruction. Their efforts were in vain, the study of secular subjects was forbidden, and the teachers were excommunicated. The school benches remained empty. There were no Jewish skilled workers. There was vague talk of the arrival of Jewish immigrants, Russians chased out by the persecutions of czarism who were coming to take refuge in the land of their ancestors, the messianic country of History and of Humanity. They were going to earn their bread by working the land. *Mikweh Israël,* that first hope of Palestinian Jewry, was growing stagnant, fighting against the discouragement of its students, the harassment of its neighbors, and the distrust of the authorities. With neither education nor resources, few in numbers and weakened by persecution, hated and despised, confined by the limits of fanaticism, and left only with their religious practices for strength, such were the Palestinian Jews of the time, of 1875 and even of 1880 . . . But they had hope. Their hearts full of memories of the greatness of their people, they wanted to believe in the return of the exiles to Zion . . . Was there not talk of settlements, were there not whispers about a benefactor who promised to cultivate the plains of the Sharon and to plant the mountains of Galilee and Judea with trees? . . . It was the beginning of an era of achievement. Netter offered the sacrifice of his life, leaving the memory of his self-denial and his endurance as comfort to the first settlers.[4] Certainly, the enemies were masked; the Orthodox Jew and the

4. Charles Netter was the founder of *Mikweh Israël.*

jealous neighbor were lying in wait. But these visionaries were not frightened by the obstacles in their path . . . The brave must hasten the arrival of these times to come in spite of all risks, braving the curses and cries, disregarding the excommunications and the threats. A modern school, with an organized program, respectful of tradition but introducing progress—this is what was needed . . .

Today Jerusalem has forty-two Jewish schools for boys and girls, which give instruction to more than 5,500 students and have an annual budget of 1,300,000 francs. The *heder,* that final reactionary and fanatic citadel, now accepts the teaching of some secular subjects and of the language of the country. What district does not have its own nursery or kindergarten? Three seminaries, one German teachers' college, one music school, one French secondary school, one *ivri* [Hebrew] secondary school; physical education and singing courses, libraries and clubs, organizations and groups. We have four hospitals of ophthalmology, one asylum, three homes for the aged, six orphanages, six or seven clinics, a hygiene center with a bacteriological laboratory, and an anti-rabies institute. Have we finished? Why not mention the lending institutions, the housing developments for workers, low-cost housing, the unions and associations, the banks and finance companies? . . .

And Jaffa is in no respect second to the religious metropolis. Its Jewish population has quintupled in these last fifteen years, and its educational, charitable, and social institutions and organizations are proportionally greater than those of Jerusalem in both number and variety. Consider those beautiful districts and the perfume of their orange trees, the beautiful homes of "Tel-Aviv," referred to, with reason, as the Jewish Heliopolis. And the Rishon, Petah-Tikvah, Ness Ziona, and Rehoboth settlements, with their wines, oranges, almonds, and variety of fruit, have in less then ten years increased the export figure in Jaffa from 8 to 14 million francs per annum. What wealth for the country. The Treasury receipts have tripled and it is with pride that the Jewish taxpayers figure their taxes, sending the Treasury 60 to 70 thousand Turkish pounds per year of the 250,000 total annual taxes collected in Judea. Some think that Galilee—with Caiffa and Zicron and the settlements of Tiberias and Safed—rivals our own region . . .

Can we make similar favorable observations concerning moral character and attitudes? Yes, the Jew is rarely accused, even more rarely condemned, lives in peace, and seeks tranquility. There are no criminal suits and never any civil or commercial conflicts. He has shed his humility. Ready to fulfill all his duties, he can demand that his civil and political rights be respected. He wants to live, grow, and develop wholly as a Jew. In this age of awakening of nationalities and of the affirmation of the rights of individuals and collectivities, who can reproach him the desire to discover his aspirations and his ambition? More than any other of his fellow citizens, he has understood the blessings of the constitution established in Turkey through the struggle of the champions of freedom. Grateful to the country which opened its doors when he was forced into exile from Spain, he waits and hopes. He calls in his turn to his persecuted brothers in Russia and Romania, offering them freedom and life-giving work.

And the Alliance was the precursor to this prodigious achievement, the leader of this fruitful activity. Some reproach the Alliance for its present timidity and want to see it swept along in the current movement. It is forgotten that it was through the prudence and political neutrality of the Alliance that the Ottoman government became amenable to the regeneration of the Jews. Today some are trying to move too quickly, to make changes before their time has come. Progress obeys the laws of nature. The Alliance continues to follow the path it has forged and opened to all similar organizations. Not to continue in its steady, regular course would be to compromise the success already in motion. Recent dissensions have proved this all too true. We must not dismiss the experience and counsel of an organization that has already been put to the test and that has already proved itself . . . [. . .]

A. Antébi

Archives of the AIU, France XI.F.20.

An Overview of the History of the Alliance's Activities in Tunisia, 1929

Sousse, 7 October 1929

THE SCHOOL IN SOUSSE

[. . .]
Founded in 1860, the Alliance opened its first school in Tetuan in 1862. In 1865, similar institutions were established in the fortunate communities of Tangier and Baghdad. Adrianople followed in 1867, and in 1873 a boys' school was opened in Salonica. Constantinople first greeted a representative from the Alliance in 1875; and it was not until 7 July 1878 that the unforgettable David Cazès inaugurated your first institution in Tunis, which has the largest Jewish community in all of North Africa.

The number of students served by this school hovered at around 800 during the first two years. A few years later it reached 1,300. The Central Committee resolved to extend its program in Tunis to its full capacity. On 1 June 1882, a girls' school was opened with about 50 children initially. There were 150 by 1 January 1883, and by 1920 there were 612. A kindergarten was added in 1891; it cared for 380 children. This brought the actual number of children served by the girls' school in 1920 to 992.

Your boys' school became unable to hold without difficulty such a considerable number of students, 1,300, and the Alliance decided to open a second school in 1910. This institution was located in the very heart of the major Jewish district, in the Hafsia. It was immediately filled with students and continued to grow, so that by 1924 (I do not have the figures for the last five years) the two boys' schools had 1,662 students. The girls' school, including the kindergarten, had 1,120. Together they add up to the imposing figure of 2,782 schoolchildren.

In the meantime, although its principal efforts were directed toward the capital, the Alliance did not lose sight of the communities in the interior. So it was that on 1 January 1883 a boys' school was opened in Sousse and another in Mahdia. The Alliance had proposed establishing schools in other communities, Djerba and Monastir, but the rabbinical corps, which was very influential in these centers, was very resistant. They saw a threat to religion in any and all innovation. It was not until 1905 that the Alliance came to Sfax, where, in contrast to the single boys' school in Sousse, a school complex was established.

The charitable action of the Alliance was not to stop there. In 1880, it founded a vocational training program for boys in Tunis, followed in 1890 with a similar program for Sousse. The program in Tunis was expanded in 1895 to include girls. All of these organizations, as each of us proudly recognizes, have served and continue to serve the Jewish population with distinction.

Crowning these achievements in education and training, a new and important undertaking was to further expand your field of activity and to open unexpected horizons for the Jews of Tunisia: the Alliance began its work in agriculture, which fostered great hopes and was welcomed with profound satisfaction by the Jewry of the Regency. In 1895, you purchased the Djedeida property (1,500 hectares) 25 kilometers from Tunis, and on 1 November a farm school was opened there to provide the Tunisian Jews with instruction in farming and agricultural methods. In 1898, your goal being to instill a lasting attachment to working the land in the Jewish youth, you did not hesitate to make the heavy financial sacrifice necessary to purchase two more parcels of land adjacent to Djedeida: the Bijaoua (2,200 hectares) and the Bassins (600 hectares). There you decided to settle those of your students who, after having completed their five years of practical and technical training, wanted to continue to make their living by farming.

To be thorough, I must add to the list the opening in Tunis in 1907 of a rabbinical school to train teachers of Hebrew and notaries sufficiently qualified for their functions.

After following this history of the diverse institutions, organizations, and programs which the Alliance has brought to the most populous communities of Tunisia, one cannot but admire the ideal of humanity and civilization which brought its leaders here. They have neglected nothing in enabling the Jews in Tunisia to occupy the rank to which their number, their social position, and their activity entitle them.

Your first representative in Tunis, . . . whose name is still pronounced with admiration and affection, had the eye of a master.[5] He presented you with the program that had to be followed in preparing our fellow Jews to meet the moral obligations they were destined to face in light of the country's new political situation as a French protectorate under the Treaty of Bardo of 12 May 1881.
[. . .]

L. Loubaton

Archives of the AIU, France VII.F.14.

5. See the letter of David Cazès dated 10 July 1881 (first letter in this chapter).

PART III

THE ALLIANCE TEACHER AS POLITICAL ACTIVIST AND POLITICAL OBSERVER

The Alliance, true to its statutes, was active in the defense of Jewish rights throughout the world and worked for the granting of equality to the Jews in countries where they had not yet been emancipated. The interventions by the organization in the national and the international arenas, its appeals to various governments to correct abuses, and its dynamic presence in international congresses such as the Berlin Congress of 1878, the Madrid conference of 1880, and the Versailles peace conference of 1919 were significant contributions to the Jewish cause.[1]

The activities of the Alliance schoolteacher in the local context mirrored those of the organization in international politics. The teachers were quick to report local troubles and antisemitic incidents to Paris and, if necessary, ask for the intervention of the Central Committee with the appropriate authorities. The teacher, especially in areas removed from the influence of central administrations, was the only person to whom a Jewish community could appeal, short of asking for the help of Jews overseas. His response (always the male teacher, because local communities and authorities would not tolerate females playing political roles) in periods of crisis was often decisive. He had many options for handling a problem. He could intervene directly with the local authorities. If this did not yield results, he could ask for the intercession of the European consuls. If the problem appeared to be intractable, he could leave it up to the Alliance, which would write directly either to the Quai d'Orsay or to the central government of the country concerned.

In short, in the locality in which he found himself, the Alliance teacher played the classic role of the Jewish *shtadlan*. Indeed, the figure of the *shtadlan*, the intercessor with the authorities on behalf of the

---

1. The official histories of the organization describe its political activities. See Leven, *Cinquante ans d'histoire,* esp. vol. 1; and Chouraqui, *Cent ans d'histoire.* Further studies based on diplomatic archives would be extremely useful to clarify many important episodes of the Alliance's work in the arena of international relations.

community, was in fact a fixture of Jewish diaspora existence, particularly in Central and Eastern Europe in the premodern period. Eventually, the role of the *shtadlan* was fulfilled by a wealthy man who enjoyed some degree of prestige within both Jewish and Gentile circles and had some links, business or otherwise, with the authorities. Jewish notables came to play this highly important role in their communities.

The emergence of the Alliance teacher as a *shtadlan* in certain areas was the sign of a new power configuration both within the Jewish community and between the Jews and the Muslims. The Alliance teacher owed all his influence to his association with the West, to the direct link he could establish with what was deemed to be an important power center in Europe. In a time of increasing European penetration of the Middle East and North Africa, this was an invaluable link for the Jewish community to maintain. Although local Jewish notables remained powerful in their essentially oligarchic societies, the authority that the Alliance teacher could bring to bear was considered to be more effective. The centers of power in the Muslim world at large, for the Muslims and the Jews, had begun to slip away from their traditional loci, whether these were central administrations or elites within Jewish society.

The roles that the Alliance teacher could play as the protector of the Jews and the champion of their interests also pointed to the slow but steady erosion of the traditional status of the Jew as a *dhimmi* in the lands of Islam. Jews and Christians were protected groups according to the *dhimma,* the covenant that had regulated their life under Muslim rule since the early days of Islam.[2] They could freely practice their religion and would be protected; in return, they had to pay a special poll tax and obey discriminatory legislation in various areas of life. The latter, such as the prohibition against building new synagogues and churches, the requirements to wear clothing of certain colors and to dismount one's horse in the presence of Muslims, the ban on the carrying of arms, were enforced with greatly varying degrees of severity in different periods and in different areas and were all designed to underscore the inferior status of the *dhimmi*. The Jew and the Christian depended on the goodwill of the rulers, with no recourse possible.

The entry of European interests into the picture upset this traditional arrangement. The Europeans protected the non-Muslims, especially the

2. For the *dhimma,* see Bernard Lewis, *The Jews of Islam* (Princeton, N.J.: Princeton University Press, 1984), 3–66; and Norman Stillman, *The Jews of Arab Lands* (Philadelphia: Jewish Publication Society, 1979), 167–68, 255–58. The work of Bat Ye'or, *Le Dhimmi: Profil de l'opprimé en Orient et en Afrique du Nord depuis la conquête arabe* (Paris: Editions Anthropos, 1980), though polemical, supplies many important documents.

Christians, and put pressure on Muslim states to treat their non-Muslim subjects on an equal footing with their Muslim ones. The Reform Decree of 1856 in the Ottoman Empire and the Fundamental Pact of 1857 in Tunisia, both of which addressed this issue, were passed under coercion from Europe. The incessant interventions by a growing number of European consuls in favor of non-Muslims also added a new dimension to Muslim/non-Muslim relations in the lands of Islam. The *dhimma* was no longer operable once the balance of power had shifted in favor of Europe, which had embarked upon an increasingly activist policy of penetration into the lands of Islam.

The protection granted by consuls to local non-Muslims had its origins in the Capitulations agreements signed between the Muslim powers and European states from the sixteenth century onward. These treaties allowed Europeans working and traveling in Muslim countries to enjoy extraterritorial privileges such as the right not to submit to native tribunals but to be tried by European courts. Gradually, this and other rights were extended to natives, overwhelmingly non-Muslims, who worked for the European consuls or for European merchants. These natives, the *protégés* of the consuls, escaped local jurisdiction altogether and enjoyed most of the rights given to Europeans. In the course of time, many were naturalized without ever setting foot in their countries of citizenship. The widespread abuse of the ancient system by both local personalities and the consuls had become a thorn in the side of the Muslim rulers by the mid-nineteenth century.

The *protégé* system flourished not only because of the material gains rich merchants enjoyed by its exploitation but also because entering under the protection of a European consul was often the only means of escaping the arbitrary jurisdiction of local courts or acts of petty oppression by capricious governors. In times of anarchy, it was often the only guarantee of a secure existence. But it also fueled the animosity of the population against the non-Muslims, who were now increasingly associated with the victorious West, and in a vicious circle, this response drove the non-Muslims to seek further protection. With the growing Western presence in the Muslim world and the consequent protection extended to non-Muslims, the *dhimma* ceased to be operative, and a new set of realities, in which the Muslim was the loser and the non-Muslim was the victor, emerged in the lands of Islam.

11
The Task of Protection

The activities of the Alliance teacher, who had connections with the European consuls and was in direct communication with Paris, extended Western protection to the Jewish community as a whole. This was a de facto protection and was dependent on the mobilization by the teacher of the European consuls and European institutions each time an incident occurred. Nevertheless, acting as a shtadlan, *the teacher's political position in the locality was objectively that of a consul of the Alliance, the power most concerned with the Jews. The fact that the teacher did not have the influence of a state behind him but rather depended upon the representatives of Western states to protect the local Jews meant that his efforts were not sure to succeed, though they frequently did. Ultimately, the help that the Alliance teacher could give to the local Jews was part and parcel of the process of the growing ascendance of the West in the affairs of the East.*

The role of the Alliance teacher as protector of the local Jewish community, important in all of the countries where the organization was active, was particularly significant in an area such as pre-Protectorate Morocco in the second half of the nineteenth and early twentieth centuries.[1] During a period of weak central power, tribal anarchy in huge areas of the country which threatened even the urban centers under the Sultan's control, and growing destabilization by European intrigue, protection by a European force was seen as the only guarantee of security:

Tangier, 25 August 1864

[. . .]

The protection granted by the British government to the Jews of Morocco is either not at all serious or is misinterpreted by its consular agents. One of Her Majesty's illustrious subjects, Sir Moses Montefiore, comes to Morocco with the recommendation of Lord John Russell. The British Minister himself accompanies him throughout his trip and the Sultan gives a *firman* [decree] in favor of the

---

1. This role has been studied extensively by Michael M. Laskier; see his *The Alliance Israélite Universelle and the Jewish Communities of Morocco.* For North Africa as a whole, see Roland, "The Alliance Israélite Universelle and French Policy in North Africa."

Jews. Who is responsible for seeing that this decree is enforced; who is responsible for opposing all acts of injustice if not the British Minister? But Mr. Hay does not like the Jews. That is why he fails to protect them in spite of the orders and instructions which he receives from London . . . When the other consuls lodge a protest in defense of our fellow Jews, he refuses to support them on the pretext that a revolution might break out . . . The one protection that the British Minister believes he has granted is very vague and of no real value. Therefore, it is urgent that the school be placed without delay under French protection. I ask that you please take the steps necessary to obtain this protection. I ask also that you pardon my vehemence; I could not resist the force of my sentiments and the love of my country[2] . . . If ever an uprising against the Jews happens here, it will be through the fault of the British Minister, who will lend his hand and provoke it. He is a very dangerous man. Everyone recognizes this privately, but all are afraid to say it, let alone write it. But I am a member and a representative of the Alliance. I fear only God and my conscience.
[. . .]

                                                                          B. Lévy

Archives of the AIU, Maroc I.C.1–2.

As was discussed earlier, the Alliance schools were not officially protected by France until well into the twentieth century, and the teachers relied on the goodwill of local consuls. In this case, Sir Drummond Hay was no great lover of the Jews and worked actively, though without success, for the dismantlement of the protégé *system. However, the mere association with Europe was often enough to give a certain power to the Alliance teacher in the eyes of the Muslims:*

                                                    Marrakesh, 13 August 1902
[. . .]
    . . . In our correspondence of this past year, I have spoken on several occasions about the abusive conduct of the *Pasha* of the *kasbah*[3] toward the Jews of the poorer classes; the more wealthy usually escape difficult situations by offering gifts. There was an urgent necessity to use any means available to make the *Pasha* a little more fair in his treatment of our fellow Jews. In this country, it suffices to be

    2. Lévy was French.
    3. The part of town inhabited by the representatives of the central authority, as well as by other Muslims.

called European or to be known as a *protégé* of some Western power to command a certain measure of respect on the part of the indigenous population. This is enough to guarantee the security of a foreigner in Marrakesh. But by our title of Alliance teachers, we are called to the more humanitarian task of guaranteeing the security of the great majority of our fellow Jews, who find no favor with the *Pasha*. The justice of the latter is very arbitrary. Any dispute submitted to the judgment of the *Pasha* is settled only through a "recompense," a suspicious affair involving a gift and always decided in favor of whoever is most generous. The position of a local governor here is paid for in cash; it is a commercial venture. Whoever buys such a title expects to derive his livelihood from it. This practice is widespread at every level: the *Sheikh* of the *Mellah,* like the *Pasha,* employs the same system to make his living. Woe to the poor devil who falls into the hands of a governor: he will be jailed or beaten if he has nothing to lay at his master's feet . . .

The notables had become quite disturbed about this after several incidents and had come to ask me to do something on behalf of my fellow Jews. I felt powerless as I had no official authority. A few of the notables had, without my knowledge, threatened the *Pasha* with the "wrath of the director of the Alliance School" if he did not show some humanity. The *Pasha* answered them that the director should see to his own affairs as he, the *Pasha,* saw to his. Since we did not have recourse to the support of a consul here, and since the Central Committee's efforts with the French Minister in Tangier had not been successful, you thought it best to address yourself to the central government so that they might intercede for us with the local authorities. You wrote to the Sultan's Minister in Tangier about this and your request has had its effect. The recommendation of Si Torrès to Hadj-Abd-El-Selam has already produced the desired result.

Consider the proof: on 28 July at around four o'clock in the afternoon, a soldier was sent on behalf of the *Pasha* (the *Pasha* of the *kasbah,* Se-El-Ar'bi-ben Abbou, not of the *Medina,* Hadj-Abd-El-Selam) to bring an order to the *Kaid* [governor of a town or area] of the *Mellah* that no Jew was to be allowed to go out of the gate of the Jewish district unless he first take off his shoes. As chance would have it, the first person to come to the gate of the *Mellah* was Mr. Trudjmann, one of the notables. He was obliged to take off his shoes before passing through the gate. The poor man, with tears in his eyes and the word *galut* on his lips, came to recount the incident to a few of the most respected Jews. In the meantime, there was increasing unrest in the *Mellah* . . .

[The school director and a delegate of the Jewish community went and complained to the Muslim judge.]
[. . .]

The following day, 29 July, at six o'clock in the morning, Mr. Corcos [the president of the Jewish communal council] sent for me, informing me that the *Pasha* himself had come to his home, which had never happened before, and that he wished to speak with the "director of the French school." For the *Pasha,* this was almost a humiliating act. I should add that the notables had advised the *Pasha* on several occasions, among friends, that he should be more fair in his actions toward the Jews, otherwise he would have to deal with the director of the school, "an influential person with the government of the French republic and with the *Makhzan.*" When I was introduced to the *Pasha,* I expressed my regret at not having been able to meet him the previous evening and that he had had to come in person "perhaps to apologize." The *Pasha* swore by all his prophets that the rumors circulating throughout the city were pure lies and that were there any basis to them, he would not have come so early in the morning to the *Mellah,* which he does very rarely . . .

It is thanks to the presence of the schools in the *Mellah* that a riot was avoided. Under the influence of your institutions, the situation of our fellow Jews in Marrakesh is improving day by day.
[. . .]

M. Lévy

Archives of the AIU, France XIV.F.25.

In times of tribal revolt, such as in northern Morocco in 1903, the Alliance teacher was often all that remained to give some help to the local Jews. As the vivid report below shows, the Central Committee always stressed the need for the teachers to stay put in times of warfare and disaster and to be of concrete use to the Jewish population:

Tetuan, 11 May 1903

[. . .]

Things are moving very quickly here; yesterday morning, Sunday, sixty families left the city; they had to be accompanied as far as the beach by a hundred soldiers, who opened a path for them amid the enemy . . . Toward evening, an English warship came for the consul and the British subjects; they are leaving now, to the great despair of those who remain and who are exposed to the most horrible tortures.

As for me, I have nothing more to do here; the schools are empty, the notables of the community have left; for whom shall I sacrifice myself then! It is a question of saving my wife and my daughter, who refuse to leave alone. We will all leave together tomorrow morning . . . We will stay in Gibraltar until I receive word. I will telegraph you from there.

[. . .]

12 May 1903

I am writing to confirm my letter of yesterday and the telegram I sent this morning expressed in these terms:

"Departure impossible, bloody combat at city gates, massive panic, situation desperate."

. . . Yesterday morning . . . we were all preparing to leave for Martin (the beach), where we were to wait for the ship owned by the Tonache Company; your personnel made this decision because there was nothing more for them to do here; indeed we had no more students, there is no longer a community, and the Chief Rabbi himself was leaving his post . . . The governor . . . forbade our exit, saying that there was no way to leave, that we were closed in on all sides, and that we would certainly be massacred en route before reaching the beach, two hours away. We went back to the school, therefore, and had no sooner returned than the sound of gunfire could be heard. The Kabyles were attacking the city after having set fire to the groves and homes in the surrounding countryside. In our closed-off Jewish district the people were in an indescribable state of panic; they did not know where to run or where to hide, certain they had already fallen prey to the savages. So I opened the gates to the school and gave refuge to those desperate women and children who felt safer on the Alliance premises. I had also posted armed Arab guards at the doors and windows. From our balcony we could see a terrifying spectacle: the Kabyles were scrambling over the walls like cats, and the Arabs, our defenders, were shooting them down with their rifles. The rounds of fire persisted but did not do much to deter the Kabyles, whose rage seemed only to increase. While this was going on, fires were blazing all around us. A cloud of smoke enveloped us as the sound of whistling bullets continued. This went on for four hours . . .

13 May 1903

[. . .]

. . . An official of the French Consulate has received . . . instructions concerning the personnel of the Alliance from the Legation in Tangier. His instructions read more or less as follows: "Although the Alliance teachers are not officially protected by the French govern-

ment, it would be advisable to come to their aid under the present circumstances. You should see that they leave the area as soon as possible and facilitate their evacuation by sea . . ." This official asked me whether it was my intention to leave the city, and I answered him: "No, since you are staying. Later, we'll see."
[. . .]

15 May 1903

[. . .]
. . . I answered that my duty held me here but that my assistants were free to go . . . I hope that no harm will come to us; in any case, we have the satisfaction of carrying out our mission to the end and of acting in conformance, not to your instructions, for your circulars do not address circumstances of this sort, but to your letter no. 4313 of 6 May and to the spirit of solidarity and charity in the work of the Alliance.

The schools are still open, and our students are still being fed through our program. Beginning Sunday, we plan to offer daily meals to the widows and orphans left with no other resources . . .
[. . .]

25 May 1903

[. . .]
. . . Tangier lies on the coast and is in constant communication with Europe and only two hours from Gibraltar, from which help can be sent at the first alert. Moreover, that city is defended by a sizable garrison. Such is not the case for Tetuan, which is eight kilometers from the coast. Its unprotected harbor is visited only once every two weeks by a French vessel. Furthermore, Europe has no vested interest in Tetuan; the city could be destroyed and its inhabitants massacred without causing the slightest distress among the Western powers. The Europeans who were staying in Tetuan have left long ago; the Jews under foreign protection and the wealthier families have found safe haven. There remain only the poor among the Arabs and Jews. There is no chance that compassion will be shown to them or intervention made on their behalf . . .

. . . Our existence has become intolerable. There is no one with whom to speak; we are prohibited from taking walks. It is stifling in the *Mellah*, having constantly before our eyes the pitiful spectacle of the blackest poverty. There are thousands of hungry poor here; there is no one left to whom they can address their pleas. They live always

with the prospect of falling into the hands of the savages from the mountains, who are impatient to finally seize their prey.
[. . .]

E. Carmona

Archives of the AIU, Maroc I.C.1–2.

The siege was eventually lifted and things returned to normal in Tetuan.

Paris, May 1903

[to Monsieur Carmona]
    . . . In spite of the seriousness of events and the suffering you are being made to endure, we believe more than ever that your duty is to remain in Tetuan among your fellow Jews. You write, "There is nothing more for me to do here, the notables of the community have left; for whom shall I sacrifice myself then?" If the notables have left, the poor remain. It is to them that you must give support, encouragement, and comfort. We consider the departure of Mr. Falcon [the assistant to the school director] a desertion and a most serious breach of professional honor.
[. . .]

J. Bigart

Archives of the AIU, Maroc I.C.1–2.

The above stance was taken consistently by the Alliance leadership, who always insisted that the teachers remain at their posts in times of trouble to help the Jewish community.
    J. Conquy, the school director in Rabat in 1903, was quite successful in securing speedy help for the Jews, thus fulfilling the expectations of the Alliance:

Rabat, 20 October 1903

[. . .]
    The events that have been unfolding in Morocco over the past year [tribal revolt and warfare] have had their effect on the Jews of Rabat. Trade has come to a halt, and at the same time necessities have become very expensive. Wheat has doubled in price; all foodstuffs have become much more costly. As a result, there is great suffering in the city.
    To make matters worse, the security of the *Mellah* has always been tenuous. The wall surrounding us had gaping holes in several places and was guarded by only one soldier; in several places it was on the verge of collapse. It was through these holes and at these weak points

that our fearsome enemies, the Zairs and the Zemmours, planned to rush in and sack the *Mellah*. We spent several very anxious nights. A few of the pregnant women nearly miscarried. The situation had become extremely critical. The community had brought this state of affairs to the attention of the government on several occasions, but its call went unanswered. When we were gathered for a general meeting one day, the members of the community earnestly implored me to intervene on their behalf. I told them they should rely on me to do everything I could.

That same day I visited the English Legation and lodged an energetic protest with my Consul against the position of the Governor, with whom I placed the responsibility for my personal safety. I did the same at the French Legation, where I was well received by Mr. Leriche, the Vice-Consul. From there I went on to see Mr. Méana, the Spanish Consul and the senior member of the diplomatic corps in Rabat. Mr. Méana is a good man, very charitable, a protector of the weak, and a friend to the Jews, in whose lot he takes a heartfelt interest; he is gifted with a certain modesty, which increases the charm of his character. Once he had been informed of the reason for my visit, this honorable diplomat promised me his full cooperation. He immediately sent his officer to the Governor, insisting that the latter send at once the necessary guards to protect the Jews and the employees of the Spanish Consul living in our district. The other Vice-Consuls, answering my plea, followed this example. On that day and for several months thereafter there were a dozen guards in the *Mellah,* where there had previously been only two.

Mr. Méana later made pressing demands through the Spanish Legation in Tangier, and our walls were restored to good condition.

After that, we were able to maintain a certain peace of mind.
[. . .]

J. Conquy

Archives of the AIU, France XIV.F.25.

The protective role of the Alliance teacher in a country such as pre-Protectorate Morocco is highlighted with concrete examples from A. Saguès, the director of the Casablanca school:

Casablanca, 28 November 1909

[. . .]

Relations between the community and the school. As divided as they may be among themselves, our fellow Jews have always been unanimous in their recognition of the advantages derived from having a representative of the Alliance Israélite present in Casablanca to serve as a qualified and official defender of their legitimate rights. The confidence they have placed in every representative of the Alliance has always been fully justified by the frequent interventions with public authorities made on behalf of the community.

As is the case in every backward country where the Jews are merely tolerated rather than given any recognition, the director of an Alliance school in Morocco assumes an arduous and selfless task; his role is not exclusively pedagogical. It is he who presents the grievances of the Jewish community to the local and consular authorities. As director he holds a unique position which is at the same time independent, disinterested, and endowed with a certain prestige; he alone is in a position to improve the situation of our fellow Jews. He defends their rights when they are ignored. As deaf as one may be to the voice of Justice, she always manages to make herself heard in the end.

Your representatives have always been concerned with the affairs of the Jewish community in Casablanca; their influence has even been felt beyond the walls of the city. It would take too long to list every affair settled through the intervention of our representatives, but I will cite two such incidents in order to reveal the kind of service their activity has brought to the Jews of Chaouia.

The Jews of Settat were cruelly afflicted during the time of Mr. Guéron's directorship. Thanks to him, these unfortunate souls were able to find a safe refuge in Casablanca and were fed and housed for several weeks through public charity. Through his insistent urgings, Mr. Guéron managed to interest all of the Consuls in the plight of these Jews, and particularly the British Consul. Even the non-Jewish merchants were generous in their contributions to the charity that your representative had organized; he saved an entire population.

The events that took place in Casablanca are still very vivid in our memories and there is no need to recount them in great detail. The Jews owe a debt of gratitude to the Alliance for making emigration possible during the unrest of 1907 and for protecting and caring for those who chose to remain here. With a truly maternal solicitude, the Alliance sent all the monetary support that was requested. A large part of this debt of gratitude must also go to Mr. Pisa. In these critical circumstances, my predecessor demonstrated a profound devotion to our brethren, much courage, and a remarkable *sang-froid*. It is not my place to distribute awards and honors, but I felt it my duty to make these observations.

It is once again thanks only to the protection which the Alliance

accords them, to the support the Alliance gives them both directly
and through the intermediary of its representatives in Casablanca, and
to the frequent interventions on their behalf which the Alliance has
undertaken with the French minister that the Jews have received
equal, if not superior, treatment to that granted the foreign nationals
in the distribution of indemnities allocated to the victims of the events
of 1907 . . . Besides the benefits of the instruction it has provided,
the Alliance has thus ensured the material well-being of the Jews of
Casablanca.
[. . .]

A. Saguès

Archives of the AIU, France XIV.F.25.

The same protective role was particularly significant in Iran:

Shiraz, 3 August 1910
[. . .]
Role of the Alliance in the protection of the Jews. . . . Subjected to
the proverbial rapacity of the Persian authorities as well as to the
implacable religious fanaticism of the Shiite priests, the Jews had only
one hope for safety. This hope was for the generous intervention of
their brothers from the West who had undertaken the providential
task of, wherever possible, coming to the aid of those who were made
to suffer for being Jews. Their hope was not disappointed. In spite of
various difficulties and a few errors in the beginning—and no such
daring undertaking when confronted with countless obstacles and difficulties can be exempt from error and vicissitude—you have obtained
admirable and encouraging results in every regard within a few years.

In my last yearly report, I wrote the following about the situation
of the Jews in Shiraz. It could equally be applied to any community in
Persia in which one of your schools is found:

"This odious regime of intolerance and oppression has become appreciably more gentle since the day you first opened your schools
here. Taking advantage of a certain prestige and influence, the
strength of which can only be explained by the ignorance and spine-
lessness of the local authorities, your directors have succeeded in putting a stop to the fierce malevolence of some and the insatiable greed
of the others. Our communities have benefited from the respect and
consideration with which we are viewed in the eyes of the Persian
world. Your representatives, here designated by the title *Reis
Yahudah* (leaders of the Jews), are looked upon as agents of considerable power. This power seems all the more formidable as no one

knows its exact nature. This is the fortunate mirage which your directors have skillfully exploited to the greater good of those whom they protect. The latter have seen their existence become immeasurably more bearable." And as happiness is a relative thing and a thing of contrast, it can be said that you have provided the majority of the communities of Persia a state of well-being which they had never before imagined. Even better than this, your regenerative undertakings, when joined to the new liberal spirit behind the government today, have allowed these people to hope for a future that will be better than the present. They can finally glimpse the comforting prospect of complete emancipation, which is the legitimate compensation for the suffering that has defined their existence until now.

But as I mentioned earlier, and as is demonstrated by events currently unfolding, the old empire of the Shahs is undergoing the most serious crisis ever known to a nation thirsty for freedom, independence, and progress. As should have been expected, all of the attempted reforms of the liberals have been met with stubborn resistance on the part of all the reactionary elements in the country—and they are legion. These reactionary elements include all those who found certain advantages and prerogatives in the old order of things which are incompatible with the new regime; all those who, whether through purely political or religious convictions or through calculated material interests, cannot accept a popular, egalitarian government without risking the loss of their own influence and privileges in the general process of equalization.

In this struggle, which threatens to continue all the longer because the advocates of the constitution and the reactionaries seem to be evenly matched, the fanaticism of the clerical party will necessarily be aroused and will experience a violent upsurge, whose terrible effects will be felt first among our fellow Jews. The sad events that have recently taken place in Kermanshah, in Seneh, in the interior of the Fars, and in Shiraz, all caused by the explosive virulence of Shiite fanaticism, demonstrate just how necessary our intervention now is and with what vigilance we must keep watch over the communities in our charge.

Our role has become all the more awkward and difficult today as we must employ the most adept diplomacy not only to remain unattached to any one party but also to obtain the sympathies of each and every party, especialy those that oppose our rights. We must handle the civil authorities carefully. We must deal carefully with the liberal party because of the good they are disposed to undertake in favor of our fellow Jews; we must deal carefully with the religious authorities

as well as the clerical party because of the harm which they might seek to inflict upon the Jews. In short, we have to navigate between two powerful and conflicting currents, and our efforts must be directed toward bringing our fragile skiff safely to harbor.
[. . .]

E. Nataf

Archives of the AIU, France XII.F.22.

The teacher's role as protector was much less significant in areas such as, for example, the Turkish parts of the Ottoman Empire, where most Jewish communities were located in the major centers, where security prevailed, and where the government was, on the whole, favorably disposed toward them. In the more distant provinces, where petty acts of oppression were more common, the teacher often acted as the conduit through which complaints flowed to the appropriate authorities either in the locality or in Istanbul.

12
The Teacher as Patriot
and Advocate of the Jews

With the final consolidation of French colonialism in North Africa follow-ing the proclamation of the Protectorate over Morocco in 1912, and the consequent increase in public security, the role of the teacher shifted from that of protector to that of advocate. The new agenda that emerged for both the Alliance and the teachers in the Maghreb concerned the legal and political status of the Jews.

The issue had been resolved for Algeria in 1870 with the granting of French citizenship to the Jews with the Crémieux decree.[1] However, the rise of a vocal antisemitic movement among the French colonists of Alge-ria as well as the fact that Tunisia and Morocco had not been annexed to France, but were Protectorates, made the French authorities unwilling to replicate the Algerian example in those two countries. The Jews were treated, from the legal point of view, as indigènes and were made to submit to native tribunals, much to the chagrin of the Alliance and the teachers. Individual Jews could be naturalized on a fairly restricted basis, but mass naturalization was out of the question. Indeed, as the French abolished the Capitulations system, first in Tunisia in 1897 and in Mo-rocco after the creation of the French Protectorate in 1912, thousands of protégé Jews were returned to the status of indigènes.

The Alliance did its best to remedy the situation, and attempted at least to have the Jews removed from the jurisdiction of native tribunals, which operated on the basis of Muslim law.[2] The teachers, most notably Y. D. Sémach, the inspector of the Alliance schools in Morocco after 1924 and the delegate of the organization in charge of relations with the Protector-ate authorities, went much further and launched a campaign for the rapid

1. For a study of the way this decree was promulgated, see Michel Abitbol, "La citoyenneté imposée: Du décret Crémieux à la guerre d'Algérie," in Birnbaum, ed., *Histoire politique*, 196–217.
2. For one such attempt, see the 1913 letter of Narcisse Leven to Résident Général Lyautey reprinted in Chouraqui, *Cent ans d'histoire*, 440–42.

naturalization of Jews in greater numbers.[3] The political entry of the Jews into the orbit of the colonizer, ardently desired by the radical westernizer, received perhaps its classic formulation in these texts, which rehearsed and reconfigured all the components of the Alliance moralizing mission to bring about the final union with the metropole.

Tangier, 7 August 1923

[. . .]

An employee of the French government sees the current social status of the Moroccan Jew, his particularistic customs, the habits of his family life, and his code of ethics and judges him to be diametrically opposed to the European, tending to confuse the Jew with the Arab. This is not the case. The Arab has a plodding mind and is slow to comprehend; his religion and traditions make him a creature of habit and his ideas are desperately slow in changing. The Jew, on the other hand, now that he has been freed of the chains that had reduced him to the status of pariah through the ages, has suddenly taken flight. Yesterday he was wallowing in his ignorance and humiliation, and here he is today, a free man, capable of keeping step with the European in his dress, manners, and the development of his mind . . . He was able to make this transition smoothly and without trauma. The photograph that you published in the most recent issue of *Paix et Droit* is a striking testimony to this power of assimilation in the Jew. Those young girls in shorts preparing to run in a public event, what an impressive example! These are the children of those veiled women who, even ten years ago, did not dare to venture outside the *Mellah*, who lived a cloistered life of silence in their homes, and who in their ignorance and superstition fled at the sight of any foreigner . . . the Jew capable of such an awakening may well aspire to a full and complete education within the framework of a European life . . .

On the other hand, the Protectorate, which seeks to instruct and educate the Jew, is not considering that it might one day profit from him in the strengthening of its own political situation; the Protectorate wants the Jew to maintain his native status. In choosing this course of action, it remains haunted by what has quite mistakenly been referred to as the error of the Crémieux decree. The memory of this past is the dominating influence on policy concerning Moroccan Jews and Tunisian Jews alike. Those who govern us are afraid of the grumbling and protest to which the emancipation of the Jews might

3. On the naturalization issue in Morocco, see Laskier, *The Alliance Israélite Universelle and the Jewish Communities of Morocco,* 163–71.

give rise. And yet, the patriotism demonstrated by the Algerian Jews should put their minds completely at rest. The Jew who has been given his freedom and raised in the French mentality becomes a true Frenchman; he becomes totally devoted to the development of the strength and power of his country.

In Morocco, where the Muslim population is more dense and more fierce and where the spirit of revolt and independence is stronger even than in Algeria, France must work toward increasing the number of French nationals. While proceeding with prudence and avoiding the displeasure of the Arab population, and even more that of the antisemitic colonies, France must work toward the eventual naturalization of the Jews. This would not happen immediately, of course, and not without certain trials and hardships. The Young Tunisians already create enough worry for the French administration; one need not have particular foresight to predict that in a few years a Young Moroccan party will be formed, a much more dangerous party. When this day comes, France should be able to look for support to the educated and completely liberated Jewish population.

Regarding education in the primary schools, it is the Alliance school that seems to us to be most capable of developing the intelligence and cultivating the awareness of the Jewish children; the teachers themselves are only recently emancipated. In their childhood memories and in their understanding of the lives of their ancestors, they will find powerful reasons to open the hearts of their students and to create in their students the desire to be worthy of their past. Once the child has learned these lessons of pride, energy, and emulation at the Alliance school, he should go to the public secondary school so that he might share in the lives of children of other beliefs and might establish those solid bonds of friendship so rarely broken in later life. There he will also find access to the immense body of knowledge necessary for the modern man.

[. . .]

Y. D. Sémach

Archives of the AIU, France XV.F.26.

Tangier, 11 May 1924

. . . The Jew is not a native in the sense this term is used by the colonists. From the moment he started attending school, he was completely transformed; he has become a European and deserves to be treated as such. And when I say European, I am using . . . a general term in order to avoid offending certain sensibilities; I should say a Frenchman. The children in the Alliance schools acquire French ideas and learn to love France; their entire upbringing and all of their traditions lead them to look to the ideas of justice, equality, and freedom, and so naturally to a liberal and republican France . . .

I am convinced that France's policies in Morocco are governed by the belief that the Crémieux decree was, at the time, an error. And yet, the Algerian Jews have since demonstrated that they deserved the favor granted them. There should be some men today who can set superstition aside and who can see all that France has to gain by bringing the Jews of Morocco to her, by assimilating them over a more or less long period of time; granting no special favor for the moment but a just reward for duties accomplished and responsibilities accepted. All of the efforts of the administration, all of the work of the community leaders, and all of the ambition of the educators should be directed toward this goal: naturalization of the Jews. The day this goal is reached, what an impressive force there would be in the service of France. One hundred and fifty thousand, and perhaps more, active, intelligent, educated Jews spread throughout the empire would constitute an effective contribution to counterbalancing Muslim action. The more education the Muslims receive, the more they become conscious of their unity and isolate themselves in their fierce nationalism.

France should have adopted this policy toward the Jews thirty or forty years ago. If France, like Spain or Portugal, had widely granted French citizenship or protection to the Jews, the question of Tangier would have been more easily resolved in her favor today. France has come to the aid of the Jews each time they have been odiously persecuted; she has educated them and given them a feeling of dignity. But when they have asked her for political protection, she has refused them in order not to antagonize the Arab world! . . . How many Jews under foreign protection would have been happy to be French! The past must serve the present in developing a Jewish policy in Morocco. [. . .]

Y. D. Sémach

Archives of the AIU, Maroc I.C.1–2.

Rabat, 31 January 1931

[. . .]

The *Résident Général* did me the honor of granting me an audience this morning. I once again discussed with him the issue of the naturalization of the Moroccan Jews, and I submitted an official note to him, a copy of which you will find enclosed.

He told me that he knows the Jews of North Africa well; he sees those in Morocco at work and believes that already many of them, very close to the French in their mentality, would deserve to be naturalized. But this was not the opinion of the Minister of Foreign Affairs.

I replied that the Central Committee of the Alliance knows that it can count on his goodwill and his great sense of justice. Beyond individual interests, it sees in this issue a question of purely national interest. These educated Jews would serve to strengthen the French element of the population and allow it to exercise a greater influence on the indigenous masses.

[. . .]

NOTE: Presented to Monsieur le Haut Commissaire Résident Général de France au Maroc.

[. . .]

The Central Committee of the Alliance Israélite is deeply interested in the issue of naturalization of the Moroccan Jews. This is in keeping with its tradition. In working toward the emancipation of the Jews, the Alliance means to serve France and to prepare dedicated citizens for her future, citizens who will help maintain French ascendancy in this country.

It is not at all a question of a request for mass naturalization, or even of naturalization of certain groups, but there seems to be no reason to reject the examination of individual cases.

Already certain completely evolved Jews have adopted French as their language in the home; they live in the French manner and have devoted their efforts to the triumph of French influence in this country. They are free, they live in safety, and they are satisfied with their material situation. But they are driven by one ambition: to see their nationality put in harmony with their sentiments. They are not seeking any personal advantage; rather they ask to take on the appropriate duties and responsibilities, the first among which is military service.

The head of the administration deems these Jews worthy of entering the family of French citizens. They love France. How could they feel otherwise? They owe everything to France: freedom, respect, material well-being. They know that they should expect nothing . . . : but when their request for naturalization is refused, they are disheartened. Might it not be that, without intending to do harm, they express their disappointment in certain hostile company in the following terms: "We have done everything, yet they reject us." We represent a few French Jews here who are aware of that danger, who want to help the administration, and who ask you, *Monsieur le Résident Général,* to grant certain requests, to favor a few outstanding individuals so that it might be said among the Jews that France knows how to recognize and reward services rendered her. The laws permit, in certain cases, that French nationality be granted in return for devotion and merit.

The question of the political status of the Jews would not be affected by such action; that question would be resolved when circumstances permit.

[. . .]

Y. D. Sémach

Archives of the AIU, Maroc I.C.1–2.

The arguments made in Sémach's letters echo those of his colleagues in Tunisia:

Tunis, 15 January 1917

THE CONDITION OF THE JEWS
BEFORE THE PROCLAMATION OF THE PROTECTORATE

[. . .]

As in all Muslim countries, [the Jews] were tolerated but had no political rights . . . There were no constraints on their economic activities, and so in Tunis they controlled all commerce . . . In short, they knew how to work with those in authority, and their situation, especially among the bourgeoisie, was not at all intolerable. The only serious difficulty was the system of justice, which was organized on religious principles, notoriously corrupt, and thus did not offer the desired guarantees of fairness. But there again, the Jews were able to manage the situation by soliciting the protection of foreign consuls. Through the Capitulations agreements, the latter were able, under certain conditions, to offer letters of protection to any of the Bey's subjects, Arab or Jew . . . But it was especially to the French representative that the Jews chose to turn in seeking European protection. Thus, at the time of the occupation in 1881, a considerable number of Jews were *protégés* of France. All of the important merchants, land and business owners, and those who had to defend sizable interests against the rapacity of the *Kaid*s and their employees managed to acquire security against such excesses by seeking the protection of the consul . . .

[. . .]

It was then that the great event took place, the establishment of the French Protectorate over Tunisia. The Jews enthusiastically welcomed the arrival of the French soldiers, who were to liberate them after years of slavery; a new era was beginning for them, an era of tranquility, justice, and freedom, which gave them reason to hope for moral and political emancipation. What has become of all these dreams? That is what we will now discuss.

[. . .]

During the first few years the Jews and the Tunisians asked for absolutely nothing; it was enough to take advantage of the order and security which prevailed in the country under the new regime and which greatly facilitated their economic activities . . . Until 1897, that is to say for the first sixteen years, nothing was changed under this regime regarding the status of the Jews; those who did not have the benefit of a letter of protection remained under the jurisdiction of the Arab tribunals, whose functioning was maintained by France exactly as it had been before the occupation.

[. . .]

In 1897 the prior treaties which the Bey had signed with the European powers expired . . . But when the time came to renew these treaties, France persuaded these foreign powers to cancel the prerogatives established in the Capitulations agreements . . .

Although it was indispensable for the normal development of the Protectorate, this measure . . . nevertheless did great harm to the Jewish population, which was the beneficiary of 90 percent of the consular letters of protection granted in Tunisia.

. . . Between 2,000 and 3,000 Jewish *protégés,* representing between 10,000 and 15,000 individuals, were suddenly deprived of French protection and thrown defenseless into the system of Arab tribunals.

[. . .]

It was in response to the suppression of the letters of protection and especially of the striking of between 2,000 and 3,000 Jews from the list of *protégés,* an act as arbitrary as it was pointless, that the question of the status of Jews in Tunisia was raised in all its urgency. The Jews quickly realized that the new conditions under which they were living represented a step backward from what had been the situation before the Protectorate . . . The younger generation was receiving a French education in the Alliance schools and in the schools run by the government; they had been introduced to the ideas of justice and liberty; and so they found especially abhorrent the idea that they were now to be treated as a race of pariahs. This generation began to make its objections heard. The young people formed groups in which the situation was debated and discussed, Jewish newspapers were founded, and public opinion was influenced by the airing of their grievances.

[. . .]

Thus, by requiring that the judges be Muslim and either teachers or graduates of the Great Mosque, the government was making a formal declaration that the *ouzara* [civil court] was to keep its religious character; the Jews, with good reason, objected to this religious character of the courts . . . As it is, the judges who have studied at the Great Mosque hold strictly to the teachings of the Koran, in which they have been trained, and consequently inspire no confidence in anyone of a different religion who must appear before them.

[. . .]

The Jews also accuse the government of having sabotaged the law concerning the naturalization of the Tunisians that the Parliament, in a spirit of generosity, had passed in 1910. The goal of this law was to make French naturalization accessible to the educated elite of the Jewish population and to those in commerce and industry who had contributed to the economic development of the Regency . . .

. . . Had it a little spirit of goodwill, the government of the Protectorate could have found from among the hundreds of applications it received a good number of petitioners who fulfilled the conditions outlined by the Parliament, which, let us remember, required of these petitioners not exceptional service rendered to the government but considerable service. Those applying the law, however, took advantage of the vagueness and imprecision of the term and found in all of Tunisia only two or three Jewish candidates who were worthy of joining the family of French citizens. What better way to make a mockery of the Parliament, which, for its part, had been making a sincere attempt to open the way to naturalization for hundreds of Tunisian Jews . . .

[. . .]

And is that all? Unfortunately, no. The Tunisian Jews have voiced even more grievances against the government. They reproach it for having systematically excluded them from all public employment. The French administration employs a good number of Arabs. It is true that the latter fill only subordinate positions, but the young Jews here would be perfectly content to accept such positions for they find themselves obliged to find employment in commerce, where they receive only between forty and fifty francs per month. The administration of the postal service, which employs many Muslims as mail carriers and in other positions, has not hired a single Jew. In the educational system there are numerous Arab teachers, some of whom are school directors, but there is not a single Tunisan Jew employed as a teacher by the government . . .

[. . .]

CONCLUSION

The Tunisian Jews are justified in calling themselves victims of the Protectorate. Their most legitimate aspirations have been thwarted, their hands tied by the narrow limits of legislation worthy of the Middle Ages. They, who so openly welcomed modern ways and ideas, have been excluded from positions in public service, administration, and the magistrature. The Arabs, who saw the establishment of the new regime with fire in their hearts in 1881, now bless its advent, for France—to her eternal glory—has managed to attract them to her with a limitless and constant solicitude. On the other hand, the Jews, who greeted the institution of the Protectorate with enthusiasm, are today taking stock of advances made in the last thirty-five years. They find that on certain issues, they are still where they were when they started; on other issues, any movement has been in reverse. This is because France, too busy currying the favor of the Arabs, has not only neglected the Jews but, what is more, has often sacrificed the latter in order to better please the former.
[. . .]

C. Ouziel

Archives of the AIU, Tunisie II.C.5.

Sfax, 18 February 1932

I respectfully submit the following report on the situation of the Jews in Tunisia.

I can relate an incident which typifies the legal status of our fellow Jews in spite of fifty years of French occupation.

This happened one evening last December in the *souk* where fabric and cloth are sold in Sfax. It was late. All of the merchants were closing up their shops. Two Arab women . . . had gone from one shop to another without finding what they were looking for. Finally they stopped in front of a small shop run by a Jewish merchant, who was just putting the lock on his door. Next to him was his "tailor."

I should tell you that every cloth merchant whose shop is frequented by the local population reserves a tiny space at the entrance to his shop: just enough room for one man and his sewing machine.

This is a very clever partnership: the merchant measures the calico or the satin and passes it to his tailor. The client sits right down on the floor across from him or in the entrance to the shop and waits as he makes a magnificent shirt with multicolored stripes, a light coat, or billowing trousers. Then the client pays one man for the cloth and the other for the tailoring.

Our merchant, then, accompanied by his tailor was ready to leave
the *souk* when he saw two Arab women approaching. He could not
resist the temptation to try to make one last sale that day. Business
had been so slow! He reopened the store and he and his associate
followed the two women back in.

These late-coming clients found the cloth they wanted but the price
was not to their liking. They began to barter aggressively, as is the
custom, and their raised voices could be heard at some distance.
Night was falling. The remaining daylight dimly lit the interior of the
store. A few Arabs, intrigued, passed back and forth in front of the
store. One of them finally stopped, and banging on the half-opened
door he called to the women: "Fallen women, what are you doing at
this hour in the store of this dog born of a dog! And you two, you
choose women of my race to satisfy your evil desires! And where do
you do this? In a store, in front of everyone, so near to the Great
Mosque!"

The man left the shop, pulling the door shut behind him, and began to call out. The whole Arab district was thus drawn in a crowd
outside the shop of these poor Jews. Had it not been for the intervention of the *Sheikh* (leader) of the district, they would have lynched
them. And our two fellow Jews were rescued from the anger of the
populace, but . . . sent to jail, where they remained for six days. It
was finally admitted that they were innocent; but why were they held
in jail for so long? Because they are Tunisian Jews, subjects of the
Bey, and as such they fall under the jurisdiction of the native courts,
which are always too slow in investigating these matters.

I can tell you another little story about a conversion.

The young Esther Cohen of Sfax, the daughter of a rabbi—and
what an orthodox rabbi!—became smitten with a Muslim. Her head
full of cheap literature praising the charm and mystery of the harems,
this was inevitable. In any case, she ran away with her friend and
came before the *Kadi* [judge] in Tunis, asking to be allowed to embrace the religion of Mohammed. This was granted her immediately,
in spite of the vigorous protest on the part of her mother, her sisters,
and the entire Jewish community of Sfax that she was acting without
proper judgment, being a minor.

"She is a minor and here is the proof," the mother clamored. "A
few months ago she sat for the exams for the primary school diploma.
Two Jewish notaries, two sworn notaries appointed by decree of the
Bey, wrote up the certificate: here it is."

"Your paper is not admissible as valid," replied the *Kadi*, "because
it is based on the testimony of Jewish witnesses. Under my jurisdic-

tion, the testimony of a non-Muslim is worthless. Furthermore, your daughter is of age. This paper proves it."

And the *Kadi* showed her a certificate written up by two Arab notaries on the testimony of two Muslims who swore that they had been present at the birth of Esther, daughter of Rabbi Cohen, some twenty years ago.

And the mother took her revenge with this response: "You are too naive or too intelligent, O *Kadi,* to believe that as I was giving birth I allowed two Muslims to come into my room."

A question arises: if the mother of Esther Cohen had been French, in possession of a certificate signed by a French justice of the peace, as is the custom here, would the *Kadi* have dared say that the justice of the peace was lying and that only his certificate, drawn up on the testimony of two Muslims, was the pure expression of the truth? I don't think so.

Many people in this whole affair of conversion of minors have been painfully surprised by the neutrality maintained by the French authorities.

Once a person becomes French, he escapes this native system of justice. But not everyone can become naturalized. The great majority of the Jews cannot take advantage of the Morinaud law of 1923[4] because they cannot meet the required conditions. Can we reasonably hope to see every one of our students receive the baccalaureate or some other secondary school diploma? Can it reasonably be required that every Tunisian Jew work for at least ten years for a French company?

When the Morinaud law was first promulgated, it was greeted with such enthusiasm that hundreds of applications were filed with the administration. But the law was applied so poorly and in such a narrow spirit that the majority of the applications were rejected, dismissed *sine die,* and now it is in a slow trickle that French nationality is granted to Tunisian Jews—scarcely four or five families a month in all of Tunisia. Is this so as not to offend the sensibilities of the Arabs and of the Bey? If not that, the government employees responsible for investigating the applications for citizenship are inspired by a certain animosity.

The Morinaud law of 1923 is absolutely inadequate, for it rejects any request for citizenship submitted by a minor. Yet it is the young people, fresh out of school and still feeling the influence of the lessons of their teachers, who would bring the most interested, most

4. The law facilitating the naturalization of the educated and wealthy segments of the Jewish population.

vital, and most enthusiastic contribution to the support of French influence in this country.

My brother-in-law is eighteen years old. He went to the *Contrôle Civil* and asked to become French. He was told, "You are a minor. Wait until you are twenty-one or else join the Foreign Legion for three years."

"But if I want to serve in a different army corps?"

"No, foreigners are not allowed in French units."

Even supposing someone has spent three years in the Foreign Legion, he is not certain of obtaining his naturalization papers, for that is a favor which is granted, and that favor can be refused based on any trifle.

And so when my brother-in-law reaches the age of twenty-one and once again goes to the *Contrôle Civil,* they will reproach him for not having joined the French army and for trying to enjoy the rights of French citizenship without having fulfilled the duties of a citizen. Vicious circle.

The Jew born in Tunisia cannot escape native jurisdiction except by becoming French. He cannot become Italian, English, or Spanish. But an Italian, a Maltese born in Tunisia, can instantly have his papers put in order by going to any consulate. That is why such a scandal is commonplace: poor Sicilians, pitiful Maltese who do not know the first word of French, obtain their naturalization papers without delay, while Tunisian Jews with excellent French and who are honorable men are refused this favor.

For a long time there has been the question of an option of legal jurisdiction for the Jews of Tunisia. This sort of law would render an immense service to our fellow Jews. The Jews of Tunisia must be given the right to choose French jurisdiction until a more generous law allows them to become part of that great guardian nation in large numbers.

I will not go on further about the advantages it would present for the Protectorate if the eighty thousand Jews of Tunisia were gathered under the French flag. This would not happen all at once, of course, but over a period of ten to fifteen years. The problem of the security of the Protectorate, the Italian issue, would appear less critical or would disappear altogether. It is not a strictly personal opinion that I am presenting here. The events of the future will determine its validity.

[. . .]

V. Danon

Archives of the AIU, Tunisie I.C.1.

*These views and the activities of the teachers and the Alliance not-
withstanding, the situation did not change substantively. The law passed
in 1923 for Tunisia did permit the elite of the Jewish community easier
access to French citizenship, but it did not alter the status of the masses.
The aspirations of the Jews had become increasingly oriented toward
France while their personal legal status, by and large, remained that of the*
indigènes.

*This disjunction rarely led to soul-searching among the Alliance teach-
ers, most of whom had themselves become naturalized in the Maghreb as
French citizens. In spite of the antisemitism so much in evidence among
the French colonists, the Alliance teachers had complete and total faith in
France, in the ultimate justice that the principles of 1789 incarnated. If
they were to blame any party, they tended to focus on the local French
colonists and local French administrations and to project onto metropoli-
tan France all the positive attributes they had imbibed through their education.*

*The teachers who were operating in countries under direct or indirect
French rule, such as those in North Africa, were convinced that the fate of
the Jews was inextricably linked to that of the French and interpreted their
task as one of aiding the local Jews in their acculturation, assimilation,
and integration into the "famille française." The propagation of French
culture through the Alliance schools to speed this integration hence appeared of cardinal importance.*

*This activist stance by the teachers to promote the political and cultural
assimilation of the Jews to France in the French colonial context is absent
in other areas where the organization maintained schools. The fact that
the teaching body was largely Francophile and identified with France is
undeniable. Nevertheless, the ideology of the Alliance was that of emancipation. The Jews had to be emancipated and integrated into the societies
of the countries in which they lived and fulfill all the duties of citizenship.
In North Africa, the Central Committee and the teachers were convinced
that the French presence was a permanent, irrevocable one. In spite of the
obvious difference between the form of French rule in Algeria and in the
Protectorates, the Alliance assumed that France was there to stay and that
the future of the Jews, sooner or later, converged with that of their "libera-
tors." Since these lands had now become French, the emancipation ideology called for integration with the French, not with the local Muslims,
who themselves, once sufficiently "evolved," could become French.*

*The situation was very different in the Levant, especially in the Otto-
man Empire and its successor states. These lands remained outside direct
French rule or entered it late, as in the case of Syria and Lebanon. The
aim of the Alliance was to make the Jews equal and worthy citizens of*

their countries, just as in Western Europe. And when new states emerged as a result of the weakening of the Ottomans, the Jews had to accept the realities and work for integration.

Tunis, 26 March 1878

[. . .]

The work of the Alliance in the Balkan Peninsula is characterized by two goals, one of which is the consequence of the other: 1. the mission of obtaining equality for the Jews and their assimilation to the other inhabitants of the country; 2. the mission of spreading instruction and education among them so that they will be able to profit from this equality of rights . . . A congress of the Great Powers may soon take place; it is the duty of the Alliance to represent our fellow Jews at this congress or to see that their cause is represented . . .[5]

[. . .]

. . . Our fellow Jews are faced with a very pressing duty: in spite of the debt of gratitude they owe the Ottoman government, they must openly accept the outcome of events and fully enter into the ideas of the rest of the population; they must not present themselves as partisans of the old regime. I can understand that this course of action may be difficult to follow, especially in Bulgaria, where the memory of recent massacres is still much too vivid to be erased, but sooner or later, this is the course of action which must be followed. The Jews cannot do better than to take the path chosen by their fellow citizens, from the very beginning, if they would not risk becoming isolated within their country.

[. . .]

. . . Should the Alliance maintain its schools in the new state or should it leave to the newly forming governments the organization of the education of their citizens and the instruction of their youth? Will the Alliance schools be considered establishments whose goal is to improve the intellectual conditions of a part of the citizenry, or will it be feared that these schools, sponsored by a foreign organization, may serve as a pretext for considering the Jews an isolated population, forming a state within the state? I am certain that all of these questions have already been formulated by the Alliance and that various solutions are currently being studied. Allow me, however, to sub-

5. The Berlin Congress of 1878, following the Russo-Turkish War, recognized the newly independent states of the Balkans—Romania and Bulgaria—and set the new status quo. The Alliance did indeed intervene actively in the Berlin Congress and was instrumental in making Romania promise to give its Jews equal rights.

mit another solution to you, one which my knowledge of the people and places of the East has inspired. I will speak in particular about the schools in Bulgaria: Rustchuk, Shumla, Varna, Samacoff, Widdin.

The government of Bulgaria will want to prove to Europe that it was worthy of the freedom which was the reason for so much spilling of blood; it will work hard at educating its people, as did Greece after the war of independence. But it will soon be lacking in funds. Now, if at that moment the Alliance schools were not only put back in place but also perfected, if the Bulgarian language were being seriously taught in these schools, the Alliance would then have the opportunity of making both a magnanimous and a political gesture, one that would win the government over to the Jewish cause. The Alliance would open its schools to children of all religions, would honor the government in so doing, and would entrust the final control and authority in these schools to the government. In a word, the Alliance would make true community schools of these establishments . . . [. . .]

As concerns the schools in the cities which will remain under Ottoman rule (Constantinople, Adrianople, Smyrna, Baghdad, etc.), they must be the object of very close attention. The Turkish government will want to compensate for its disasters through reforms, as did Austria after Sadowa. The Jews will be given the opportunity to profit from these reforms, but if they are not capable of holding their own against the Armenians through instruction and education, the latter will quickly take over all employment and take control of the direction of the movement of reform, seeing to it that only they profit. Our schools must be good schools, and there must be courses for adults organized in the evenings for those who feel the need to further their education after the day's work.

One reform which the Alliance should seek to obtain is official recognition of the organized Jewish communities by the governments of the Balkan Peninsula. This would make it possible for these communities to develop resources and to take upon themselves the responsibility for the functioning of the schools within a short period of time. This would relieve the Alliance of that responsibility and allow it to carry the torch of civilization into the interior of Morocco and into Persia. [. . .]

D. Cazès

Archives of the AIU, Tunisie I.D.1.

However, the Central Committee did not heed the advice of Cazès and was quite slow in increasing the number of hours devoted to local languages in these schools. French remained the primary medium of instruction. Still, on the whole, the Alliance did its best in the Levant to keep its distance from French political interests. The kind of close collaboration that existed between the French consuls and the teachers in North Africa was much more subdued in the Middle East until the end of World War I. Indeed, as was mentioned in Part I, only the Ecole Normale Israélite Orientale *was an officially recognized French institution. The Alliance itself was an international body and did not enjoy official French protection.*

Hence the tone of the teachers' letters from the Levant lacked the political identification with France so much in evidence in the Maghreb. The Jews had, on the whole, a positive relationship with their Turkish rulers and had more to fear from the rising nationalities within the empire. They were in constant economic competition with the Greeks, which, as this letter from Salonica demonstrates, often led to outbursts of antisemitism among the local Greek populations:

Salonica, 1 December 1909

Mr. President,

You requested in your letter of 8 November, no. 7973, that I give you certain information concerning a period of antisemitic disturbances provoked by the Greek population in Salonica.

The following is a succinct account of the events that occurred and the causes, nature, and import of these events.

This period of unrest lasted from September 1908 to June 1909. A backlash was also felt in September of 1909.

The most intense phase of unrest was in September of 1908, and again in March and June of 1909.

It had both a political and an economic nature.

It took the form of an attempted boycott of the Jewish work force and Jewish merchants and of a press campaign.

[. . .]

. . . It seemed inevitable that Bulgaria would one day take control of Macedonia. Had it not begun its takeover of Eastern Rumelia by introducing a system of financial control and a reorganization of the civil police force on the European model?

The most intelligent and active agents of this propaganda were sent to Macedonia, and particularly to Salonica.

The Greeks who would lay claim to the Macedonian empire soon realized that the Greek sector of the population in this region was very small in number and that it counted little as an economic factor.

They tried to improve the economic conditions of the Greeks in Macedonia, and naturally they came into conflict with the Jews.

Economic conditions. The greater part of commercial activity in Macedonia and in Salonica is in the hands of the Jews. The smaller merchants from the interior of Macedonia who need to do their buying in Salonica go through the brokers in Salonica. No significant business can be carried out without one of these brokers as an intermediary agent. It happens that almost all of these brokers are Jews. They are rather well-off; often they advance funds to the merchants and they almost always act as guarantors for their clients in their dealings with the large commercial enterprises. Even the banks sometimes grant credit to the merchants only because of the recommendation and the guarantee of the brokers.

The Greeks wanted to supplant the Jewish brokers and replace them with Greek brokers. And as the Greek brokers did not have the necessary funds to replace the Jewish brokers, the Greeks began by founding Greek financial institutions in Salonica; it was thus that we witnessed the successive openings of the Mitylene bank, the *Banque d'Athènes,* and the *Banque d'Orient.*

More precisely, the development of commerce in Macedonia led certain merchants from the interior to send their children to Salonica and establish them there as correspondents. The Greek financial institutions gave credit to these young men and tried to attract the Greek clientele from the native cities and surrounding areas of these correspondents.

The Jewish brokers began to sound the alarm, and, in a spirit of solidarity, the Jewish merchants refused to grant these brokers the payment and credit terms they granted the Jewish brokers, so that, in spite of the intervention of the Greeks, businesses were still obliged to work through the Jewish brokers.

Let us mention in passing that this was not the first time that the Greeks had endeavored to bypass the Jews in commercial dealings. In the spring of 1908, a similar action had been attempted on a smaller scale and had failed.

The owners of the groves in the area surrounding Salonica are almost all Greek; the fruit and vegetable merchants in Salonica are almost all Jewish. The intermediaries between the producers and the merchants are Jewish agents. In the spring of 1908, the Greek producers made it known that they would sell their fruit—it was cherry season—only through Greek agents. The Jewish fruit merchants came together and decided they would buy fruit only through the Jewish agents.

For three days the producers held their ground, but when they began to see their cherries rotting in baskets, they gave in.

This failure of the Greek agents exasperated the promoters of the "Great Idea."[6] They were trying to establish a boycott against the Jews when the Ottoman Revolution occurred.

The revolution [of 1908]. For a few days all quarrels were forgotten; there was general celebration and calls for union and brotherhood. These calls were all the more numerous and strong because they represented new and superficial emotions. A certain incident was soon to demonstrate the fragility of these new sentiments.

In the days after the proclamation of the constitution, Turkey's neighbors hurried to come and salute the "Heroes of Freedom" and to make the pilgrimage to the "Cradle of Freedom." It was first the Greeks, then the Serbs, then the Bulgarians, not to mention the Turks themselves, who came from all of the cities of the empire.

Each time a new group of visitors arrived in Salonica the cafés and restaurants glowed with activity; music of every ethnic group in the population could be heard in the public squares; the delirious crowds greeted the friendly visitors as they entered the city.
[. . .]

It is a secret to no one that the Greeks did not look kindly upon the installation of the new regime in Turkey. As long as disorder had reigned in this country, they had hope of realizing the Great Idea. If Turkey was to undergo a regeneration, if it was to become strong and gain the sympathies of European nations, the Great Idea would have to be laid to rest. Although they could not openly express their disappointment, they bore resentment against all those who had taken a major part in the establishment of the new regime, and particularly against the Jews. Thus . . . the Greeks lashed out against the Jews, claiming to find in their attitude an insult directed against the Greeks and a manifestation of the hatred which the Jews, according to them, bore against the Greeks.

On Tuesday, 15 September, the *Pharos tis Thessaloniquis,* the Greek newspaper in Salonica, published a virulent article against the Jews. This article was full of venom and hatred and, among other things, asked the Greeks to declare economic war against the Jews and to stop buying from the Jewish merchants.

The Jewish papers responded, revealing the true sentiments of the

6. The Greek nationalist ideal of re-creating the Byzantine Empire on the ruins of the Ottoman state.

agitators, who, only a few days before, had been calling for brother-hood among the races. The *Pharos* published an even more violent article the following day, in which it accused the Jews of having sold out to a foreign power that was seeking to suppress the Ottoman constitution . . . Trouble was brewing; both sides were reduced to pulling childish, ridiculous pranks. The Greek fire fighters refused to come put out a blaze in the Jewish district, and the conflict worsened. Finally the Committee for Union and Progress, fearing the trouble would spread, intervened and reconciled the Greeks and the Jews. [. . .]

The masses, however, were unrelenting. And when in July 1909, the Cretans declared their desire to unite with Greece, the Jews joined with their Muslim fellow citizens in protesting this threat to Turkish unity. At that time there was a repetition of the same injuri-ous articles accompanied by ludicrous caricatures and the same at-tempted boycotts.

The current situation. For the moment, the relations between the Greeks and the Jews are good. The slightest provocation, however, could create another confrontation, and the same scenario could eas-ily be repeated tomorrow.

The Greeks who have not brought themselves to accept the Jews as leaders of commercial activity in Macedonia and in Salonica, and the Jews who feel that their interests are threatened, all continue to work in silence.

The Jews are organizing; the merchants now know what the dan-gers are and they have formed coalitions. They have founded the "*Cercle Commercial Israélite*" (May 1909), which works to protect the interests of the Jewish merchants. [. . .]

Conclusion. The agitation and unrest never took on a truly serious character; nevertheless, it was caused by deep-seated political and eco-nomic factors. These factors are still in operation. The Greeks are still using any and all methods to achieve commercial domination; the Jews are organizing a defense. And if a lesson must be learned, it is clear that the Jews must be united and must work toward the strength-ening of Turkey. When the day comes that Turkey is stable and strong, the political causes for these disruptions will disappear and, along with them, the economic causes. [. . .]

M. Benghiat

Archives of the AIU, Grèce I.C.48.

As events unfolded, bringing with them the disintegration of the Otto-
man Empire, the attitude of the teachers toward the departing Turks, the
rulers of the area for centuries, was one of regret, as is shown by this letter
from Salonica at the time of its conquest by the Greeks in 1912 during the
Balkan wars:

Salonica, 12 November 1912

[. . .]

I have been lying low until now. You have been much better informed in Paris than we were here. We were only receiving very
vague and contradictory information about the terrible events taking
place. Today it is a *fait accompli:* the Greeks, Bulgarians, and even
the Serbs are occupying our city. There are several thousand of them
here and they fill the streets with their proud and defiant *zitos* [hur-
rah]. The cafés are packed with soldiers in caps. All over the city
there can be seen only soldiers and the Greeks, our fellow citizens,
giving them a warm reception. The city's inhabitants hide, keeping
out of the way. The Turks, the *Dönme,*[7] and the Jews know that for
the time being their heretics' beards would be quickly spotted among
the clean-shaven victors. Justifiably cautious, they prefer not to draw
attention to themselves.

The tremendous numbers of the Balkan troops here, increased by
the many Ottoman soldiers who were disarmed and forced back into
the city, have caused prices to rise considerably. It is impossible to
buy bread; the bakeries are taken by storm as soon as they open. No
eggs, vegetables, or milk are to be found.

And life has come to a complete halt. All of the stores are closed;
all movement has stopped. The trains are no longer running. Salonica
is cut off from Europe. It has become an island visited by ships only
at rare intervals. The greater part of our population is living from
hand to mouth, in miserable conditions.

Since the arrival of the Greeks, the Jews have been confronted with
a problem. Our Greek fellow citizens, as you can easily understand,
are jubilant. They now greet each other with the words *O christos*
anesti (Christ is risen). They fire guns as a sign of their joy, shout
songs of triumph in chorus at every street corner. They have covered
all the walls of their homes with banners in the Greek colors, white

---

7. The *Dönme* were the descendants of Jews who followed the false messiah Sabbetai
Sevi, converted to Islam in the seventeenth century, and yet maintained secret, messianic
practices and rites. Most moved to Turkey during the Greek-Turkish population exchange
that followed the Lausanne treaty of 1923. The term *dönme* comes from the Turkish verb
"to turn."

and blue. When there was no more cloth they began using paper, paint, and whitewash. There is a profusion of blue over a white that is not quite pure because of the haste with which the flags are painted. And here is the problem with which we were wrestling: should we join in the general rejoicing? Should we deck with flags the more visible clubs, shops, and homes? Of course, there was no question of sharing the greeting of Christ's resurrection; we are, as you know, descendants of those Jews who held strong against the Inquisition. Nor was there question of firing off guns; we had long ago changed our instruments of war into plowshares and our plowshares into well-made strongboxes. But it remained to be seen if we should bring out the flags and cry *zitos!*, if we should walk through the streets with ecstatic contentment shining on our faces. That is it! What was needed was a watchword, a slogan, a political stance. It goes without saying that we, the Jews, never act without calculation and political maneuvering. But, here is the problem, we were overlooking the sentiments of the people. We, the oracles, the representatives of the six Jewish societies in the city forming the *Interclub,* held serious discussions and gravely weighed the historical, sociological, economic, patriotic, philosophical, mystical, and humanitarian arguments; we learnedly quibbled over the pros and cons, and we bickered. In the meantime, the common people, with surprising unity, refrained from cheers and applause. They maintained a most dignified and proper attitude. Certainly they showed no hostility; but neither did they show satisfaction.

After two days of deliberations, the *Interclub* decided to refrain from all demonstration of support and the communal council had resolved to send word to all establishments under its direction—schools, hospitals, hospices, and others—to hang the flags of the four Balkan states. But the two resolutions came too late. We had barely finished drawing them up when the Greek princes were already establishing themselves in the city; the king of Greece and Prince Boris of Bulgaria had already made their triumphal entries. We will have plenty of time later to play tug-of-war over such decisions. But by that time the wellspring of jubilation among our turbulent Christian population will certainly have run dry and whether or not the Jews demonstrate will be immaterial.

But the Jews are currently in a critical situation. The Greeks from our region envy our commercial success and would like to supplant us for good. They believe the time for their reign has come, and they want to rule the city alone. They ignore the Turks, few in numbers and nonexistent as commercial competitors, and move directly to attack the Jews. They spread absurd rumors against them. Since last night, more and more incidents have occurred. In one part of the city a few poor stall merchants had their stands overturned; in another part of the city several poor souls were taken to the police post for trifling reasons. Among the Greek population, people are talking about a Jewish massacre. The community council called an urgent meeting this morning to decide what steps to take in approaching the Greek authorities of the city. Is it possible to keep contained the hatred of these agitators who stir up trouble against our unfortunate fellow Jews? We hope so.

What will be the new conditions created for our fellow Jews by the events now unfolding? Some fear the worst. Some expect irreparable losses and there is talk of a mass exodus, to which the Jews will be compelled as much by antisemitism as by the new economic conditions resulting from the war.

Bakalum![8] as our masters of yesterday would say, and let us add as they did, always wise and confident, *Allah kerim!*[9]

[. . .]

J. Nehama

Archives of the AIU, Grèce I.C.51.

The teachers, like the local Jews, clearly preferred Turkish rule. Indeed, Salonica Jewry lost its sparkle under the Greeks and faced considerable economic dislocation and antisemitism.

A journal kept by the Alliance headmistress of the girls' school of Adrianople during the siege of 1912 reveals a full awareness of the coming to an end of the old world in the Balkans and exhibits considerable Turkish patriotism:

Adrianople, 30 October 1912

[. . .]

I wrote to you on the twenty-fourth of this month and spoke to you about the closing of the school and my desire to render myself useful to the motherland since I was then free of my duties as headmistress. That letter left with the last train to Constantinople and since then we have been unable to have any communication with the outside. I intend to keep a journal, in which I will record for you the political occurrences and events involving the school as they happen. I will

8. *Bakalum [bakalım]*, "we will see" in Turkish.
9. *Allah kerim*, "God is kind" in Turkish.

send this journal with the first mail to leave the city. When? Each of us anxiously asks that question.

It is almost two weeks since war was officially declared, exactly one week since the first shots fired from the fortifications in the city caused a great commotion in the population and increased the emigration of the women, the elderly, the sick, and a part of the able-bodied population.

[. . .]

5 NOVEMBER

The situation has become decidedly alarming. It seems we are completely cut off. I say "it seems" for we can only guess. No news is certain; nothing is confirmed. The telegraph office refuses even the most urgent messages and for twelve days now we have received no letters and no newspapers. A siege. How horrible it is when real. It is all very well to read about in fat history books; but to live through a siege, with the prospect of famine, poverty all around, and the frightening music of machine guns and cannons!

How I regret not having left Adrianople!

I am afraid not of death, for I do not know what it is, but of the silence that has set in all around us, of the monotonous and disheartening wait; I am afraid of the slow agony of starvation.

And yet, they say that Adrianople can hold for a long time. It has 100,000 containers of cheese, enough wheat and grain for three months, and a large supply of meat.

Think of it: from all the surrounding villages the peasants have come with their livestock to take refuge in Adrianople. They sell them at very low prices for they have no pasturage. The poor farmer, his heart breaks as he gives up the animals he loves and which represent his entire fortune.

[. . .]

SUNDAY, 24 NOVEMBER

[. . .]

Today we went through some moments of anguish. The shelling of the city continues relentlessly day and night. After it has been fired, a shrill whistling announces the imminent arrival of the Bulgarian shell. It then hits the victim which misfortune has chosen. Some shells fall on soft ground, sink into the earth, and cause no harm, but others strike solid objects, explode into bits, and the fragments spread death for meters all around, starting fires . . .

The Bulgarians are cowards to attack a peaceful population in this way and to strike women and children without mercy.

TUESDAY, 26 NOVEMBER

The shelling continues. I am beginning to see my energy fade and my child, whom I am breast-feeding, suffers for it. Yesterday evening there was a big fire near the Sultan Selim [Mosque]. What is going to happen to us? I don't know why, but I find myself constantly thinking about the *Titanic* disaster, and I shiver (my faith calls out "higher, higher!"). My faith still has hope in life, and I am afraid to die. It's true, I am afraid. In the face of danger we are driven by a strong and unconscious egoism, while so near to us cruel death works her well-sharpened scythe.

[. . .]

And what will become of our poor country with so many enemies united against it and Europe indifferent! And they dare call this theft of territory and this carnage through modern machines the civilization of the twentieth century. I have read volumes full of praise and enthusiasm for the benefits of progress, and now I smile bitterly when I think of them. They would like to tear our country to shreds, like another Poland, and Europe sits quietly and finds this just, for she whispers to herself: there will be something there for me, too.

Barely recovered from the internal battles over the constitution, Turkey gets into trouble with Italy, who judges it appropriate, I don't know how, to steal one of her provinces.[10] She struggles with the bellicose people of Yemen, problems are created for her in Macedonia, and finally, enemies invade her territory from four directions at once.

The rules have not changed since Frederick the Great. The windmills are left unharmed, but provinces are stolen.

[. . .]

Foodstuffs are in short supply. Up until now we have lacked paraffin oil, sugar, salt, alcohol, and charcoal. Now we have to struggle at the bakery to get a loaf of bread, happy enough not to return home empty-handed. Fortunately, we had stocked a little flour and we knead our own bread at home.

I smile sometimes when I recall how, as a young girl, I used to recite my *Siège de Paris* of 1870 without giving it a thought. The Parisians had written over the entrances to their restaurants "*rat goût de*

---

10. A reference to the Turco-Italian War of 1911, which ended with the Italian annexation of Libya.

mouton."[11] What a *ragoût!* And will that be our fare a few weeks from now?

17 JANUARY 1913

[. . .]

. . . Patriotism could find less bloody ways to manifest itself. The goal of a war may be noble and generous, but the war itself is a call to violence; and violence awakens emotions in man which are too cruel and too instinctively fierce. Tamed by laws, religion, and ethics, it is the animal in man which takes over when hatred between the races is given free rein.

Thinking only of saving himself in defeat, man forgets his duty toward his fellow man and leaves a friend of twenty years to drown without reaching a hand out to him, for fear of losing a moment in his flight. Without a hint of remorse soldiers and officers have told us stories of abandoning their friends along the way without reaching a hand out to them.

[. . .]

1 MARCH 1913

[. . .]

Then has Ottoman pride and glory truly vanished? And the proud Janissary of the Mohammeds and the Solimans, has he grown pale and weak before the savage deeds of these new nations? The illusions our soldiers held only six months ago are gone, destroyed. I can still see him—is he still alive?—that old officer, saddened at the fateful news of the declaration of war but still filled with enthusiasm as he came to pay his debts and tell us with naive vanity, "I'll have my beard trimmed in Sofia." Today enthusiasm has given way to despondency and to that indifference natural to the Turks. "So it was written," they are resigned to it. It hurts to see the sickly, thin soldier. His uniform now fits him too loosely and he wears it wearily, as one carries a cross, tired and suffering. He thinks about his plot of land, his small house, his animals now fallen prey to the enemy. He thinks about his mother, his wife, and his children. He wonders about a country that has not cared for his wounds and his sickness, that does not give him enough to eat, that has reduced him to begging for his bread and has pushed him to exhaustion; he wonders if such a country merits so many bitter sacrifices. The hospitals are full of sick men

11. A play on words in French in which *rat,* "rat," and *goût,* "taste," are put together to approximate the word *ragoût,* "stew." Thus, whereas *ragoût de mouton* normally means "mutton stew," here it means literally "rat tasting like mutton."

who, for lack of care and medication, are dying by the dozens every day. Scurvy, pneumonia, physiological deficiencies, and cholera are rampant in these hospitals.
[. . .]

3 MARCH 1913

We will continue to talk about our siege for a long time to come. The memory of our hardships, of our violent emotions, and a little of that virile energy which led us to look upon the shelling as an old, familiar acquaintance, I almost said friend, will remain engraved in our hearts. We remain proud and strong in the face of the enemy shells, like children who hold back their tears when submitting to an unjust or overly harsh punishment. In fact, you Bulgarian soldiers, what right did you have to strike at us blindly, to mutilate women and children, and to burn without mercy our hearths and our homes? Is this how you handle the Christians, whom you claim you wish to protect from cruel Ottoman exactions? And you who naively strike off heads, do you think you will frighten us and break down our resistance? You will not! You are playing all or nothing in this clashing of swords. You have now called schoolboys of fifteen to seventeen years to defend your flag; their mothers had perhaps planted sweeter illusions in their hearts. Do you think we have less resolve . . . ?
[. . .]

WEDNESDAY, 26 MARCH

I have come to the last page of this appalling tragedy and from the tangle of my emotions I will try to extract something clear and coherent to describe for you this solemn day of 26 March, sadder with its music and dance, with its movement and holiday spirit, than the darkest days of famine and shelling. The Bulgarians had been preparing for a decisive attack for the last two weeks. They had had 150,000 fresh troops brought in with 600 cannons; energetic and determined, they attacked our strongholds from all sides at once, principally through Marash and the Keyik. The assault lasted forty-eight hours without one minute's interruption. For forty-eight hours, a hail of bullets fell upon us and we were deafened by the noise of 1,200 cannons all firing at once. The Turkish soldiers opposed the enemy with a startling resistance, if one considers their declining and weakened state. Their blood was spilled for their country; perhaps they were happy not to survive to feel the pain of surrender.

And now, alas, that the sacrifice is consummated, now that so many brave men have fallen without sparing Turkey this painful amputation, the wound will long continue to bleed in the hearts of all the Ottomans.

I too knew this misfortune was inevitable. I knew that one day our Adrianople, so valiantly disputed, would finally fall prey to the enemy. And still, when that had been accomplished, when I saw our soldiers unarmed and heard the Bulgarian soldiers, laughing and triumphant, fill the air with their rough Slavic speech, I felt a wrenching in my heart. My indignation was at its peak when I saw the whooping, cruel joy of the [local] Greeks and the Bulgarians as they ran to meet the victors. It is not right to laugh before those who are crying and when so many Ottoman hearts are bleeding; they should not have shown so much joy. It seems that this is the law of war, and in war one speaks more of gunpowder than hearts. As I am writing this to you I am sitting on the steps to my house. In front of me there is a large field where a Bulgarian company is preparing to camp for the evening; they are talking noisily and singing together. They generously distribute sugar and salt and ask for flowers, which they wear in their kepis. They have stripped the city of its springtime.

Yesterday, in the morning, some of the soldiers who had been captured announced that the enemy was going to enter the city today. We laughed at what we considered vain boasting. We were wrong.

Nevertheless, it is natural that men who have been educated and imbued with liberal ideas and who are strong in patriotism should prove to be, if not more courageous than professional soldiers, at least more resolved and determined in their resistance. Their devotion is more the result of reflection. It is because of the obscurantism of the *hamidian*[12] that Turkey is surrendering today. She had her cannons, but she had no schools, and that was her great misfortune. May she learn from this cruel trial, may it be a useful experience for her future, and may she actively put into practice that happy phrase "Union and Progress."

Work alone regenerates and rejuvenates. "So it was written": that mentality is the poison of the Eastern nations, and the only antidote to that poison is progress.

[. . .]

I see breaking on the horizon a worry that greatly concerns us. This morning a few Jewish families watched as their homes were pillaged by the Greeks and the Bulgarian soldiers; a dozen of the instigators were caught in the act and put in jail. What is most disappointing

---

12. A reference to the despotic regime of Abdul Hamid II, which ended with the Young Turk Revolution of 1908.

about this is that only Jewish homes were pillaged, not only with the goal of stealing but with thoughts of hatred and vengeance. The furniture which the thieves could not carry with them, they destroyed and broke into pieces.

The story is spreading, started by the Greeks, that we Jews supported the Ottoman resistance with our efforts and our money and that, were it not for us, Adrianople would have fallen long ago. And even were that true, is it not more of a joy for the victors to have conquered a population capable of showing energy and patriotism in times of danger? But can one reason with antisemitism?

This page in history comes to a close with dark omens. No doubt the Bulgarians will make our cities beautiful and construct magnificent buildings; they will give us a taste of Europe. But we Jews have an enormous debt of gratitude to this Ottoman population, so far from progress, it is true, but nevertheless so humane.

Who knows after how many days of suffering we will regret the guiding hand of the Turks, so gentle to the Jewish population!
[. . .]

Mrs. A. Guéron

Archives of the AIU, Turquie I.C.1.

In spite of these outbursts of patriotism, the paradox of preaching loyalty and emancipation in a locality while at the same time dispensing an essentially French education in the schools was not apparent to the leaders and teachers of the Alliance. French was the language of civilization par excellence *and was deemed crucial for the work of "regeneration." This premise remained fundamental. French was considered superior to the local languages, which were seen as incapable of transmitting the spirit of "modern civilization." Ultimately, the ideology and perceptions of the pre–World War II Alliance leadership and personnel remained firmly moored in the colonial and imperialist presupposition of the superiority of European civilization over all others. The Alliance was caught unprepared for the world of independent nation-states in Muslim lands.*

13
The Age of Nationalism

The nationalism unleashed during the twentieth century did not prove kind to the Alliance. The organization was challenged from within the Jewish community by the emergence of Zionism and from without by the intransigent anticolonialist nationalism in the Muslim world. Its schools could eventually reach a modus vivendi *with the former, but they could not survive the latter.*

From an ideological standpoint, the Zionists and the Alliance had diametrically opposed worldviews. The Alliance was passionate in its belief in the importance of the emancipation of the Jews wherever they lived and saw its central task as helping the Jews achieve equality with their fellow countrymen throughout the world. In this it reflected the mid-nineteenth-century optimism of Western Jewry. It viewed antisemitism as a throwback to the Middle Ages and was never in doubt about the ultimate victory of the principles of emancipation. Zionists, on the other hand, believed that emancipation was an illusion and that antisemitism could not be eradicated. Assimilation would lead to the eventual disappearance of the Jewish people as a distinct entity. The answer to the Jewish question was the creation of a Jewish state in the ancestral homeland of the Jews and the revival of an authentic Jewish culture with a rejuvenated Hebrew language as its foundation. The Alliance was constantly criticized by the Zionists for neglecting the Hebrew language. The teachers were quick to defend their position:

Safed, July 1898

ZIONISM AND THE QUESTION OF PEDAGOGY
[. . .]

In the present state of affairs, should the youth of Palestine be taught exclusively in the *Hebrew* language or in the *French* language?

Those who have never been to Syria[1]—a province which is part of the Turkish empire—will be surprised at my question and may ask,

---

1. Parts of Ottoman Palestine were considered to be in the region referred to here as Syria.

with good reason, why we would not sooner adopt the language of the country, *Turkish* or *Arabic.*

As far as *Turkish* is concerned, this is out of the question. What good can come of wasting the too short time the children of Palestine spend at school in teaching them an absolutely useless language, especially given that even most government employees in this region do not speak this language and that all official documents, including judicial cases and all business documents, are written and conducted in Arabic? It could be mentioned in passing that throughout Syria more people understand French and English than Turkish.

Should we have recourse to *Arabic* and use it as an instrument of instruction in the primary schools? This would be madness. Even if all the Jews of Palestine knew this language to perfection, and it is a magnificent language, they would not be any further ahead. This is not the language that, in our times, is a vehicle for the conquest of modern civilization. Nor is it due to their knowledge of Arabic that the Jews will procure a few positions in the government: consider the Jews of Damascus, Aleppo, and Baghdad, who have always cultivated this language. Finally, judging from the way things are going, it is not the Arabic-speaking nations that will soon control the destinies of humanity.

Nonetheless, it is right to teach a correct Arabic to the young Palestinians so they can manage in their dealings with the indigenous population.

As for the teaching of *Hebrew,* seeing that Arabic is the mother tongue of these children, experience will prove to everyone that in a school with any organization at all, in an educational institution where the Hebrew teacher uses a rational method—the *Carré* method, for example, which is based on the principle that the teacher refrains from all translation into another language and only translates *Hebrew into Hebrew*—the children express themselves fluently in Hebrew after only two or three months. Note that if the child is in school for two or three years and continues, according to this excellent system, to speak in Hebrew—*three hours* per day if only three hours are devoted to Hebrew—and if he continues to study intelligently not only postbiblical history but spelling, style, grammar, and a little literature, in short the *language* itself and just that, and especially if you inspire in him an interest in that admirable book which is the Bible, you will have provided ample response to emotional and sentimental concerns. By this I mean the idea of Jewish nationalism, of Zionism; you will have provided all that is necessary to remind the Jew that he is a Jew. If you also take into account the traditional religious piety of this

country and its atmosphere, which can be said to be laden with historical memories in all the areas inhabited by the Jewish population; if
you consider that in this country everything—the Jordan, the Lebanon, Mount Carmel, Lake Tiberias, and the tombs of the saints and
the kings—is a constant reminder to all of the ancient homeland, the
country taken by force from the Hebrews; you can be sure that the
Palestinian Jew will not forget for one moment those *sentiments* which
the Zionists are afraid will fade away in him.

But, my good Zionists, you are not unaware that an individual, and
much less a people, cannot live on *sentiment.* One must win his daily
bread to survive. It is necessary above all that the children of Palestine be taught to earn their living with honor and dignity and to survive by means other than the *halukah.*

[. . .]

Nowadays, Caesar's domain is that of constantly developing contemporary civilization, that is to say *European* civilization. What better
way to introduce a population into this civilization than to explain its
principles in a *European* language?

Because the Latin races played such a great role in this civilization,
one powerful Jewish organization, which is currently planning the
work of spreading education throughout Palestine, has judged it appropriate to use a language of Latin origin as the instrument of this
education: French.

To get to the heart of the matter, if the Zionists of Palestine were
sincere, they would readily admit that the Hebrew language, an instrument which dates back two thousand years, is becoming impractical
for the assimilation and comprehension of modern civilization. You
can secularize and enrich the sacred language all you please, there
remain, I will not say subtleties, but common ideas which the ancient
Word of the Prophets will never be able to render. And who does not
know that every language, or every family of languages, has its own
genius? The languages of Latin origin have their own; Slavic and Ger-
manic languages each have their own. This is so true that even with
the best translations a Frenchman can never capture the beauty of a
work of Shakespeare, of Goethe, or of Tolstoy, to cite only a few
examples.

[. . .]

Zionists, my friends, cultivate neo-Hebraism, create a new language, write works in Hebrew about all modern science, in short,
continue your work! But, please . . . do not compromise the future of
a single Jew; that would be unforgivable.

It may be useful to say in passing that the Jews who are natives of the Holy Land do not look with much kindness upon the Zionists, whom they see as freethinkers, going too far in the secularization of Hebrew. From this we can learn that the teacher working in Palestine has a duty to preserve a religious character in his teaching.

I will also add that not until the day when the pious Jews of Palestine realize that they have been overburdening their children in forcing them to learn the Talmud—that is to say, the Jewish civil and criminal code—in their plodding *heder* from the age of seven, until the day when they understand how impractical this education is, until the day when they begin sending their sons at least by eight years of age to well-organized schools, until this day no *modus vivendi* could ever be reached between the Zionists and the non-Zionists . . .
[. . .]

M. Franco

Archives of the AIU, Israël, II.C.10.

These arguments, however, did not satisfy the Zionists. The school network was hurt badly in Bulgaria, where in the decade preceding World War I, all but one of the Alliance schools were closed by the communities now dominated by the Zionists.[2] *This situation made the organization extremely careful in its dealings with the opposing movement, and the teachers were quick to report Zionist activities in their communities:*

Salonica, 9 January 1903

Mr. Secretary,

A society for Jewish studies that was founded in Salonica a few years ago has recently taken a certain turn . . .
[. . .]
. . . Not long ago—in 1899—a few of R. Ottolenghi's students,[3] after having lived several years in the *yeshivot* . . . began the study of French, which was a veritable revelation for them. They took an enthusiastic and unsystematic interest in all secular subjects, . . . they wanted to convert their fellow Jews to science, and . . . they conceived of a project which would spread to the masses, in Hebrew, the sum of the knowledge they had found in French books. They founded a society, to which they gave the ambiguous name of *Kadima* (forward, or toward the state, in Palestine) . . .

The recent renaissance in Hebrew letters, by profusely spreading

2. See Rodrigue, *French Jews, Turkish Jews,* 139–40.
3. The Livornese rabbi who reformed and headed the communal *Talmud-Torah* of Salonica.

the ideas acquired through modern science in numerous books and periodicals, has given rise to an important development in the *Kadima* Society . . .

[. . .]

With the neo-Hebraic literature full of Zionist aspirations, ideas from other realms have been filtering into the *Kadima*. The Hebrew newspapers carry Zionist articles and manifestos which, through their talk of honor and their great humanitarian airs, easily seduce these naive and impulsive minds. The members of the *Kadima* look on the pompous proclamations of the speakers at these meetings as the Word of the Law and the Prophets. The visit to Salonica by Mr. Deinar, a fiery Zionist and a polemicist of some talent from New York, served to exalt the fantastic hopes of these young, modernized Hebraists, who now have frequent meetings during which they sing Zionist songs in full chorus.

This extravagant excitement is all the more dangerous in that it may arouse legitimate concern on the part of the police. Already in high places certain malevolent voices have been raised concerning these Zionist tendencies. This was precisely the principal cause for the suspension of a very interesting, popular Judeo-Spanish publication that the *Kadima* had tried to take over to use as an instrument of propaganda.

Let us hope that sound common sense will soon return to banish these nationalist preoccupations of the *Kadima,* which, when it has sobered, can once again devote itself exclusively to the very sensible and useful program it had chosen to pursue in the beginning.

[. . .]

J. Nehama

Archives of the AIU, Grèce I.G.3.

Salonica, 19 May 1916

[. . .]

. . . The Ottoman revolution was breaking out. Once the initial embracing and celebration had passed, everyone realized that this Ottomanism of redemption, the force that would bring all races together and unite all the inhabitants of the empire in a common cause, was but an illusion. Each population freely and openly stirred up nationalism for its own interests. Beginning in 1910, Zionism raised its voice for all to hear.

Various societies were founded for the propagation of the new faith. . . . The members . . . set themselves up as prophets, their prophesies were heard on every street corner, and they spoke in every synagogue and in every place of prayer. The Young Turks tried to quell the passion of these neophytes. With their usual blundering ways, their lack of political finesse, and the brutality of their threats, they managed only to frustrate the desires and make more passionate the hopes of the Zionists.

. . . When the Turks had gone and the Greeks arrived, the first reaction of the Jewish population was one of revulsion for the new rulers . . .

This was a period of immense renewal for Zionism. Its leaders experienced intoxicating popularity, its institutions flourished . . .
[. . .]

. . . In the meantime, in the press and among the middle classes, the Zionists engaged in a bitter campaign against our schools. They attempted to represent us as the despicable instruments of de-Judaization and impiety. We had to face, as you know, many difficult moments . . . Our schools were certainly not deserted, but they were no longer tremendously popular. We were neither Zionists nor Germans; quite the contrary, we represented the ideas of the French Revolution; we did our teaching in French. We were deserving of nothing but scorn and hatred. No opportunity was missed to point this out to us.
[. . .]

J. Nehama

Archives of the AIU, Grèce I.G.3.

The same cry of alarm had been heard a few years before in Constantinople:

Constantinople, 16 November 1910

Mr. President,

Zionism is gaining ground rapidly in Turkey. If the Zionist idea is, in the goal it pursues, essentially chimerical, the Zionists are eminently practical when it comes to the means they use. Whenever they want to act, they choose a man and create an organ of propaganda. Hence their relative success.

In Turkey, the man is called Lucien Sciuto, and the organ [his newspaper] *L'Aurore*. The man and the organ are in the process of transforming the Jewish population of the empire. Soon we will be able to measure the ravages of the Zionist idea, and we will be stupefied in the face of the disastrous consequences which will follow.

The Jewish youth in Turkey are not yet Zionist, far from it. Generally they even manifest some repugnance for throwing themselves into the movement. But left to themselves, deprived of guidance and advice, they will not delay—taking noise for success—in joining the side of those who act and shout. These youth, educated in our schools, are still hesitant . . .

The Alliance confines itself to its role as educator. It rejects direct action. It expects all from education and trusts good common sense too much. While others act, it waits, hopes, and is content to hope. Attacked, calumnied, it does not deign to defend itself, refusing to adopt the tactics of the adversary. This is all very well. But with such tactics, one loses battles. And the Jewish population of Turkey will all become Zionists tomorrow, as is the case in Bulgaria, because of the absence of a man and an organ of the press.

The hour is decisive. All can still be repaired, and our youth can be easily brought back. We need a man and an organ, an organ to restrain our population from falling into Jewish nationalism and to maintain it within the limits of national Judaism. Otherwise, tomorrow will be too late.

[. . .]

J. Loria

Archives of the AIU, Turquie I.G.1.

This call to arms was not heeded, and the Alliance refused to create a newspaper and to put Loria in charge as he had asked. Rebuffed, Loria resigned a few years later and joined the Zionist ranks, becoming the editor of the Zionist newspaper La Nation, *published in Istanbul after World War I. Other teachers continued to sound the alarm:*

Constantinople, 21 March 1912

[. . .]

The Jewish community of Constantinople is threatened in its very existence. A handful of men from the outside have thus far been bold enough and fortunate enough to sow complete disorder in the very heart of Ottoman Jewry . . .

[. . .]

The Zionists . . . have chosen the Ottoman Empire as their field of battle; and it is the Alliance that they are attacking. It is the Alliance which was established here long before they arrived and whose immovable position, in everyone's opinion, has a tendency to exasperate the more volatile of them . . .

[. . .]

. . . They have decided to move heaven and earth to have the Alliance put out of the principal Jewish centers in the East; and so it is

up to the Alliance to stave off the blows they are trying to strike. In so doing the Alliance would strengthen the force of its work and, at the same time, perhaps render a most valuable service . . .
[. . .]

E. Nathan

Archives of the AIU, Turquie I.G.1.

Tunis, November 1920

[. . .]

Zionism still continues to make progress in Tunisia. In all the major cities of the Regency, Zionist committees have already been established. In Tunis itself there are three distinct Zionist groups which are at this time seeking to unite. Also in Tunis, we have five Zionist newspapers, three of which are published in French and two in Judeo-Arabic. But all of this movement seems to me to be superficial for the moment. It is a question of a few devoted militants and a good number of opportunists who are only using Zionism to forward their own personal interests. The majority of the population, although they are interested in the Zionist idea, do not yet have the faith that leads to action. Furthermore, none of the notables join any of the Zionist associations, and it is only, for the most part, the less influential who form these groups.
[. . .]

C. Ouziel

Archives of the AIU, France VII.F.14.

Tunis, 5 March 1938

ANTISEMITISM AND ZIONISM IN TUNISIA: HOW THEY AFFECT THE SCHOOL
[. . .]

. . . Yes, antisemitism exists in the Regency. The relations between Jews and Arabs are certainly satisfactory, but there are certain indications which do not escape the notice of those who are aware and which suggest that there are currents of discontent on the part of the Arabs toward the Jews. This discontent is especially caused by the jealousy of the Arabs when they see too many Jews succeeding in commerce and in the liberal professions (most of the businessmen, lawyers, and doctors in Tunis are Jewish) and little by little taking over the life of the nation. The Destourian movement[4] serves only to increase and spread this discontent. They resent not only the French but also the Jews. Obviously, antisemitism does not figure directly in

4. The Tunisian nationalist movement.

the program of the *Destour,* but it is implied. A violent spirit of chau-
vinistic nationalism and a call for "National Awakening" animate the
Tunisian youth of today and dictate to them quite unfavorable sentiments toward the Jews.

[. . .]

At the same time, it is no less certain that Zionism, too, exists and
is rapidly developing. The Jewish daily newspapers, *La Nouvelle
Aurore, Tel-Aviv,* and *La Semaine Juive,* regularly devote long articles
to this topic. They comment at length on the activities of the Zionist
movement, its efforts, its successes, the obstacles it faces in Palestine;
they keep the public informed of the situation of the Jews in the various countries and show how that situation is daily growing worse.
What is most distressing is that this movement is not simply a Zionist
movement but rather a party with clearly Revisionist tendencies: often it is only a question of Mr. Jabotinsky and his projects. And this
movement has grown even among the Boy Scouts. It is saddening to
observe that these troops of Jewish Scouts are becoming involved in
politics. This is damaging not only to the Scouts themselves but to the
entire population.

Thus the two movements growing stronger and stronger in Tunisia
are Zionism and antisemitism. Are these two movements opposed?
Should we believe that the former encourages the latter or that it is a
remedy to it? Is it because of Zionism that antisemitism is developing? Is Zionism the solution to antisemitism? Are the Jews here justified in lending themselves to such a degree to political preoccupations
of this nature?

Without trying to give a direct answer to such delicate questions, I
will limit myself to applying these questions to what can be seen in
the school.

[. . .]

In general terms, all of our students, like most young people
today—this is the *"mal du siècle"*—are taken with politics, and this is
regrettable. Under the pretext of keeping informed, they scour the
newspapers and become passionately involved in public and international issues. In this way, they waste a good portion of their time,
often to the detriment of their studies and sound thinking. Indeed,
through this kind of reading they acquire a mass of misguided opinions, which they take for Gospel and of which it is very difficult to rid
them.

This is also true for my pupils, who are older adolescents preparing
for the *brevet élémentaire.* Among them are several Muslims affiliated
with the Destourian party . . . When I am giving my course on civics

(in the second year of preparation for the diploma), there are always a few of them who point out certain so-called inequities or injustices which make them indignant. I cannot help but notice that the same idea is always behind these remarks: "make room for the Tunisians who are living in the streets and dying of hunger while scores of Frenchmen and Jews occupy all the respected positions."

Although I never allow myself to become involved in politics in the classroom and I do not tolerate the slightest allusion to this subject, I make it my duty to reply to these remarks, to analyze them, and to refute them. I believe that if these young people have been led astray in their circle of family and friends, it is up to us to show them the truth. Most often I succeed in convincing them and in disposing them toward higher sentiments and more just ideas.

The Jews live side by side with the Muslims, and on excellent terms. The Jews too, in their way, take an interest in politics. Obviously in their circle of family and friends, the sole topic of conversation is Zionism. How could they keep from talking about it, from discussing it at length, from considering all the possibilities and all the theories, and from enumerating all the solutions? Their minds are so steeped in these ideas that they cannot help but expose their personal sentiments, sometimes even in their compositions. Allow me to tell you about one case:

I had assigned the following topic (again it is a question of the students in the second year of preparation for the diploma), which is, as it happens, a regular topic in the program: "What emotions, what dreams does the word *partir!* [to leave] suggest to you?" A few spoke about Palestine and discussed the ideal of every Jew, to leave one day for the Holy Land. Thus far there could be nothing more legitimate and natural. But they did not stop there. "Why should I work for this ungrateful land?" I am quoting word for word from one composition, "Why pour out my efforts here while my country awaits me? I do not want to live in exile and sacrifice myself for foreigners . . ."

Such ideas denote a special mentality. If the students speak about this even in their school compositions, that means that they certainly talk about this among themselves and with their Muslim friends. What might happen when these Muslims, strongly influenced by Destourian ideas (therefore nationalistic and antisemitic ideas), revolt and challenge their Jewish friends so full of misunderstood Zionist ideas? This is what will happen: the relations between them, which have been excellent up until now, will become more and more strained and will contribute to profound dissension between the two sections of the Tunisian population. On the one side, the Arabs will spread the word that the Jews are foreigners, who have only to leave, that this is not their home, and that they are living as parasites. On the other side, the Jews, continuing along these lines, will neglect even their most basic civic duties.

Such is, then, the precise state of mind of our students today, and such are the serious consequences in which it may result.

[. . .]

How can we struggle effectively against such a situation? Should we systematically speak out against both the Destourian movement and Zionism? Is it wise to tell our students, even in an indirect and discreet manner: "You are both wrong; give up these ideas." In so doing, would we not risk shocking them and deeply wounding the sentiments they hold most dear?

It would appear that the solution lies elsewhere; this solution is twofold: 1. It is our duty to strengthen the civic and moral education of our students. They should understand that the first duty of the Jew is to the country in which he lives. Because they have the privileges accorded all citizens, it is right that they also accept the duties of citizens and carry them out fully. Even more than this: the Jews must always regulate their behavior and their lives in such a manner that they not become targets for those malicious minds who are always looking for faults and who never fail to generalize them. I would like to quote here a few of the noble words spoken by the Chief Rabbi of Geneva, Mr. Poliakoff, who visited our school when he was in Tunis and left an elevated moral teaching in the minds of our older students: "My dear children! Never forget that the Jews are closely bound together. The slightest fault, the slightest questionable affair on the part of one, is quickly generalized and attributed to all . . . We have a heavy burden to bear: for centuries the name Jew has been a synonym for coward, thief, usurer; this name represented all moral baseness. It is through our actions and our conduct that we can show the world the injustice that has been done to us and that we suffer still today. You must lead lives that are dignified, irreproachable, and exemplary from a moral, civic, and religious point of view. Then those who seek only to denigrate and belittle us, to deny us our very existence, will be able to find no fault in you . . ."

And so the first duty of any Jew is to be a "good citizen," worthy of the country in which he lives and worthy of his glorious heritage.

2. But it is not enough to give the students a solid civic and moral base. They must also be turned away from politics, which is the source of contention, disorder, and so many fruitless, if not tragic, discussions. The mind of the adolescent, just beginning to awaken,

has need of nourishment. He seeks it out, and because most often he is surrounded by discussions of politics, he turns to politics himself. But could not this active mind and this hunger for learning, which are typical of the adolescent, be put to other, more profitable use?

Since he has this passion for all that is new to him and for all that is capable of awakening, strengthening, and developing his most pure and noble sentiments, why not warn him against the wrong road and show him the right path, the path rich in positive results?

And what path could this be?

This path has just been discovered by the students at the *Lycée Carnot* in Tunis: they founded a paper, which they write, edit, and publish entirely on their own. All questions of politics are excluded; the paper treats topics in literature, the arts, the sciences, sports, and anything that has to do with daily life. The first issue has already come out, and to judge by the favorable opinion of the public and the encouragement offered by the authorities concerned, this paper promises to prosper for a long time to come.

Does not an initiative such as this deserve to be imitated? Could we not do something along those lines, obviously on a more modest scale, with some of our students? We could encourage the students in their French (a subject in which they are generally quite weak), lead them toward sound and instructive reading, introduce them to literary masterpieces rather than insipid serial novels, develop in them artistic taste and sensibility (some of them are gifted in this area; they have shown me their sonnets and their sketches, and they are quite good), talk with them about sports, which so fascinate them, and speak to them of friendship and brotherhood between Arab and Jewish classmates. And as we do all this, we would be stimulating a spirit of healthy competition, which could bring only good results. Is not this the most effective way to turn them away from politics completely and to channel their growing energy in a manner that is both instructive and enjoyable? . . .

These are the solutions resulting from my reflections on antisemitism and Zionism and their effects on the school.

[. . .]

M. Cohen

Archives of the AIU, Tunisie I.G.3.

The standard response of the teachers to Zionism was that it was utopian and dangerous, as it threatened to undo all that had been or was to be achieved by emancipation, on which the very edifice of westernization had been constructed. It was seen as impractical and destined to lead to a dead end. In this the teachers echoed Jacques Bigart, the secretary general of the Alliance.

Paris, 30 July 1919

To the Association of Former Students of the Alliance in Sousse:
Mr. President,

In response to your letter of 5 July, we deem it appropriate to send you the enclosed copy of a resolution passed by the Central Committee of the Alliance on 16 April 1919.

This document does not, strictly speaking, address the issue of the Zionist movement itself, but it does give an indication of the point of view held by the Alliance. We do not wish to engage in debate over the advantages and disadvantages of the Zionist doctrine. Remaining strictly within the bounds of facts and possibilities, however, we do have the duty to direct the attention of all Jewry toward the effects which the Zionist movement may have on the Jewish people of Eastern Europe:

The situation of the Jews in Poland, in the Ukraine, and in Lithuania (the former Russia) is currently such a precarious one that hundreds of thousands of Jews—we could say millions—are now hoping to leave their countries and to emigrate as rapidly as possible. Not only was this drive toward emigration provoked by the anti-Jewish policies of the Russian and Polish governments, but it is to a certain extent one of the effects of the glowing promises which Zionism has held up before the Jewish imagination. As it stands, however, America and England have all but made the official decision to close the door to immigration for a time. Other countries do not have an appreciable capacity for the absorption of immigrants. What remains for these unfortunate people is the mirage of Palestine. Let us suppose that England, which will most likely be the protective power in Palestine, does fulfill in some measure the promise of a national homeland. What will be the result? The Jewish masses, who aspire to a peaceful life far from the violence of antisemitism, will arrive in tumultuous waves in Palestine. There, nothing has been readied to receive them and there is the risk that they will find even greater hardships than those they are suffering at present. The situation is such that the poor will not be able to stay there. The settlement of a single family today costs 50,000 francs. Where could the necessary funds be found to settle a considerable number of families? And in any case, has anyone truly reflected on the kind of welcome these Jews would receive in

Palestine? The total population of the country is 600,000, of whom approximately 10 percent are Jewish. Do people think that the Arabs will renounce their rights and privileges? Would not England hesitate to carry out its own plan of action when it is faced with the hostility that the Arabs will unfailingly demonstrate the moment it proposes any semblance of autonomy for the Jews?

Certainly Palestine is capable of absorbing new life and energy; certainly Palestinian soil could be cultivated by a considerably greater number of farmers than are currently working the land. Nevertheless, the possibilities are again limited. The most optimistic of the people who really know the country estimate that between 10,000 and 20,000 new arrivals per year is the very maximum immigration possible. You can see, then, how long it would take for an appreciable number of our fellow Jews from Eastern Europe to be settled in Palestine. Some very competent sources have indicated that Palestine will never be able to support more than 800,000 to 900,000 inhabitants. The Zionist leaders themselves, now that they have been forced to put their words into actions, have begun to advise against a rash mass exodus. And yet there are now millions of poor Jews who cling to the thought of Palestine as the last hope remaining to them, as the only possible relief from their misery. When so many wretched people awake from their dream only to see the cold reality, with what bitterness will they reproach those who encouraged them in such fantastic ideas? This is what we greatly fear; this is what we feel it is our duty to say, not because of hostility toward Zionism itself, but because we see a grave peril on the horizon. We too have no more fervent hope than to see thousands and thousands of Jewish families leave the Russian and Polish ghettos and find freedom. But we believe that the path being shown and the hopes being given to millions of our brethren will lead them to disaster.

This is why we also believe that the reasons are pressing for the immense majority of the Jews to remain in the countries where they are currently established, to adapt to the context in which they live while maintaining their own identity, in particular their own traditions and religious hopes. The primary duty of Jewish organizations interested in the fate of these people is to obtain for them the recognition of their rights and the suppression of all legal barriers limiting their activities and their liberties. This is the task which the Alliance has always sought to fulfill. This is the goal which the Alliance sought to achieve during the Peace Conference. The agreement signed there by Poland is witness to how effective we have been in achieving this goal. We hope that other agreements, which will be submitted to

other states of Eastern Europe, will confirm the same principles in
favor of the Jews.
[. . .]

J. Bigart

Archives of the AIU, Tunisie I.G.1.

*The teachers remained true to this emancipation ideology they had
imbibed at the ENIO, although a few, such as Sam Hochberg and Jacques
Loria, became Zionists and left the organization, albeit more for career
than ideological reasons. Some, however, became convinced of the necessity for the Alliance to reform and democratize itself in order to co-opt
Zionism:*

Isphahan, 12 August 1917

Dear Mr. Leven:[5]
[. . .]
. . . Following the explosion of antisemitism at the end of the nineteenth century, the Central Committee believed it wise, if not to abandon completely its political activities, at least to assign primary importance to the task of instruction, which seemed, at least on the surface,
to absorb all of its energies. This voluntary retreat of the Alliance
certainly counts for much of the success of Zionist propaganda . . .
Many Jews in the West followed Herzl especially because he offered
them the opportunity to affirm themselves as Jews.
    It would seem that the Central Committee is now trying to change
its policy, especially if one is to judge by the dispatch it sent to Prince
Lvoff in the days following the Russian Revolution, in which the Central Committee spoke in the name of Jews the world over. I have also
read in the *Jewish Chronicle* of 4 May that a congress of Italian Jews
decided to ask the Alliance to call a congress of Jews from all the
Allied countries, that is to say, from the greater part of Jewry. I hope
that the Central Committee did not fail to seize this unique opportunity to step back into its former role. Circumstances would appear
favorable. France's defeat in 1870 was one of the principal causes for
the decrease in the international stature of the Alliance. This was due
first to the foundation of the Anglo-Jewish Association and later to
Prussian predominance and the decline of humanitarian ideas. The
present war, whatever the final outcome may be, has returned to the
country which gave us the Rights of Man that grandeur which the
pedants from beyond the Rhine had tried to take from her. It is natu-

5. Georges Leven was the son of Narcisse Leven, the deceased president of the Alliance.

ral that the Alliance profit from these circumstances, all the more so as the Alliance is well situated as an equal with the United States and liberated Russia, which hold the two largest Jewish populations.

But there is a first condition which the Alliance must meet if it is to once again take its place as the leader of Judaism: it must introduce more freedom and more clarity into its organization and structure. Even when the Second Empire was in its least liberal stage, the founders of the Alliance based this organization on universal suffrage. I remember having read a discussion on the mode of Central Committee election in an old bulletin of the Alliance. If I am not mistaken, it was your late father who eloquently defended direct election by all members of the Alliance, opposing Mr. Oppert in this. And it is now, when rivers of blood are flowing to ensure the triumph of democracy throughout the world, that the Alliance would maintain a mode of election that is scarcely appropriate even for academic societies or those outdated charitable organizations where charity is synonymous with alms.

I fully recognize all the difficulties involved in establishing a system for voting in an organization whose members are scattered throughout the world. Elections through a congress or general assembly would perhaps be preferable, but it would still be necessary for all members to be represented; this would be quite difficult. But whether the election be carried out through universal suffrage or through the intermediary of a congress, over two or three days, it is certain that the electors cannot know the candidates and that they must therefore vote for ideas and issues rather than for individuals. Furthermore, if the Alliance hopes really to be international, it must be able to welcome in its midst all those who are not ashamed to call themselves Jews.

Thus, already in 1902, in a study that I sent a copy of to Mr. S. Reinach[6] two years ago, I had proposed that proportional representation be introduced into the system of elections to the Central Committee. I was treated as a dreamer. Perhaps now, however, the members of the Central Committee will consider that the moment has come to reestablish elections by adopting a system that, while allowing for the expression of all opinions, will guard against the kind of sudden revolutions that may put the very existence of the Alliance in danger, such as the one nearly provoked by the Germans during the last elections.

One consequence of the adoption of the reform outlined above will be that the Alliance must abandon the openly anti-Zionist attitude

6. Salomon Reinach was a vice-president of the Alliance.

which it has adopted. This attitude has distanced the Alliance from a great number of Jews from both the East and the West, who, if they do not wholly accept the credo of Basel—which many do not know— have preserved the ideal of a return to Zion, which has for so many centuries given strength to their fathers. Personally, I am opposed to Zionism if it must necessarily entail a dispossession of the Arabs and create a Jewish nationalism which would be even more fanatical than the others. For history has shown us (we need only look at the recent example of Romania and perhaps of Poland) that the first act of freedom by peoples newly released from oppression is to persecute the foreign elements among them. We have seen that they exercise a tyranny which is in direct proportion to that which they were made to bear: and it would be hard to refuse to the people of Israel the record in persecutions suffered.

It would be an abuse of power to stop those Jews who wish to return to the country of their traditional hopes, and in avoiding a break with the Zionists, there will be more chance of avoiding nationalist excesses. The future will certainly bring a solution, probably on the Canadian model, which will reconcile the interests of the two great peoples called Semites.

In any case, whether there be only a Jewish state in Palestine or a moral and intellectual center, which even the fiercest anti-Zionists accept, only a minority of Jews will return to the land of their ancestors. The Alliance will still have quite enough work to do in maintaining the unity of Judaism and in ensuring the protection and the moral and economic development of the Jews. We would be wrong to let down our guard; the enemy is always armed and waiting. It may be that the revolution in Russia will bring to all her minorities not only religious freedom but even their freedom as nations, which the West did not necessarily see the need for. There is no less reason to fear, however, that another result of the war will be an increase in narrow nationalism and hateful xenophobia. All those who are in any way different from the majority of the inhabitants of any country would be made to suffer. It could be hoped that having shared life for three years, exposed to the same dangers and demonstrating the same heroism, a great majority of the people of each nation will maintain a sacred unity after peace has come, but it is also possible that social issues and the differences in opinion inherent in them will become increasingly significant. As we have often seen in the past, many people find in antisemitism a release for the anger caused by frustrated demands and social unrest. Already some of the so-called serious newspapers are printing attacks against our fellow Jews; even England, champion

of freedom, has been the scene of anti-Jewish riots. It will take no less than the union of all the sons of Israel to ward off the attacks of the reactionaries, or rather (for after the war there will be very few who will dare to openly declare themselves against democracy) to stop the virus of antisemitism from penetrating the ranks of the defenders of freedom and to unmask the Tartuffes who, hiding behind demagogy, will seek to destroy all that the modern spirit has achieved. I hope that you will agree that the best way to preserve the esteem and the support of our non-Jewish friends is not to hide our colors, not to deny international Jewish solidarity.
[. . .]

A. Brasseur

Archives of the AIU, Iran I.C.3.

This politically astute and uncannily prescient appeal remained unanswered by the Central Committee.

Zionism did make considerable inroads among the Sephardi and Eastern Jewries, especially among the youth. However, the movement was not strong enough in most countries to dismantle the work of the Alliance, though it did succeed in weakening it.[7] *The schools eventually reached a* modus vivendi *with the Zionists and, while increasing the hours devoted to Hebrew, did not fundamentally alter their programs until after World War II. The Alliance and the teachers tried to appear officially neutral vis-à-vis Zionism in order to prevent conflict, though considerable ideological and practical reservations were aired publicly. The official position hid a determined anti-Zionist stance among the leadership and the great majority of the teachers. The emancipationist ideology of the Alliance could not but remain diametrically opposed to a movement espousing Jewish nationalism. Only after World War II and the Holocaust would the organization adopt a pro-Zionist orientation.*

Predictably, the emergence of nationalism among the Muslims was also greeted with disquiet by the Alliance personnel. The teachers had always had ambivalent attitudes toward the Muslim population. Echoing accepted Western opinion of the time, they thought that the Muslims remained the biggest obstacle to progress, imbued with a fanaticism difficult to overcome. This perception was less prevalent among teachers working

7. For a case study of the rise of Zionism as a potent political force in a Sephardi community and the problems that this caused for the Alliance, see Esther Benbassa, "Haim Nahum Effendi, dernier Grand Rabbin de l'Empire ottoman (1908–1920): Son rôle politique et diplomatique" (Thèse de doctorat d'état ès lettres, Université de Paris III, 1987). See also idem, "Le Sionisme dans l'Empire ottoman à l'aube du 20ᵉ siècle," *Vingtième Siècle* 24 (1989): 69–80.

*in the Turkish parts of the Ottoman Empire and was more common in
Iran, Iraq, and North Africa. Writing from Baghdad in 1909, A. Franco
was deeply contemptuous of the local Muslims:*

Baghdad, 28 May 1909

[. . .]

The Christians and the Jews both gave a very enthusiastic welcome
to the new regime.[8] The Jews especially had anxiously followed every
turn taken in the combat being waged between autocracy and freedom; they knew instinctively that their fate depended on the outcome
of this battle. For them the triumph of liberty was not simply the
fulfillment of a spiritual and intellectual aspiration; it was a question
of life itself. This triumph represented a safeguard against an arbitrary
government and protection against the fanaticism of the population,
which, from that moment, lost all official sanctioning of its harassment of the Jews.

Although the non-Muslims joyously greeted the news of the constitution, the majority of the Muslims were cold and hostile. The reason
for their discontent must be attributed to various causes:

The Muslims already sensed that the new regime would strike
heavy blows against their fanaticism. The dream of a good Muslim
would be to see Islam triumph throughout the world, and toward this
dream he must eliminate the infidel, whatever the means. With the
freedom granted by the constitution, the good Muslim finds himself
obliged to hold his hatred in check, and he can no longer indulge in
methodical persecutions. The Muslims cannot conceive that the infidels should benefit from the same rights as they. Jews, their equals,
brothers of the Muslims: what an upheaval in their way of thinking!
To their eyes it is quite audacious to consider treating Muslims on an
equal footing with the infidels; the latter are for them *kefir*s, impure
beings, execrated by God, and must disappear from the face of the
earth.

By protecting the Jews from the ill-will and injustice of the Muslims, the constitution has exasperated them. They find their hands are
tied and they are forced to maintain a certain respect, at least an
apparent respect, for the infidels.

[. . .]

During the long months which followed the promulgation of the
constitution, and especially during the recent unrest in Constantinople
after the coup d'état of Abdul Hamid, the non-Muslims were not always

8. A reference to the Young Turks, who came to power in 1908.

certain of what tomorrow would bring. They feared renewed aggressions and their fear contributed quite a bit to the spreading of alarming rumors. Among themselves they were saying the Muslims would certainly be moved by what was happening in Constantinople and that, reactionaries by nature, they would lend a hand to the reactionaries in the capital in striking a decisive blow to the liberal institutions.
[. . .]
Since the definitive victory of the Committee for Union and Progress, there has been more light on the horizon and more sense of security in the city. As the reactionaries are no longer in a position to take advantage of an equivocal situation, they are forced to resign themselves. They did not receive the news of Abdul Hamid's ousting with great enthusiasm, but they could not manifest their discontent very openly. They no longer have the support of the government, which had no other choice but to take a liberal attitude.

Will the new regime have a profound effect on the conscience of the population? Is it an answer to the hopes of the people? Will they know how to put their new rights to good use? The Christians and the Jews, although they have not been well prepared for liberty, have fervently aspired to it. They have suffered tyranny too long not to embrace liberty fully. Their spirits are finally released; their lives and their possessions protected. It is only a question of time and education before they are able to profit from the changes which have taken place in the country.
[. . .]
In no other country are the laws more in advance of habits and customs than in Mesopotamia. The social condition of the Muslims is very backward, and as the Muslims are the majority, the backlash is felt among the Jews and the Christians. One example of this is the extreme scorn and disdain which the Muslim feels toward women; to him they are inferior beings who must be left to wallow in ignorance and in tedium. Women are made to take care of the home and to be slaves to the masters . . .
[. . .]
And so we see that the Muslims are the stumbling block to all progress; they are a dead weight which also drags down the rest of the population. Since they are enemies of all innovation, they look with a critical eye upon any effort on the part of the others to create a better life. Thus, they would like to stop the others from wearing European dress. This is considered a sign of civilization to them. They also want to put a stop to the habit of caring for one's personal appearance. They are capable of stoning a Turkish subject should he

wear a hat. The others must model themselves after the Muslims, and even remain at a lower level than they.

To bring down this bastion of fanaticism and ignorance and to bring thousands of individuals back to life and to action, the new government must put all of its efforts in the instruction and education of the masses. The only way to purify the contaminated air which stifles the city is to allow new air to come in. Thus, they should organize a system of instruction which answers modern needs and is based on modern ideas. The government will no doubt meet with stubborn resistance on the part of the *ulema*s [Muslim clergy], who run the Islamic schools and who see to it that the Koran is not open to close examination. But the government is stronger than they are, and it must firmly impose its will.

[. . .]

The victory won by the Committee for Union and Progress will be a simple illusion if the Committee does not manage to institute an educational system throughout the empire. Liberty will be simply a word devoid of meaning, and even a source of danger, if the population is not prepared to deal with it wisely. This preparation will come only when the population becomes aware of its own rights and potentials.

[. . .]

A. Franco

Archives of the AIU, Irak I.C.4.

The teachers, together with most Jews, looked to the West to stabilize the anarchic situation prevailing in most Muslim lands. They interpreted the arrival of Western rule as a very positive development. The enthusiastic letter of Loubaton from Agadir, Morocco, in 1913 was, in this respect, quite representative:

Agadir, 14 August 1913

[. . .]

The years 1912–1913 mark an important stage in the history of the empire of the Maghreb. After ten years of constant effort, after a series of incidents and numerous problems, after long and painful negotiations which ended only with painful but inevitable sacrifices, France has obtained *carte blanche* in Morocco and has proclaimed its protectorate. The government of the Republic has realized its dream for the colonies: there is a direct link from North Africa to West and Equatorial Africa, and French influence has been solidly established from the Mediterranean to the Atlantic.

[. . .]

In order that this account may be complete, I must point out the advantages which our community has already drawn from the new organization of the city. The French authorities (the consul, the mayor, the police commissioner, and the medical officer) established contact with the leaders of the community. The consul office, and Mr. Lebé [the mayor] in particular, are quite well disposed to the interests of our community. Mr. Lebé has invited the members of the local committee to meet with him regularly, once a week, to discuss the needs of the community and to submit proposals to him concerning actions which may be taken to improve their condition. From the very first meetings it was agreed that the municipality should promptly undertake an initiative to clean up the *Mellah;* toward this goal important steps for maintenance and rehabilitation of the area will soon be implemented. In addition, it was decided that the committee would take necessary measures toward the elimination of public begging. Finally, it was recognized that there is an urgent need for a facility for the incurably ill and a hospital for the Jews.
[. . .]

L. Loubaton

Archives of the AIU, France XV.F.26.

The passion for the West and the extraordinarily high hopes for "progress" pinned on Western rule are nowhere more in evidence than in the wildly jubilant and ecstatic letter penned in 1915 from Basra in Iraq by the Alliance teacher Zilberstein upon the arrival of British troops:

Basra, 20 August 1915
[. . .]
22 November 1914, the day the English entered Basra, is an important date in the colonial history of England. It was on this day that the great British dream was accomplished, the dream of half a century, whose realization Great Britain had been working toward for many years.

To take possession of Basra, which is the entrance to Iraq and to Mesopotamia and thus the key to one of the richest regions on earth, and from there to command one of the most important trade routes in the world: this had been the ambition of all the powerful Englishmen involved in colonial affairs. And the shores of the Shatt-al-Arab in their turn saw the waving of the British flag, the flag which flies over one-quarter of the earth. And this was accomplished without much spilling of blood and without much sacrifice of human life, without a great war, as the result of a simple expedition.

If at the moment I am writing only a few cities are under the rule of the English, within a few weeks, a few months at most, all the rest of this rich region, the first cradle of humanity, will come under English domination.

Forever released from the oppression of the Turks, which has weighed upon this privileged land for centuries, this country will see the return of the prosperity it knew 2,000 years ago. The ruins which have accumulated through centuries of Turkish barbarism will be restored; new communication routes will be constructed; the rivers will be made into navigable waterways for ships; canals will be built to fertilize regions that have been left barren and unproductive; and Mesopotamia will see a prosperity that was not possible under the Turks. It will flourish under the new regime.

[. . .]

In predicting the progress which Basra will make in the future, it is helpful to know who the peoples are who inhabit the city and which ones will be called to play an important role in the economic development of the city and of Iraq.

According to the last statistics compiled before the Turkish government took flight, the city of Basra (with its surrounding areas) held around 40,000 inhabitants divided as follows: 33,000 Muslims, 6,000 Jews, 1,000 Christians. But over the course of this year the number has increased considerably, so that one may now estimate the population at 50,000 (not including the army).

[. . .]

If there is a people who, for its endurance, its perseverance, and its skills, is called to play an important role in the development of Mesopotamia and of Basra, it is certainly the Jewish people, one of the oldest on earth . . . There are 70,000 Jews in all of Iraq; these will be joined by others from Persia and from Hindustan. And even today long caravans of Jews are coming down over the plateaus of Iran, fleeing an intolerant government and seeking refuge in English territories. One could estimate at 1,000 the number of Persian Jews who have come to settle in Basra and in other regions occupied by the English troops . . .

[. . .]

The Jews in the city can be divided into three very distinct groups: 1. The immigrants from Baghdad, who control all of the commerce and who are the most advanced and most educated members of the Jewish population. These are the former students of our schools in Baghdad who settled in this city after the opening of the Suez Canal and who have, through their instruction, come to exercise a great influence on their fellow Jews. 2. The oldest inhabitants of the region, who are for the most part extremely rich landowners. 3. The immigrants from Persia, who are, in any case, quickly assimilated.

All of the Jews of Basra witnessed the entry of the English troops into the city with joy. The long nightmare and worry over being robbed and murdered were finally dispelled. England had just pulled them out of the long misery in which they had been plunged, but they did not want to express their sentiments too freely in order not to overly shock the sentiments of the Muslims. In spite of some pillaging and the death of several Jews, they did not for a moment sympathize with their former fatherland, for which they had no feelings at all. They knew that once the occupation was complete, perfect order and calm would be restored. Before the war many of the Jews who had traveled in Europe or visited India and Egypt and who had been able to compare their countries to the countries occupied by European powers were hoping for and impatiently awaiting the arrival of the English . . .

[. . .]

As I have said, Basra has a great future ahead. When the railroad line Constantinople–Aleppo–Baghdad is completed in a few years, Basra, the last stop on the line, will profit enormously from this new link with Europe.

We hope that the bloody war currently being fought in Europe will soon come to an end and that all of the peoples of Europe, delivered at last from the scourge of war, can in peace rebuild what has been destroyed and work for the progress of civilization, which has been at a standstill for more than a year now.

[. . .]

A. Zilberstein

Archives of the AIU, Irak I.C.5.

The same teacher was as optimistic about Western control fifteen years later in Syria:

Damascus, 25 May 1930

[. . .]

As for the Jewish population, it is concentrated in the big cities; the Jewish population is more numerous in the south, in Palestine; the total Jewish population does not exceed 100,000.

I do not need to remind you how precarious the situation of this population was toward the middle and even at the end of the nine-

teenth century; no instruction; the population was poor, the most impoverished Jewish population in all of the East. In Palestine, and even
in Syria, the greater part of this population lived on charity and was
subject to the abuses of the authorities.

It was to improve the moral condition of this population that the
Alliance founded its schools. Schools were opened almost simultaneously in all of the cities. In the beginning it was difficult; there was
much resistance. But with tenacity and perseverance, nothing is impossible. The first generations began to go out from our schools, generations of students who were proud and bold. The Jews began to be
workers; they were already, thanks to the schools, intellectually and
morally superior to the Arabs. Their eyes were already turned to the
West; French books were being read and the French language was
being spoken in many Jewish families . . .

The Alliance Israélite is not French! The Alliance is international!
But are we considering the attraction France already had for those of
the students who had begun to learn to speak French? France had
achieved the moral conquest of the Jews in the East. We already felt
that everything that concerned France concerned us. In my distant
childhood years, at the beginning of the twentieth century, it was the
issue of Alsace-Lorraine which excited the majority of my classmates,
just like the children in France. During recreation, how many times
did I see the young students divide into two groups, the *Triple Alliance* and the *Triple Entente*. There were always greater numbers in
the *Triple Entente* and their games always finished in victory for the
latter, that is to say for France!

Through the French language learned at the Alliance school, the
young Jew could more easily earn his living. The unskilled trades,
which the Jews had practiced for centuries, were abandoned. They
began to work in commerce; they took over the banks. Because the
Jews had become more intelligent, the Turks had more need of them
and they began to work in the government. Those young people who
could not find a position went to the neighboring country, Egypt, a
rich country. From each successive class leaving the school, hundreds
of young men went to Egypt. The Syrian and Palestinian Jews today
number in the thousands in that country. This emigration to Egypt is
truly a return to Egypt.

It was during the year 1908, at the moment of the Young Turk
Revolution, that the wind of nationalism blowing in from European
Turkey shook the Arab populations. It was the year of emancipation.
The most noble promises were made to every element of the popula-

tion. Freedom, equality, and brotherhood: this was the slogan of the
new Turkey. Muslims, Christians, and Jews were fraternizing. Great
banquets would bring thousands of inhabitants together. Once the enthusiasm had passed, we were left with the same divisions.

Then came the war; the Jewish population paid dearly for its attachment to France. The Turks, supported by Germany, which had for
some time been seeking to establish its domination in Turkey, began
to turn on certain harmless populations. The deportations began.
Those who had been on friendly terms with the French were hunted
down and hanged in the public square. Lebanon was surrounded and
an attempt made to starve its inhabitants! Thousands and thousands
of innocent victims were dying as sickness and epidemics ran rampant. France vowed to rescue this population and to have it placed
under her protection . . .

A few words were spoken in London, and the Zionist movement
had begun. Only England could create a national Jewish homeland;
and so England was to be given control of Palestine. And England
needed Palestine because of this country's location on the route to
India. So Palestine was now a Jewish land, and thousands of Jews
returned to the land of their ancestors.

The Arab world had been sleeping for centuries. English money
and propaganda awakened it; the Arab movement was created. In
response to the call to arms and the sound of gunfire, there was a
rebirth of fanaticism in the Arabian Peninsula. Thousand of Arabs
came on their fleet horses from out of the desert, brandishing lances
and sabers. The Arabs set off to conquer the world. Led by Faysal,
hordes of Arabs entered Palestine and Syria; Damascus was occupied.
Syria was set up as an Arab kingdom, and an Arab government was
formed. Arab newspapers began to be published. The Syrians were
reluctant to accept the counsel of the few French officials responsible
for guiding Syria to independence. French influence seemed to have
been irrevocably compromised. Plotting and intrigues against the
French became so serious that France was finally forced to take action. Damascus was occupied in 1920. Faysal, in flight, demanded another crown from England for the help he had given the Allies during
the war.

[. . .]

Any foreigner who had known this country under the Turks and
who sees Syria today cannot help but be struck by the progress which
has taken place here in the last ten years. Justice, which was once
only accorded the strong and the powerful, is now equally available

to all. The *fellah* [peasant] can now work in safety and is not subject
to the demands and exactions of greedy government representatives.
He is no longer exploited by powerful landowners. Whole expanses of
land in the area surrounding Damascus, which were once covered
with swamps and were breeding grounds for malaria, have been
cleaned up and made safe. Wondrous roads and railways have been
planned and constructed, equal to the best in Europe.
[. . .]

As for the Jewish population in Damascus, a population of barely
8,000, over the course of the last few years it had been under heavy
Zionist influence. Promises of the establishment of a national Jewish
homeland in Palestine had inspired enthusiasm in Jews throughout the
world. Assured of their domination in Palestine, the Zionists were
working at extending that domination into the neighboring countries.
Two Hebrew schools were founded in Damascus. It was especially
those living in poverty who sent their children to these schools. There
was little place in the Hebrew schools for the teaching of Arabic and
French. In those schools the same teaching methods were used as in
the schools in Palestine; the same exaltation could be found among
the young people. But when faced with the hostility of the Arab population and a lack of money, these schools were forced to close their
doors. The societies which had formed them remained, however, and
continued to work to keep the Zionist movement alive. It has been
five years since the Hebrew schools were closed. The numerous societies, formed on the model of the societies in Palestine, have begun
to dissolve. In the last two or three years new societies have been
organized; their members are young people brought up in our
schools, whose aspirations are already different from those of the generation preceding them.

The Jewish population of our city is in some ways lost amid an
Arab population fifty times its number, yet the pan-Arab movement
has had very little influence on it. The Frenchman, civilian or military, is enchanted when he reaches the Jewish district, having passed
through the *souk*s of Damascus and the masses of Arabs, who will
never be touched by French influence. When he first sets foot in the
Jewish district, he sees groups of children in the streets or playing in
front of their homes, speaking a very pure French. If he approaches
these children to ask them for information or directions, he is amazed
to hear with what ease these young children express themselves. Several administrators and officers whom I have had occasion to meet
have spoken to me with enthusiasm about the Jewish district. They

have told me that in Damascus the Jewish district is the only area of the city where French is widespread and spoken by so many young people.

A knowledge of French enables many Jews from Damascus to make a living or to hold a position of importance when they emigrate to America, and this is thanks to the Alliance schools. The Alliance school is the grand fortress of the Jewish district. All of the foreigners agree that it is the best primary school and that the teaching done there best fulfills the needs of the population. We do not neglect the teaching of Arabic; on the contrary, we know how important this language is for our fellow Jews, who are in daily contact with their Arab neighbors. But the Jews of Damascus would do well to become bilingual, to also speak a language that is used internationally and that may permit them to expand their commercial interests and to have some contact with French civilization.

Those of the Jews here who experimented by sending their children to the Hebrew schools learned that the Zionist movement is not useful for them. This movement succeeded only in exciting hostility from their neighbors. The Jewish community of Damascus is poor and few in numbers; hence it has neither the money nor the influence to support the Zionist movement. The Arab nationalist movement would equally be a step backward for this community. Our fellow Jews here must follow the example of their brethren in North Africa, who, under the aegis of France, have made enormous progress in every domain.

As for the Syrian population proper, it is only with the support of France that it will be able to achieve emancipation and follow the road to progress.

France did not come into Syria in order to colonize the country. No French farmers have settled in any part of the country. The French and European population in Syria is very small, and Syria will never see the immigration of southern Europeans on a large scale.

Communication among the five regions of the globe has become very rapid and economic interests tend to bring peoples closer together. Isn't there talk of the United States of Europe?

Because Syria is a poor country and is for the moment incapable of its own administration, it is in Syria's best interests to join that assembly of peoples who, under the aegis of France, constitute the vast empire of French overseas territories.

This population speaks a language that has minimal influence in the outside world, and it would do well to adopt the French language, the language of ideas *par excellence,* the language of good taste and refinement. Lebanon seems to be moving in this direction. Now it is up to Syria to find its own way. In a few years, Syria could well become a forward outpost of France in the Near East with far-reaching influence.

[. . .]

A. Zilberstein

Archives of the AIU, Syrie I.C.5.

The rise of local nationalist movements challenging this optimistic worldview, which presupposed a continuing strong European presence in the Middle East and North Africa, constituted a rude shock to the teachers. The fate of the Alliance schools in Turkey after the coming to power of a nationalist regime provided a cautionary tale: with the emergence of the Turkish republic out of the ashes of the Ottoman Empire in 1923 and the creation of a highly nationalistic secular state, a foreign organization in charge of the education of a section of the citizenry was no longer tolerated. The schools were nationalized by the mid-1920s and ceased to function as Alliance institutions:

Galata (Istanbul), 14 May 1935

[. . .]

It was around 1923 when governmental actions began to take on a precise and deliberate character.

Hence . . . a notice dated 20 May 1923 announced that "courses in the Turkish language and in the history and geography of Turkey must be taught in Turkish and by Turkish instructors. The Ministry reserves the right to select and to appoint these instructors."

According to my passport, I may be as Turkish as Mehmet or Ahmet; according to my diplomas and my general background, I may be well qualified to teach children. None of this matters. I am eliminated *de facto* since the selection of an appointee to any post is the right of the administration responsible for public education. This administration has already received a list of young men from among whom it must make its selection, to the exclusion of all other candidates. Automatically eliminated, then, are many teachers who have been filling these positions brilliantly for many years.

It should be noted that the word "Muslim" is never mentioned in the different documents which I am sending you, although this is the word that comes regularly to mind . . .

The measure enacted by the aforementioned notice was not enough to satisfy its promoters: Jewish educational institutions were still very much alive. The reason for this was that contact had been maintained with the Alliance, whose personnel were running these institutions. These personnel had been specially trained for a mission which required tact, a certain psychological instinct, and a devotion which sometimes bore the mark of heroism; behind these personnel was the Alliance, financially supporting the schools and permitting them to hold steady.

That was no problem, a new *irade* [decree] would do the trick: the Civil Code had long been gathering dust; these good Jews would be given the order to cease all relations with the Alliance. It made no difference that neither the law nor its representatives should have had anything to do with these relations . . .

On 21 June 1924, a new blow was dealt us, and this one was fatal.

The Alliance had been eliminated, true, but the West continued to make its presence felt through the French language, which continued to be the language of education, that is to say, the vehicle for all that humanity holds most exalted, and of which the Jews must be deprived. The action of the Alliance was no longer being felt directly, but the personnel it had trained continued to zealously practice the methods and programs of teaching inspired by the Alliance.

The notice of 21 June 1924 . . . consummated the disaster. The upheaval would be complete.

In terms bearing the mark of the most blatant hypocrisy and cruel cynicism, we were informed that the order had come down to begin teaching all subjects in the "mother tongue of the Jewish nation," that is to say, Hebrew. The person who drew up this masterpiece knew perfectly well this was a bold-faced lie. No doubt that is why he didn't sign it but merely affixed the official seal. In fact, there is no Turk in Constantinople who does not know that the mother tongue of the Jews in Turkey is a more or less corrupt Spanish, but what difference does that make? If need be they would create a separate Jewish nation, right in the Turkish republic, in spite of identity papers and documents. Along with this new nationality, there would be imposed a language, the Hebrew language. Certainly the Jews are proud of this language but it is still not their "mother tongue." And since there is always "more than one way to skin a cat," it was made clear that in place of Hebrew, we could teach in the official language: that is to say, Turkish . . .

The substitution of Turkish (given the impossibility of adopting Hebrew) for the French language resulted in the destruction of the homogeneity which had thus far been upheld by our instructors. Experienced and excellent teachers had to be dismissed only to be replaced by "Muslims," whom we were obliged to recruit locally. This quickly

opened the door to more or less disguised interventions on the part
of government employees who were anxious to procure positions for
their friends and relations. To all of this were added several cases of
misappropriation of funds on the part of some of our own personnel, who were eager to court certain government officials and to fish
in troubled waters. The ultimate result was complete chaos among
your directors, who were in no way prepared to hold up in such a
storm.

It goes without saying that we attempted to fight back. Serious and
well-orchestrated steps were undertaken in Ankara but to no avail.
And as of October 1924 . . . the transformation of our schools, while
gradual, was a foregone conclusion . . .
[. . .]

E. Nathan

Archives of the AIU, Turquie, II.C.8.

*Troubles in Palestine, which spilled over into overt acts of antisemitism
in other Muslim countries, as well as the rise of European antisemitism
and fascism, found increasing echo in the letters of the teachers in the
inter-war years:*

Tunis, 17 October 1932
[. . .]

During my last visit to Paris we had the opportunity to discuss the
antisemitic disturbances that had occurred this summer in different
cities of Tunisia . . .

1. Were there Arab representatives from Palestine in Tunisia?

2. Is there any correlation between the visit of these representatives to Tunisia and the disturbances that occurred there?

The first question can be answered in the affirmative. There were
in fact Muslims from Jerusalem who arrived in Tunisia last July and
who were still in Tunis at the beginning of October. What is the goal
of their visit? . . . They are in direct contact with the nationalist leaders, and even if we suppose that they are not charged with any particular mission by the Mufti of Jerusalem, they must be discussing the
state of affairs in Palestine with the people they visit. But the truth of
the matter lies elsewhere. The Tunisian nationalist party, which, as a
result of weakness in the central government, has greatly expanded in
recent times, has already had relations with the Arab Executive in
Palestine for some time now. This party's attacks against Zionist
claims in its newspaper, *The Tunisian Voice,* and its energetic interventions, with threats of rioting, against Zionist lectures given by repre-

sentatives from outside Tunisia are but the execution of directives sent
by the Arab party of Jerusalem . . .

. . . But the problem is much greater and much more deep-seated.
The Arabs, stirred up by the nationalists, are above all resentful of
the French. Their attacks against the Jews are only an indirect result
of this bitterness, a kind of preparation . . .

If to this state of mind you add the general uneasiness created by
the current crisis, and the Arab population is especially suffering from
this uneasiness, you will have an explanation for the incidents of this
summer. These incidents were provoked by trivial causes, but they
suddenly took an exceptionally serious turn.
[. . .]

C. Ouziel

Archives of the AIU, Tunisie II.C.6.

Baghdad, 18 December 1934

[. . .]

At the time of the Ottoman Empire, the Jews were shut into their
district, a kind of ghetto, and had no civil rights. It would be superfluous for me to emphasize the attitude of the Turks toward minorities:
the massacres of Armenians, the expulsion of the Orthodox Greeks,
and the slaughter of the Kurds are all glaring proof of their barbarity.

And so the Jew, who was barred from public life, gave himself over
entirely to commerce. It was his knowledge of languages, acquired
through the generous efforts of the Alliance and the dedication of its
pioneers, which enabled him to excel and to dominate in this sphere
of the country's activities.

In 1920, during the Iraqi Revolution, all elements of the population
joined together in the struggle against the exactions of the British
army. Through their discourse, the leaders of the country tried to
cement this friendship by declaring to the ignorant masses that Jews
and Arabs belonged to the same race and that they should thus work
together in securing prosperity for their young country. Alas! This
brotherhood was short-lived. More than one factor contributed to its
demise. The early stages of the Mandate seemed to the Arab to entail
total subordination to foreigners. Indeed the English, who were masters of the country, had taken over all higher functions and surrounded themselves with assistants selected, for the most part, from
among the former students of your schools. As a result, the young
Jews held well-paying positions and were soon making rapid advances
in their careers, while the Arabs were overlooked and neglected.

A silent hatred began to grow between these two elements of the

population. The effects of this animosity became tangible the day
Lord Melchett (Sir Alfred Mond) arrived in 1927. Certain agitators
had inculcated in the minds of the fanatics the idea that the English
were most likely going to name this important figure king of Palestine. Bands of protesters ran through the main streets of the city,
attacking the cars coming in from the desert and mistreating the pas-
sengers, whom they took for Lord Melchett's entourage. Several people were stripped and beaten.

After Sir Alfred Mond had left, all seemed to have returned to an
apparent calm when the incidents of 1929, over the Wailing Wall,
brought the crisis to a higher pitch. Demonstrations were organized . . .

The bloody events in Safed brought even more venom to the already strained relations, for whatever happens in Palestine has its repercussions in Iraq. The Jews, in order to demonstrate their attachment to their country and its cause, contributed generously to a fund
started to aid the families of those Arabs who had been killed by the
Zionists. The Arabs found a certain hypocrisy in this generosity.
[. . .]

When Iraq became independent with the treaty of 30 June, it
adeptly rid itself of the British employees in the government. Any
Englishman whose contract expired was not rehired. The others were
invited to resign their posts in exchange for a generous breach-of-
contract payment.

The new Arab leaders were not long in letting their Jewish subordi-
nates know that their presence was undesirable.

There is nothing surprising in this; those who now hold the destiny
of the country in their hands studied in the same schools as the leaders of the new Turkey. In every domain, they follow the example of
their colleagues from across the border. The press is devoted to them.
In recent days this campaign has taken on an alarming character.

Those who had encouraged the movement against the Jews were
obliged to control the ardor of the agitators, who are legion in this
country, for this constant intoxication of the masses would have eventually provoked massacres of an element of the population which has
in all circumstances demonstrated its loyal attachment to the nation.
[. . .]

R. Mefano

Archives of the AIU, Irak I.C.3.

Baghdad, 23 April 1936

[. . .]

Agitation in Palestine. Events in Palestine have had their repercussions on the spirits of the people here. Every day the Arab newspapers devote long articles to the violent activities of the Jews in Palestine and to the so-called massacres of Arabs. The Jews here have asked the Minister to order the press to maintain the necessary calm under the circumstances and not to arouse pointless hatred against the Jewish population in this country. We would like to hope that this request will be taken into consideration and that we will not have reason to lament the consequences of this campaign of incitement and hatred which the press has been conducting over the last few days.

We cannot deny that the situation is becoming difficult. Anything the Jews here may do has become suspect. The slightest gesture is labeled Zionist or antipatriotic. And yet God knows the Jews in Baghdad are far from entertaining any Zionist ideas. Here are a few examples of the way our actions and gestures are being viewed and interpreted:

A while ago I wrote you that the leader of the community, *Hakham* Sassoon, had organized a religious ceremony in memory of Mrs. Farha Sassoon, of the David Sassoon family in London, who was recently deceased. This ceremony was held in the courtyard of our school.

A few days afterward we learned that the police had written up a statement in which the school was charged with holding a meeting without authorization . . . In order to release myself of all responsibility, I was obliged to give proof that the ceremony had been organized by the head of the Jewish community and that it was he who had issued the invitations. It would have been quite serious had I been charged with the responsibility for this affair in light of the fine which the tribunal had imposed last year as a result of the reception we had given for the students at the school . . .

You must also have heard that a short time ago the president of the community of Basra was sentenced to fifteen days in jail for having assisted several Jewish emigrants, some of whom, it was said, did not have valid passports.

[. . .]

M. Laredo

Archives of the AIU, Irak I.C.3.

However, the Europe-centered worldview and discourse of the teachers proved resistant to change even though accompanied by a great deal of prescience about the impossible position in which the Jews of the Middle East and North Africa would find themselves during the coming age of decolonization:

Aleppo, 9 June 1936

EVENTS IN THE EAST AND THEIR REPERCUSSIONS
ON THE JEWISH COMMUNITIES

[. . .]

Important events are now taking place in the Near East. Syria, following the example of Iraq, is claiming its right to independence, and the Syrians are hoping that the negotiations that have begun between the Syrian delegation and the French government will conclude in their favor.

I am anxiously wondering:

1. Would it not be more humane for the East to remain subject to the rule of a more civilized people rather than be given its freedom, considering its false conception of civilization and its often primitive instincts?

2. What will be Syria's attitude toward those who will grant this freedom?

3. What will then happen to the Jewish communities in Syria?

To give an accurate idea of the repercussions which the change of regime in Syria may have on the future of minorities in general, and of Eastern Jewry in particular, I will try to summarize the impressions, if not the judgments, that I have formed after many years in the East.

The upheaval of the Great War shook the entire world. The East in particular broke out of its lethargy and reclaimed its right to life, to that intense, agitated, and out-of-balance life left by the greatest catastrophe ever to befall humanity. This awakening of the East would have been a most fortunate thing had it been due to the positive forces of civilization—the arts, the sciences, morality, refinement of manners, unselfish ideals—in a word, had it been a kind of humanist renaissance analogous to the one that shook the Middle Ages. Unfortunately, it is the other side of civilization, that composed of pride, hatred, and national fanaticism, which brought the East out of its thousand-year sleep. If we must place part of the blame for this disastrous awakening on the guns of the Great War, we must still not forget that this monstrous seed could only have grown and flourished in the soil of the East, which has always been rich in hatred and religious fanaticism. Excited Arabs have never hesitated to kill in revenge for the slightest wrongs. Coupled with their sense of vengeance is a cowardice that leads them to attack only when they are certain of impunity. By nature both impulsive and naive, they are easily taken in and enthusiastically join in pillaging and massacring. Religious fanaticism has always been able to keep hatred strong in the Arabs; today's national fanaticism, much more dangerous, has succeeded in arousing and exacerbating that hatred. Today, whether they be believers or atheists, the Arabs have a new religion: nationalism, which translates to hatred of outsiders. Formerly, the fatalism of their religion made it possible for them to be patient and to wait for better days; the moral teachings of the monotheistic religion of Mohammed had a more or less calming effect on their otherwise totally impulsive nature. Today Islam and nationalism have become blended and confused in the minds of the believers and together have given rise to a dangerous xenophobia. Among the atheists, of whom there are any number among the leaders of the masses, racist nationalism alone has filled the immense void left by loss of religious faith. Today the Arab people aspire only to independence and to the realization of pan-Arabism rather than pan-Islamism. And so these people seek to be rid of this humiliating guardianship, all the more so because England has presented bright images of an Arab empire and because, having witnessed the deployment of Western force, the Arab people have the desire to be strong. Syria has already been promised that its requests will be granted.

And will the Syrians be content with obtaining their independence? It is certain that they will not. They will have the desire, and will make an effort, to unite. They will seek to form that Arab empire modeled after the Third Reich, the only form of government appropriate for a people in the habit of servitude and permeated with fanaticism. To Arab eyes, Hitler represents the model most in keeping with their ideas. How many swastikas are carved into the desks in secondary schools in Iraq and in the hearts of the young people in school; how much more deeply is Hitler's ideal engraved. This ideal is one of pure hatred: a hatred of Jews, to which is joined a hatred of the colonizers.

Steel gray shirts have already begun appearing in Syria. The god of the Syrian nationalists, Dr. Shahebandar, who was exiled by the French authorities and is currently in Egypt, declared recently that only the Nazi regime was suitable for Syria.

Paradox! Historical irony! It is from a socialist government, from all the anti-Fascist forces of the French people, that the Syrians hope to procure their independence. And this is an independence which will permit them one day to establish an antiliberal regime diametrically opposed to the spirit of justice animating France, the liberator. The future will bear witness to the fact that a grave error is being committed. "It is good to be charitable," but toward whom? At the time

when the French Revolution proclaimed liberty for all, was its intention to accord liberty to criminals and to those who seek liberty only
to abuse it? It is hard to understand and to accept that democratic
France would contribute to the establishment of a despotic and base
regime in the East. Have the Arabs earned the right to enjoy the
same freedom as the Europeans? Aren't the massacres in Constantine, of the Assyrians in Iraq, of the Jews in Palestine sufficient to
prove that a dangerous, impulsive people is about to be liberated?
They will, at the first opportunity and under the slightest pretext, spill
the blood of innocent people. Will thousands of lives of people in the
minorities be thrown to the savage lions, hungry for their independence?

And when the Arabs have obtained their independence, will they
be grateful to the countries which liberated them? As soon as conditions are favorable, they will not fail to throw themselves into the
arms of the greatest enemies of those who have given them their independence. It would be naive to think that Iraq feels any gratitude
toward England, in spite of the fact that it is the first Arab country to
achieve autonomy.

The king himself first obtained glory and popularity when he know-
ingly directed the massacre of the Assyrians and, *according to the
public rumors of his subjects,* dismissed the English ambassador to
Iraq, who, it is said, was trying to advise him at the time.

Two years ago I witnessed a scene which raises certain questions
about the nature of Arab sentiments toward England. I was in one of
the largest movie theaters in Baghdad. On the screen could be seen
the soldiers of the English fleet entering the Dardanelles and their
subsequent defeat. These were poignant scenes where English sailors,
many only adolescents, were falling under Turkish fire; faces covered
with blood and wrenched in pain were rolled back and forth in the
mire. These scenes would have touched the hardest hearts; they were
feverishly applauded by the Arab audience, which was beside itself
with joy. And yet these dying soldiers were the children of the people
who had granted them freedom, and the bullets killing them came
from the Turks, the eternal enemies and despotic masters of the
Arabs.

These sentiments given spontaneous expression by the crowd are
much more sincere than those of the suave and hypocritical diplomats
who make the rounds of the European capitals. These diplomats are
turning to their profit the credulity and sincere idealism of certain
important Western personalities.

Having lived thirteen years in Iraq, and having seen the Arabs from up close, I will allow myself an observation. The East has many tragic surprises in store for the West once independence has been achieved here. There will be murder, betrayal, and widespread revolt against Western countries, and there will be a racist position taken toward the Jews.

[. . .]

Geographically and historically, Palestine is but a province of Syria and is considered as such by the Arabs, who call it Southern Syria. An error was committed when they were separated by the Treaty of Versailles; the destinies of these two countries are inextricably linked. *An independent Syrian regime and a Palestine under foreign domination are not politically viable. Such a situation would both aggravate and perpetuate the troubles currently raging throughout the East, and it would be the Jews who would pay.*

What makes the future of the Syrian Jews look even darker is that they have emigrated to Palestine in great numbers. More than a thousand Jews from Aleppo have left over the course of this past year. Many Jewish families in Syria have relatives in Palestine and they will not be forgiven this crime.

The Syrian Arabs thus have a serious reason for reproaching the Syrian Jews concerning their Zionism, and for considering them partly responsible for the fate of the Arabs in Palestine.

Although the watchword in Syrian nationalist context is not to mistreat the minorities while the Syrian delegation in Paris has not yet had all its requests met, there are already incidents of agitation today. It is true that these incidents are not very serious, but they are an omen of darker days.

Around ten days ago in the district of A'zaz in northern Syria, in the village of Afrine, a public crier, beating his drum, proclaimed a boycott against the Jews.

Threatened with death, some Jews have been forcibly kept away from the weekly markets held in Aleppo. On 1 June, in Bahsita and Saha, districts that house the poor families of the Jewish population of Aleppo, windows were broken and women and children injured. The Arab agents from the police post refused to carry out an investigation; the French police intervened and arrested two Muslims.

In Djemilie, a Jewish and European district of Aleppo, a rabbi on his way to *Talmud-Torah* was attacked by Muslim youths, who tore off his turban and beat him. Schoolchildren, usually the very small children, are sometimes mistreated by Arab adolescents. Several Muslims can be heard to say, "The French will be leaving soon and you'll see what we'll do with you." The Jewish community of Aleppo is very

anxious about the fate that awaits them. A delegation of simple peddlers who had been boycotted came to see me and to ask that I intervene.

In Damascus, more serious disturbances have broken out; your representative in that city must have spoken to you about them.

CONCLUSION

Syria is in negotiations with France for its independence. France has
promised, under the threat of the general strike, to grant it a treaty
similar to that granted Iraq. The Syrians claim they are forcing France
to accept this treaty. There is nothing more dangerous, considering
the Arab mentality, than this impression of weakness in the Manda-
tory Power. For her part, France may think that by according independence to Syria she is appeasing the Syrians and gaining their friendship; in fact, France is allowing this country to grow strong and better
able to resist her. Beyond this, Syria would be the second independent Arab state in the Near East and this will increase the arrogance
of the Arabs. As soon as conditions become favorable for the Muslim
world, as soon as any difficulties arise in Europe for France and England, these new, young, ardent, and fanatical countries, who will
have their own soldiers, will easily be able to break the agreements
reached with the Western powers they abhor.

France is anxious to resolve the Syrian question for the present, but
the French must certainly envisage the possibility of Syrian betrayal.
They will probably grant independence to Syria, but they must not
fail in their eternal and noble duty to protect the weak. The French
must not abandon the minorities, who are living in torment and who
dearly love France. They must require that Syria make serious guarantees for the protection of its minorities. The presence of *the French
army is the only effective guarantee.*

Without French protection, the future of Syrian minorities appears
bleak. The Jews especially have the most to fear from this eventuality.
In the profound hatred for Zionism shared by the Arabs, the Jew and
the Zionist have become fused. The first thing the free and strong
Arabs will fight is Zionism, which stands in the way of pan-Arabism.
Will the new leaders of a fully independent Syria be equal to the
task? Will they be able to neutralize the virus of a new Arab antisemitism and to protect the Jewish communities from the probable persecutions and massacres? Will they be able to find a solution to the economic crisis in a rather poor country? Will they be able to put a stop
to the fanatic excesses of the unbridled masses, drunk with their
independence?

These are so many distressing questions that only the future can answer.
[. . .]

E. Menda

Archives of the AIU, Syrie I.C.3.

Beirut, 19 June 1936
[. . .]
. . . Our leaders are currently negotiating independence for their countries and the latest news reports tell us that the basic terms of a Franco-Syrian treaty have been agreed upon. The Mandate will soon come to an end. Both Syria and Lebanon, but especially Syria, are loudly proclaiming their joy. The Muslims of these two countries are in a frenzy of excitement. "No more Mandate, no more French. Complete, entire, absolute independence. We will be our own masters; no advice, no interference." Islam has triumphed.

The victory of the nationalists has plunged us into dark despair. Those who will lead us tomorrow are not yet prepared to shoulder the heavy responsibilities of Freedom.

The Jews in Beirut and the Jews in Syria, especially the latter, look to the future with dread. A profound anxiety grips our hearts. No more Mandate, no more control; as long as the French flag was waving over our heads, we felt perfectly safe. The French army was protecting us. The High Commissioner quickly repressed all abuse and rectified all injustice. Many times in the course of the last few years we have felt we were in danger because of events in Palestine. Each time, a simple appeal to the representatives of France was enough to restore peace of mind to the members of our communities.
[. . .]
What does fate hold in store for the minorities in Syria and Lebanon in the days to come? Tomorrow, what will be the Muslim policies concerning us?
[. . .]
We are too close to Palestine; this is what increases the uneasiness.
[. . .]
In these anxious and apprehensive moments, the Jews of Syria and the Jews of Beirut can do nothing but turn to the Alliance, which has always watched over them with a loving, maternal solicitude, and implore that it continue to think of them and of the sad fate which awaits them.

Your precious interventions on behalf of the communities of Jews throughout the world have always brought about the hoped for and expected results. May the members of the Central Committee of the Alliance today hear our SOS. They can still prevent the misfortune which may one day befall us by bringing our fears and grievances to the attention of the French diplomats who are negotiating the Franco-Syrian treaty.

The Quai d'Orsay has always given the opinions of the Alliance the attention they deserve.

In requesting an addition to the aforementioned treaty of a clause conveying this meaning "France will always be responsible for the fate of the minorities, which it hereby places under its direct protection," the Alliance will once again have served the vital interests of the Jews of Lebanon and Syria. It will have restored the peace and the calm necessary if they are to return to the lives they have been leading for centuries in these countries.

[. . .]

E. Penso

Archives of the AIU, Liban I.C.1.

The anxiety about the departure of the West was fully justified. With the foundation of the state of Israel and decolonization, the overwhelming majority of Jews in Arab lands had to migrate en masse.[9] They were too closely identified, in terms of Muslim perceptions, with both the West and Zionism.

Rampant nationalism, antisemitism, and fascism were severe blows to the mid-nineteenth-century optimism of the Alliance. The agendas and solutions of the past were no longer satisfactory. Sylvain Halff, the secretary general of the Alliance, acknowledged as much, five months before the outbreak of World War II, in his letter to Ben-Meir, a teacher in Sousse, Tunisia:

Paris, 29 March 1939

Sir,

We have received your report dated 8 March.

The dialogue between a Zionist, an assimilated Jew, and one who has been de-Judaized which you recounted in your report expresses the thoughts of three personalities now struggling within Jewish hearts, never coming to an agreement. It is easy to understand that our spirits are troubled. In the presence of unbridled antisemitism in countries where we believed civilization had at last arrived, the Jews

9. See the discussion in Norman Stillman, *The Jews of Arab Lands in Modern Times* (Philadelphia: Jewish Publication Society, 1991), 113–76.

begin to question the essential precepts of a civilization that made so many promises it was unable to keep.

The arguments put forth by the man whom you call de-Judaized are perhaps the weakest. Without even mentioning the indignity which such a renunciation entails, the option of de-Judaization has disappeared as an alternative since antisemitism has become an issue of race.

As concerns Zionism, it would seem to have led to an impasse. One would not be wrong to suggest that the choice of Zionism as a solution, a choice made by so many in the belief that no other solutions remain, is a choice imposed by a false historical perspective. To accept Zionist doctrine is to forget all of the difficulties through which Judaism has passed and over which it has triumphed in the course of its history. It may be that the misfortunes of today are but another stage in our struggle for emancipation.

Is assimilation, then, the only solution? Perhaps. But only on the condition that its fundamental theses be reexamined in the light of new facts. It was formulated in the nineteenth century and is no longer in step with the events of our times. There is here a subject for meditation; it is first an issue for private, internal reflection. And the spiritual role of Judaism, its religious mission in the world—of which there is no mention in your account—would not fail to dominate these reflections. But a doctrine of this order cannot be hastily improvised. And we are in complete agreement with you concerning the need to invite the students of the *Ecole Normale* to begin such reflection and to guide them in their search.

The Secretary General,
S. Halff

Archives of the AIU, Tunisie I.G.1.

After the shock of the Vichy regime and the Holocaust, the Alliance would indeed revise its ideology. It would not abandon the centrality of emancipation. However, like all major international Jewish organizations after World War II, it would add to the equation the centrality of the state of Israel. The age of emancipation in Jewish history with its all-encompassing worldview came to an end with the Holocaust, giving way to the age of national emancipation. The revision of the old model for Jewish modernity accepted by the Alliance was a product of this profound sea change.

Conclusion

Tangier, 2 August 1902

[. . .]

. . . Without going all the way back to the prophets, there is no question that the first of the humanists was Spinoza, whose genius of thought was able to free itself from rabbinical orthodoxy. Indeed, Jewish philosophers before Spinoza had drawn their inspiration from rabbinical dogma, and their writings are merely more or less subtle, more or less ingenious commentaries on sacred texts, most often written in the margins of these. Spinoza shook philosophical speculation free from the accepted religious tenets of the time, and the rabbis saw that he paid for this independence with the most shameful of humiliations.

. . . In the eighteenth century the situation was different. The France of the *philosophes* and the Germany of Frederick the Great broke the yoke under which the churches had sought to hold the human spirit, and humanism triumphed. This humanism meant the liberation of reason, the affirmation of free and close examination and questioning, the emancipation of the human conscience, the cultivation of the sciences, and the rejection of dogmatic values, whose strength had been worn away by years of abuse.

Moses Mendelssohn was the principal architect in this renovation of Judaism. He had gone to Berlin when he was still very young to take up talmudic studies. He was captivated by the spirit of reform and the love of science that had taken over the Prussian capital; he studied mathematics, Latin, philosophy, and he formed a friendship with Lessing, through whom he met many others . . .

Wanting to improve the spiritual condition of his fellow Jews, Mendelssohn translated the Pentateuch, whose meaning had been altered through rabbinical and cabalistic commentaries; this German translation was condemned and burned. But the students of the rabbinical schools were, in their turn, touched by the spirit of the age, and they began to study secular sciences and literature.

Following the example given by Lessing, who courageously de-

287

fended Judaism, other Christian scholars began to study the glorious
Jewish past. In his *Political Reformation of the Jews,* Dohm made a
plea for the Jews to be given the same rights enjoyed by the others
who lived in the country.

And Mendelssohn continued in his mission. In *Jerusalem,* he demonstrated that the Jewish religion granted its followers the freedom to
believe according to their conscience . . .

The freedom which the Jews of Berlin could acquire only through
the church, France was to give them without imposing humiliating
conditions or forcing them to act contrary to their beliefs and their
dignity. It was in fact the French Revolution that realized the goal of
Mendelssohn, Lessing, and Dohm: the integration of the Jewish element into the population of the nation in which they lived. There is
no doubt that this new situation had a second implication. From the
moment the Jews had a homeland that accorded them all rights as
citizens, and they had called for these rights with tenacious perseverance for some time, they could not and must not any longer look
toward other lands. And so, gone was the messianic dream which had
comforted Jewry through the course of its centuries of suffering, for
this dream had been fulfilled in an unexpected manner. Gone too,
were the Jewish laws that might appear outmoded or in contradiction
to the laws of the state . . .

The Bible is at the base of the Mosaic religion. The Bible, it is
true, is a whole, a unit that must be accepted or rejected. But the
Judaism that had been given the mission of educating humanity had
difficulty recognizing itself in the particularist tendency and narrow
conception of our ancestors at the time of the conquest of Palestine,
which perhaps answered the needs of the period . . .

How much more at ease are we in those texts of great moral impli-
cations and universal dimensions, in which are affirmed the ideals of
our Prophets; it is from their writings, in the universalism they
preached, that Judaism can and must draw its pride and its reason for
being. The Prophets, who interpreted the thinking of a universal
God, have given us, have given Israel, a mission and a duty toward
other nations; the Prophets tell us of an ideal of humanity, solidarity,
and brotherhood.

Such is the religion of our Prophets and such are the principles the
French Revolution brought to triumph in Europe, in the hope that
they would one day become the charter for all humanity. And so, if
there has been assimilation, it has been in the other direction. It is
the Judaism of the Prophets that has won the world over to its ideal
of justice and peace, either directly or through the intermediary of

Christianity, and especially through the intervention of the Reformation, which stopped halfway on the road to Judaism. Is it to be re-
gretted that other peoples have embraced our principles and have
quenched their thirst for the ideal in the waters which flow from
our religion? The Prophets are claimed—and this is the glory of
Judaism—by all of humanity, which has become assimilated to
Judaism . . .

A. Saguès

Archives of the AIU, Maroc LIX.E.943c.

*This intellectual genealogy and rationale for the work of the Alliance
outlined by one of the most important teachers of the organization during
a public lecture points to an important truth about the society in general
and its teachers in particular. The intellectual roots of the Alliance lay
indeed in the European* Haskalah *("enlightenment," in Hebrew) begun
by Mendelssohn, that body of ideas constituting the Jewish counterpart of
the Enlightenment. The movement that began in the middle of the eighteenth century in Germany and later spread elsewhere called in its various
manifestations for an overhaul of traditional Jewish culture and society in
the light of modern "universal" civilization and for the cultural and social
integration of the Jews in the countries in which they lived. The sharp
critique of traditional Jewish culture and society, especially of rabbinic
culture, the attempt to cast away what was deemed to be superstition and
to bring out more clearly the pure essence of the religion, which was
considered to be in harmony with reason, the call for productivization,
the transformation of an unhealthy Jewish social structure by the teaching
of manual artisanal and agricultural trades, the cult of modern secular
education: these were all familiar themes of the European* Haskalah *that
had been widely debated during the hundred years before the foundation
of the Alliance. The emancipation ideology of the Alliance configured all
these principles around the act of emancipation, the raising of the Jews to
citizenship and equality. In this respect, the discourse of the Alliance and
the teachers was a French expression of the wider European* Haskalah.

*Nineteenth-century French Jewry has often been characterized as the
"assimilationist" Jewry* par excellence, *a community whose Jewish identity and ties had become attenuated until they were revived by large numbers of foreign Jews immigrating to France at the end of the century.
Nevertheless, no other European Jewry produced an organization like the
Alliance in the second half of the nineteenth century,[1] an organization*

---

1. The Anglo-Jewish Association was a much weaker institution. It was created in 1870
as a sister body and always worked closely with the Alliance.

which worked effectively to improve the status and physical and moral welfare of Jews throughout the world. The existence and activities of such an institution highlight the shortcomings of the catchall term "assimilation" as an analytical tool. The current usage of the term simplifies the extraordinary complexity of a constantly evolving French-Jewish identity in the age of emancipation. This identity, rooted in a specifically French-Jewish articulation of the larger European Haskalah, called for both the "assimilation" of the Jews into the surrounding society and a strong solidarity with coreligionists throughout the world. French "republican Judaism" saw only harmony between these nominally dichotomous notions. Later historical developments should not obscure the reality and appeal of this ideology as the foundation over which was erected the Jewish identity of modern French Jewry.

Within the context of the ideology of emancipation, solidarity also brought with it a missionary zeal to remake other Jewish communities in the idealized image of modern French Jewry. In the final analysis, one can interpret the function of the educational endeavors of the Alliance in modern Jewish history as the particular conduit through which a French version of the European Haskalah reached Sephardi and Oriental Jewish communities. The Alliance teachers formed an indigenous elite imbued with the principles of this Haskalah. They created an important bridge between Western and Eastern Judaism in the modern period by popularizing through the Alliance mass educational system the message of this ideology.

But there was an added, ultimately fatal twist. This encounter between Western and Eastern Jewry occurred in the age of imperialism. With the European domination of the Middle East and North Africa, the agenda of reform became that of westernization, whether accepted as a necessity for survival by the local elites or imposed from above by Western interests. Westernized elites, fervent reformers of their societies, came into being in all Muslim lands. In this context, the Alliance teachers were also the Jewish counterparts of the Muslim reformers. The admiration for the West and a certain critique of the East were shared by both groups. But there was ultimately one major difference. The teachers were unconditional and devoted supporters of the European presence in the area, whereas the Muslim reformers eventually adopted that most European of ideologies, nationalism, to rid their countries of the imperialists.

The letters produced by the teachers closely resemble the writings of the European, especially East European, adepts of the Haskalah, the maskilim engaged in a critique of traditional Jewish society. However, because of the context in which these texts are anchored, the triumphalist discourse of European domination structures their tonality, observations, percep-

*tions, and representational strategies, revealing to the reader the universe
of the native radical westernizer in identification with the West.*

*The new orientation toward the West was eventually shared by many
Jews of the Middle East and North Africa, although rarely reaching the
ideological extremes revealed in the letters of the teachers. This was firmly
rooted in the appreciation of the precarious nature of the existence of the
Jews as a minority group in the lands of Islam. The* dhimma *that had for
centuries set the status of the Jews as a tolerated but inferior group was no
longer in operation due to European presence and influence. The political
and economic decline of the Muslim world in the preceding centuries,
with the consequent growth of chaos and anarchy, had heightened the
sense of insecurity among the non-Muslim communities. For them, the
European presence meant security first, then economic opportunity, especially for groups that had traditionally acted as middlemen, and finally
offered the promise of equality.*

*This package proved impossible to resist. For the Alliance teacher, who
as a result of his or her schooling was already ideologically predisposed to
look up to Europe as the repository of all that was positive, the commitment to the West became unconditional. Consequently, the message of the*
Haskalah *imbibed at the* Ecole Normale Israélite Orientale *was radical-
ized further by the teacher to mean total westernization, the wholesale
adoption of Western culture and way of life by Eastern Jews.*

*The role of the Alliance schools and of the education and instruction
dispensed by the Alliance teachers in shaping the contours of the Sephardi
and Eastern Jewish encounter with the West was highly significant. In the
age of imperialism, such an encounter was all but inevitable. But the
Alliance teacher mediated this encounter, presenting the West to the Sephardi and Eastern Jews in a Jewish context and making it more palatable
and attractive. Over and above this ideological model provided by the
teacher, he or she also dispensed a crucial economic commodity: the
mastery of the French language. This ability not only opened new horizons but facilitated economic links with the West, which were so important
for upward social mobility—hence the popularity of the Alliance schools.*

*The drama in which the Alliance teachers became actors was one in
which the irruption of the West led, whether in rejection, adaptation, or
assimilation, to a fundamental reorientation of state, society, and economy in the lands of Islam in the modern period. In this process, the Jews
embarked upon a path that eventually led them to a radical cultural and
political dissociation from their traditional moorings. In contrast to the
European Jewish situation, the issue of convergence with the surrounding
society did not emerge as the central challenge of the modern period. The
opposite proved the case. Sephardi and Eastern Jewries experienced the*

*vagaries of "acculturation" and "assimilation." But the matrix of Euro-
pean domination dictated that these were in the direction of a culture and
civilization distant from the locality. This route rendered them singularly
ill-adapted to survive the departure of the West from the region and the
creation of nation-states with their own conflictual approach to minorities. The Arab-Israeli conflict proved to be the last straw for an already
problematic relationship and brought in its wake the mass departures of
Jews from the lands of Islam. The letters of the Alliance teachers, themselves the products of the fundamental reconfiguration of the place of the
Jews in Muslim lands, present and re-present through one particular looking glass the landscape of the Jews in the lands of Islam in the final
decades of their existence.*

Glossary

Definitions of Arabic, Hebrew, Persian, and Turkish Terms as Used in the Letters

agha. Powerful landowner.

Allah kerim. "God is kind."

amin. Head or superintendent of a trade guild.

bakalum (bakalım). "We will see."

dar al Makhzan. Palace; the central administration in Morocco.

dayanim. Jewish judges.

dönme. Descendants of Jews who followed the false messiah Sabbetai Sevi. They converted to Islam in the seventeenth century, yet maintained their own secret rites.

drashah. A disquisition on the Holy Scriptures.

duar. Camp.

fellah. Peasant.

firman. Decree.

galut. Exile.

hakham. Name given to rabbis in the Middle East; also the name for teachers in the traditional schools.

hakham-bashi. Chief Rabbi.

halukah. Donations from diaspora Jewry to support a religious Jewish presence in the Holy Land.

Hara. The Jewish quarter in Tunis.

hazanim. Cantors.

heder. Jewish traditional school.

herem. Excommunication.

irade. Decree.

ivri. Hebrew.

kadi. Muslim judge.

kadish. A traditional Jewish prayer to commemorate the dead.

kaid. Muslim governor of town or area.

kasbah. The citadel and the surrounding area in a North African town inhabited by the representatives of the central authority as well as by other Muslims.

kefir. Someone judged impure according to the Islamic faith.

kif. Snuff.

maamad. Meeting of the Jewish community council; also used to refer to the council itself.

Makhzan. Palace; also used to refer to the government of the Sultan of Morocco.

Medina. Muslim quarter of North African town.

mehalla. A quarter in a city.

Mellah. Jewish quarter of North African town.

meshuar. Citadel.

midrashim. Jewish religious elementary schools.

muezzin. One who calls Muslims to prayer.

mursheh. Bailiff in Jewish court, who sometimes also argues cases.

mushtehed. High priest of Islam.

nedjes. Impurity ascribed to non-Muslims.

ouzara. Islamic civil court.

reis yahudah. Leader of the Jews.

sayid. Muslim clergyman in Iran.

shaliah. Collector of the *halukah.*

sheikh-al-yahud. Leader of the Jews.

shohetim. Ritual slaughterers of animals.

souk. Market.

talit. Jewish prayer shawl.

Talmud-Torah (pl. *Talmudei-Torah*). Traditional Jewish school.

taref. Ritually unclean.

ulema. Muslim clergy.

yeshiva (pl. *yeshivot*). Academy of higher Jewish religious instruction.

Bibliography

Archival and Published Primary Sources

ARCHIVES OF THE ALLIANCE ISRAÉLITE UNIVERSELLE

Files: Algérie, Egypte, France, Grèce, Irak, Iran, Israël, Liban, Lybie, Maroc, Suisse, Syrie, Tunisie, Turquie.

PUBLICATIONS OF THE ALLIANCE ISRAÉLITE UNIVERSELLE
(IN CHRONOLOGICAL ORDER)

Alliance Israélite Universelle. Paris, 1860.
L'oeuvre des écoles. Paris, 1863.
Bulletin Semestriel de l'Alliance Israélite Universelle. 1860/1865–1913.
Brochure publiée à l'occasion du 25ᵉ anniversaire de la fondation de l'oeuvre. Paris, 1885.
L'Alliance Israélite Universelle, 1860–1895. Paris, 1895.
Bigart, Jacques. *L'Alliance Israélite: Son action éducatrice.* Paris, 1900.
Instructions générales pour les professeurs. Paris, 1903.
Revue des Ecoles de l'Alliance Israélite. 1901–4.
Bulletin des Ecoles de l'Alliance Israélite. 1901–4.

Select Bibliography on the Alliance Israélite Universelle, French Jewry, and the Jews of Muslim Lands in Modern Times

Abitbol, Michel. *Témoins et acteurs: Les Corcos et l'histoire du Maroc contemporain.* Jerusalem: Yad Ben-Zvi, 1977.
———. *Judaïsme d'Afrique du Nord au XIXᵉ et XXᵉ siècles.* Jerusalem: Yad Ben-Zvi, 1980.
———. "The Encounter between French Jewry and the Jews of North Africa: Analysis of a Discourse (1830–1914)." In *The Jews in Modern France,* edited by Frances Malino and Bernard Wasserstein, 31–53. Hanover, N.H.: University Press of New England, 1985.
———. *The Jews of North Africa during the Second World War.* Detroit: Wayne State University Press, 1989.
———. "La citoyenneté imposée: Du décret Crémieux à la guerre d'Algérie."

In *Histoire politique des Juifs de France,* edited by Pierre Birnbaum, 196–217. Paris: Fondation Nationale des Sciences Politiques, 1990.

Ahmad, Feroz. "Unionist Relations with the Greek, Armenian, and Jewish Communities of the Ottoman Empire, 1908–1914." In *Christians and Jews in the Ottoman Empire,* edited by Benjamin Braude and Bernard Lewis, 1:401–34. New York: Holmes and Meier, 1982.

Ahroni, Reuben. *Yemenite Jewry: Origins, culture, and literature.* Bloomington: Indiana University Press, 1986.

Albert, Phyllis. *The Modernization of French Jewry: Consistory and Community in the Nineteenth Century.* Hanover, N.H.: University Press of New England, 1977.

———. "Ethnicity and Jewish Solidarity in Nineteenth-Century France." In *Mystics, Philosophers, and Politicians: Essays in Jewish Intellectual History in Honor of Alexander Altmann,* edited by Jehuda Reinharz and Daniel Swetschinski, 249–74. Durham, N.C.: Duke University Press, 1982.

———. "L'intégration et la persistance de l'éthnicité chez les Juifs dans la France moderne." In *Histoire politique des Juifs de France,* edited by Pierre Birnbaum, 221–43. Paris: Fondation Nationale des Sciences Politiques, 1990.

Allali, Jean-Pierre, et al., eds. *Les Juifs de Tunisie: Images et textes.* Paris: Editions du Scribe, 1989.

Allouche, Jean-Luc, et al., eds. *Les Juifs d'Algérie: Images et textes.* Paris: Editions du Scribe, 1987.

Allouche-Benayoun, Joëlle, and Doris Bensimon, eds. *Juifs d'Algérie hier et aujourd'hui: Mémoires et identités.* Toulouse: Privat, 1989.

Angel, Marc D. *The Jews of Rhodes: The History of a Sephardic Community.* New York: Sepher-Hermon Press, 1978.

———. *Voices in Exile: A Study in Sephardic Intellectual History.* Hoboken, N.J.: Ktav Publishing House, in association with Sephardic House, 1991.

Ansky, Michel. *Les Juifs d'Algérie: Du décret Crémieux à la libération.* Paris: Editions du Centre, 1950.

Arberry, A. J., ed. *Religion in the Middle East: Three Religions in Concord and Conflict.* 2 vols. Cambridge: Cambridge University Press, 1976.

Attal, Robert. *Les Juifs d'Afrique du Nord: Bibliographie.* Jerusalem: Yad Ben-Zvi, 1973.

Attal, Robert, and Claude Sitbon, eds. *Regards sur les Juifs de Tunisie.* Paris: Albin Michel, 1979.

Ayoun, Richard, and Bernard Cohen. *Les Juifs d'Algérie: Deux mille ans d'histoire.* Paris: J. C. Lattès, 1982.

Bahloul, Joëlle. *Le culte de la table dressée: Rites et traditions de la table juive algérienne.* Paris: Editions Metailie, 1983.

———. *La maison de mémoire: Éthnologie d'une demeure judéo-arabe en Algérie, 1937–1961.* Paris: Editions Metailie, 1992.

Barnett, Richard D., and W. M. Schwab, eds. *The Sephardi Heritage.* 2 vols. New York: Ktav; Grendon, Northants: Gibraltar Books, 1971–89.

Bat Ye'or. *Le Dhimmi: Profil de l'opprimé en Orient et en Afrique du Nord depuis la conquête arabe.* Paris: Editions Anthropos, 1980.

Ben Ami, Issachar, ed. *The Sepharadi and Oriental Jewish Heritage.* 2 vols. Jerusalem: Magnes Press, 1982.

Benardete, Mair Jose. *Hispanic Culture and Character of the Sephardic Jews.* New York: Hispanic Institute in the United States, 1953.

Benbassa, Esther. "Presse d'Istanbul et de Salonique au service du sionisme (1908–1914): Les motifs d'une allégeance." *Revue Historique* 276 (1986): 337–65.

———. "Haim Nahum Effendi, dernier Grand Rabbin de l'Empire ottoman (1908–1920): Son rôle politique et diplomatique." Thèse de doctorat d'état ès lettres, Université de Paris III, 1987.

———. "Israël face à lui même: Judaïsme occidental et judaïsme ottoman (19e– 20e siècles)." *Pardès* 7 (1988): 105–29.

———. "Le sionisme dans l'Empire ottoman à l'aube du 20e siècle." *Vingtième Siècle* 24 (1989): 69–80.

———. *Un Grand Rabbin sépharade en politique, 1892–1923.* Paris: Presses du CNRS, 1990.

———. "Comment être non-Musulman en terre d'Islam." *L'Histoire* 134 (1990): 86–91.

———. "L'éducation féminine en Orient: L'école de filles de l'Alliance Israélite Universelle à Galata, Istanbul (1879–1912)." *Histoire, Economie et Société* 4 (1991): 529–59.

———. "Le sionisme et la politique des alliances dans les communautés juives ottomanes (début XXe siècle)." *Revue des Etudes Juives* 150 (1991): 107–31.

Benbassa, Esther, and Aron Rodrigue. "L'artisanat juif en Turquie à la fin du XIXe siècle: L'Alliance Israélite Universelle et ses oeuvres d'apprentissage." *Turcica* 17 (1985): 113–26.

Benbassa, Esther, with Aron Rodrigue. *Une vie judéo-espagnole à l'Est: Gabriel Arié.* Paris: Cerf, 1992.

Benveniste, Annie. "Le rôle des institutrices de l'Alliance Israélite à Salonique." *Combat pour la Diaspora* 8 (1982): 13–26.

———. *Le Bosphore à la Roquette: La communauté judéo-espagnole à Paris (1914–1940).* Paris: L'Harmattan, 1989.

Berkovitz, Jay R. *The Shaping of Jewish Identity in Nineteenth Century France.* Detroit: Wayne State University Press, 1989.

Birnbaum, Pierre. *Les fous de la République: Histoire politique des Juifs d'Etat de Gambetta à Vichy.* Paris: Fayard, 1992.

———, ed. *Histoire politique des Juifs en France.* Paris: Presses de la Fondation Nationale des Sciences Politiques, 1990.

Braude, Benjamin, and Bernard Lewis, eds. *Christians and Jews in the Ottoman Empire: The Functioning of a Plural Society.* 2 vols. New York: Holmes and Meier, 1982.

Bunis, David. *Sephardic Studies: A Research Bibliography Incorporating Judez-*

mo Language, Literature, and Folklore and Historical Background. New York: Garland, 1981.

Burrows, Matthew. "'Mission civilisatrice': French Cultural Policy in the Middle East, 1860–1914." *Historical Journal* 29 (1986): 109–35.

Cabasso, Gilbert, et al., eds. *Juifs d'Egypte: Images et textes.* Paris: Editions du Scribe, 1984.

Cazès, David. *Essai sur l'histoire des Israélites de Tunisie.* Paris: Durlacher, 1888.

Chouraqui, André. *Cent ans d'histoire: L'Alliance Israélite Universelle et la renaissance juive contemporaine (1860–1960).* Paris: Presses Universitaires de France, 1965.

_____. *Between East and West: A History of the Jews of North Africa.* Translated by Michael M. Bernet. Philadelphia: Jewish Publication Society, 1969.

_____. *Histoire des Juifs en Afrique du Nord.* Paris: Hachette, 1985.

Cohen, Avraham. "Iranian Jewry and the Educational Endeavors of the AIU." *Jewish Social Studies* 48 (Winter 1986): 15–44.

Cohen, Eliahou. "L'influence intellectuelle et sociale des ècoles de l'Alliance Israélite Universelle sur les Israélites du Proche-Orient." Thèse de doctorat, Université de Paris, 1962.

Cohen, Hayyim. *The Jews of the Middle East, 1860–1972.* New York: Wiley, 1973.

Covo, Mercado J. "Contribution à l'histoire des institutions scolaires de la communauté israélite de Salonique jusqu'à la fondation de l'école des garçons de l'Alliance Israélite Universelle." *Almanach Nationale au Profit de l'Hôpital de Hirsch* 8 (1916): 97–103.

Davison, Roderic H. "Turkish Attitudes concerning Christian-Muslim Equality in the Nineteenth Century." *American Historical Review* 59 (1954): 844–64.

Deshen, Shlomo A. *The Mellah Society: Jewish Community Life in Sherifian Morocco.* Chicago: University of Chicago Press, 1989.

De Felice, Renzo. *Jews in an Arab Land: Libya, 1835–1970.* Translated by Judith Roumani. Austin: University of Texas Press, 1985.

Dermenjian, Genèvieve. *Juifs et Européens d'Algèrie: L'antisémitisme oranais, 1892–1905.* Jerusalem: Yad Ben-Zvi, 1983.

Deshen, Shlomo, and Walter Zenner, eds. *Jewish Societies in the Middle East: Community, Culture, and Authority.* Washington, D.C.: University Press of America, 1982.

Djait, Hichem. *L'Europe et l'Islam.* Paris: Collections Esprit/Seuil, 1978.

Dumont, Paul. "La condition juive en Turquie à la fin du XIXe siècle." *Les Nouveaux Cahiers* 57 (Summer 1979): 25–38.

_____. "Une source pour l'étude des communautés juives en Turquie: Les archives de l'Alliance Israélite Universelle." *Journal Asiatique* 267 (1979): 101–35.

_____. "La structure sociale de la communauté juive de Salonique à la fin du dix-neuvième siècle." *Revue Historique* 263 (1980): 351–93.

_____. "Jewish Communities in Turkey during the last Decades of the Nineteenth Century in the Light of the Archives of the Alliance Israélite Universelle." In *Christians and Jews in the Ottoman Empire,* edited by Benjamin Braude and Bernard Lewis, 1:209–42. New York: Holmes and Meier, 1982.

Ettinger, Shmuel, ed. *History of Jews in Islamic Countries.* In Hebrew. 3 vols. Jerusalem: Zalman Shazar Center, 1981–86.

Farhi, David. "The Jews of Salonica in the Young Turk Revolution." In Hebrew. *Sefunot* 15 (1971–81): 135–52.

Fattal, Antoine. *Le statut légal des non-Musulmans en pays d'Islam.* Beirut: Imprimerie Catholique, 1958.

Franco, Moïse. *Essai sur l'histoire des Israélites de l'Empire ottoman.* Reprint. Paris: Centre d'Etudes Don Isaac Abravanel/U.I.S.F., 1980.

Galanté, Abraham. *Histoire des Juifs de Turquie.* Reprint. 9 vols. Istanbul: Isis, 1985.

Gelber, N. M. "An Attempt to Internationalize Salonika." *Jewish Social Studies* 17 (1955): 105–20.

Gerber, Jane S. *The Jews of Spain: A History of the Sephardic Experience.* New York: Free Press, 1992.

Girard, Patrick. *Les Juifs de France de 1789 à 1860: De l'émancipation à l'égalité.* Paris: Calmann-Lévy, 1976.

Goitein, Shlomo Dov. *Jews and Arabs.* New York: Schocken, 1955.

Goldberg, Harvey. *Jewish Life in Muslim Libya: Rivals and Relatives.* Chicago: University of Chicago Press, 1990.

———, ed. *The Book of Mordechai: A Study of the Jews of Libya.* Philadelphia: Institute for the Study of Human Issues, 1980.

Graetz, Michael. *Les Juifs en France au XIXe siècle: De la Révolution française à l'Alliance Israélite Universelle.* Translated by Salomon Malka. Paris: Seuil, 1989.

Grunwald, Kurt. *TürkenHirsch: A Study of Baron Maurice de Hirsch, Entrepreneur and Philanthropist.* Jerusalem: Israel Programs for Scientific Translation, 1966.

Haramati, Shlomoh. *Three Who Preceded Ben Yehudah.* In Hebrew. Jerusalem: Yad Ben-Zvi, 1978.

Hertzberg, Arthur. *The French Enlightenment and the Jews.* New York: Columbia University Press; Philadelphia, Jewish Publication Society of America, 1968.

Hirschberg, H. Z. *A History of the Jews in North Africa.* 2 vols. Leiden: E. J. Brill, 1974–81.

Hyman, Paula. *From Dreyfus to Vichy: The Remaking of French Jewry, 1906–1939.* New York: Columbia University Press, 1979.

———. *The Emancipation of the Jews of Alsace: Acculturation and Tradition in the Nineteenth Century.* New Haven: Yale University Press, 1991.

Israël, Gérard. *L'Alliance Israélite Universelle, 1860–1960: Cent ans d'efforts pour la libération et la promotion de l'homme par l'homme.* Paris: AIU, 1960.

Kedourie, Elie. "The Alliance Israélite Universelle, 1860–1960." *Jewish Journal of Sociology* 9 (June 1967): 92–99.

———. "Young Turks, Free-Masons, and Jews." *Middle Eastern Studies* 7 (1971): 89–104.

———. "The Jews of Baghdad." *Middle Eastern Studies* 7 (1971): 355–61.

Krämer, Gudrun. *The Jews in Modern Egypt, 1914–1952.* Seattle: University of Washington Press, 1989.

Landau, Jacob. *Jews in Nineteenth Century Egypt.* New York: New York University Press, 1969.

Laqueur, Walter. *A History of Zionism.* New York: Holt, Rinehart and Winston, 1972.

Laskier, Michael M. *The Alliance Israélite Universelle and the Jewish Communities of Morocco, 1862–1962.* Albany, N.Y.: SUNY Press, 1983.

———. "Aspects of the Activities of the Alliance Israélite Universelle in the Jewish Communities of the Middle East and North Africa: 1860–1918." *Modern Judaism* 3 (May 1983): 147–72.

———. "Avraham Albert Antebi: Aspects of His Activities in the Years 1897–1914." In Hebrew. *Peamim* 21 (1984): 50–82.

———. "The Alliance Israélite Universelle and the Social Conditions of the Jewish Communities in the Mediterranean Basin (1860–1914)." In *L'"Alliance" dans les communautés du bassin méditerranéen à la fin du 19ᵉᵐᵉ siècle et son influence sur la situation sociale et culturelle,* edited by Simon Schwarzfuchs, lxxi–lxxxvii. Jerusalem: Misgav Yerushalayim, 1987.

———. *The Jews of Egypt, 1920–1970.* New York: New York University Press, 1992.

Lazare, Lucien. "L'Alliance Israélite Universelle en Palestine à l'époque de la révolution des 'Jeunes Turcs' et sa mission en Orient du 29 octobre 1908 au 19 janvier 1909." *Revue des Etudes Juives* 138 (July–December 1979): 307–35.

Leibovici, Sarah. *Si tu fais le bien.* Paris: AIU, 1983.

———. *Chronique des Juifs de Tétouan (1860–1896).* Paris: Maisonneuve et Larose, 1984.

Leven, Narcisse. *Cinquante ans d'histoire: L'Alliance Israélite Universelle (1860–1910).* 2 vols. Paris: Félix Alcan, 1911–20.

Levy, Avigdor. *The Sephardim in the Ottoman Empire.* Princeton, N.J.: Darwin Press, 1992.

Lewis, Bernard. *The Middle East and the West.* Bloomington: Indiana University Press, 1964.

———. *The Emergence of Modern Turkey.* 2d ed. London: Oxford University Press, 1968.

———. *The Muslim Discovery of Europe.* New York: W. W. Norton, 1982.

———. *The Jews of Islam.* Princeton, N.J.: Princeton University Press, 1984.

———. *Semites and Anti-Semites: An Inquiry into Conflict and Prejudice.* New York and London: W. W. Norton, 1986.

Lipman, Sonia, and Vivian D. Lipman, eds. *The Century of Moses Montefiore.* Oxford: Oxford University Press, 1985.

Loeb, Laurence. *Outcaste: Jewish Life in Southern Iran.* New York: Gordon and Breach, 1977.

Malino, Frances. *The Sephardic Jews of Bordeaux: Assimilation and Emancipa-*

tion in Revolutionary and Napoleonic France. Tuscaloosa: University of Alabama Press, 1978.

Malino, Frances, and Bernard Wasserstein, eds. *The Jews in Modern France.* Hanover, N.H.: University Press of New England, 1985.

Marrus, Michael. *The Politics of Assimilation: A Study of the French Jewish Community at the Time of the Dreyfus Affair.* New York and Oxford: Oxford University Press, 1971.

Marrus, Michael R., and Robert O. Paxton, eds. *Vichy France and the Jews.* New York: Basic Books, 1981.

Memmi, Albert. *The Coloniser and the Colonised.* Translated by Howard Greenfeld. New York: Orion Press, 1965.

———. *La statue du sel.* Paris: Gallimard, 1966.

Navon, A. H. "La fondation de l'école de l'Alliance à Andrianople." *Paix et Droit* 3 (April 1923): 13–15.

———. "Contribution à l'histoire de la fondation des écoles de l'Alliance Israélite Universelle." *Le Judaïsme Séphardi* 1 (July 1932): 8–9.

———. "Contribution à l'histoire de la fondation des écoles de l'Alliance Israélite Universelle." *Le Judaïsme Séphardi* 4 (November 1932): 64–66.

———. *Les 70 ans de l'Ecole Normale Israélite Orientale.* Paris: Durlacher, 1935.

Nehama, Joseph. *Histoire des Israélites de Salonique.* 7 vols. Paris: Durlacher; Thessaloniki: Molho, 1935–78.

Patai, Raphael. *The Seed of Abraham: Jews and Arabs in Contact and Conflict.* Salt Lake City: University of Utah Press, 1986.

Raphael, Chaim. *The Road from Babylon: The Story of Sephardi and Oriental Jewry.* New York: Harper and Row, 1985.

Rejwan, Nissim. *The Jews of Iraq: 3,000 Years of History and Culture.* Boulder, Colo.: Westview Press, 1985.

Rodrigue, Aron. "Jewish Society and Schooling in a Thracian Town: The Alliance Israélite Universelle in Demotica, 1897–1924." *Jewish Social Studies* 45 (Summer–Fall 1983): 263–86.

———. "The Alliance Israélite Universelle and the Attempt to Reform Rabbinical and Religious Instruction in Turkey." In *L'"Alliance" dans les communautés du bassin méditerranéen à la fin du 19eme siècle et son influence sur la situation sociale et culturelle,* edited by Simon Schwarzfuchs, liii–lxx. Jerusalem: Misgav Yerushalayim, 1987.

———. "L'éxportation du paradigme révolutionnaire: Son influence sur le judaïsme sépharade et oriental." In *Histoire politique des Juifs de France,* edited by Pierre Birnbaum, 182–95. Paris: Fondation Nationale des Sciences Politiques, 1990.

———. *French Jews, Turkish Jews: The Alliance Israélite Universelle and the Politics of Jewish Schooling in Turkey, 1860–1925.* Bloomington: Indiana University Press, 1990.

———, ed. *Ottoman and Turkish Jewry: Community and Leadership.* Indiana University Turkish Studies Series. Bloomington, 1992.

Roland, Joan Gardner. "The Alliance Israélite Universelle and French Policy in North Africa, 1860–1918." Ph.D. diss., Columbia University, 1969.

Saguès, Albert. *Deux organisations de défense du judaïsme: Le sionisme et l'Alliance Israélite.* Tunis: M. Zarcka, 1920.

Sassoon, David S. *A History of the Jews of Baghdad.* Letchworth: Solomon D. Sassoon, 1949.

Schroeter, Daniel. *Merchants of Essaouira: Urban Society and Imperialism in Southwestern Morocco, 1844–1886.* Cambridge: Cambridge University Press, 1988.

Schwarzfuchs, Simon. *Les Juifs de France.* Paris: Albin Michel, 1975.

―――. *Napoleon, the Jews and the Sanhedrin.* London: Routledge and Kegan Paul, 1979.

―――. *Les Juifs d'Algérie et la France, 1830–1855.* Jerusalem: Yad Ben-Zvi, 1981.

―――. *Du Juif à l'Israélite: Histoire d'une mutation, 1770–1870.* Paris: Fayard, 1989.

―――, ed. *L'"Alliance" dans les communautés du bassin méditerranéen à la fin du 19ᵉᵐᵉ siècle et son influence sur la situation sociale et culturelle.* Jerusalem: Misgav Yerushalayim, 1987.

Sebag, Paul. *Histoire des Juifs de Tunisie: Des origines à nos jours.* Paris: L'Harmattan, 1991.

Sémach, Yomtov D. *A travers les communautés israélites d'Orient.* Paris: Durlacher, 1931.

Shamir, Shimon. *The Jews of Egypt: A Mediterranean Society in Modern Times.* Boulder, Colo.: Westview Press, 1987.

Shaw, Stanford J. *The Jews of the Ottoman Empire and the Turkish Republic.* New York: New York University Press, 1991.

Shaw, Stanford J., and Ezel Kural Shaw. *History of the Ottoman Empire and Modern Turkey.* 2 vols. New York: Cambridge University Press, 1976–77.

Shorrock, William. *French Imperialism in the Middle East.* Madison: University of Wisconsin Press, 1976.

Silberman, Paul. "An Investigation of the Schools Operated by the Alliance Israélite Universelle from 1862 to 1940." Ph.D. diss., New York University, 1973.

Simon, Rachel. *Change within Tradition among Jewish Women in Libya.* Seattle: University of Washington Press, 1992.

Slouschz, Nahum. *Travels in North Africa.* Philadelphia: Jewish Publication Society, 1927.

Stillman, Norman. *The Jews of Arab Lands: A History and Source Book.* Philadelphia: Jewish Publication Society, 1979.

―――. *The Jews of Arab Lands in Modern Times.* Philadelphia: Jewish Publication Society, 1991.

Szajkowski, Zosa. "Conflicts in the AIU and the Founding of the Anglo-Jewish Association, the Vienna Allianz, and the Hilfsverein." *Jewish Social Studies* 19 (January–April 1957): 29–50.

————. "Jewish Diplomacy: Notes on the Occasion of the Centenary of the Alliance Israélite Universelle." *Jewish Social Studies* 22 (July 1960): 131–58.

————. "The Schools of the Alliance Israelite Universelle." *Historia Judaica* 22 (1960): 3–22.

Thobie, Jacques. "La France a-t-elle une politique culturelle dans l'Empire ottoman à la veille de la première guerre mondiale?" *Relations Internationales* 25 (Spring 1981): 21–40.

Tritton, A. S. *The Caliphs and Their Non-Muslim Subjects: A Critical Study of the Covenant of Umar.* London: Humphrey Milford, 1930.

Udovitch, Abraham L., and Lucette Valensi. *The Last Arab Jews: The Communities of Jerba, Tunisia.* New York: Harwood Academic, 1984.

Valensi, Lucette. "La tour de Babel: Groupes et relations ethniques au Moyen Orient et en Afrique du Nord." *Annales E.S.C.* 4 (July–August 1986): 817–35.

Weiker, Walter. *Ottomans, Turks and the Jewish Polity: A History of the Jews of Turkey.* New York and London: Jerusalem Center for Public Affairs and University Press of America, 1992.

Weill, Georges. "Charles Netter ou les oranges de Jaffa." *Les Nouveaux Cahiers* 21 (Summer 1970): 2–36.

————. "Emancipation et humanisme: Le discours idéologique de l'Alliance Israélite Universelle au XIXᵉ siècle." *Les Nouveaux Cahiers* 52 (Spring 1978): 1–20.

————. "The Alliance Israélite Universelle and the Emancipation of the Jewish Communities of the Mediterranean." *Jewish Journal of Sociology* 24 (1982): 117–34.

————. "L'action éducative de l'Alliance Israélite Universelle de 1860 à 1914." *Les Nouveaux Cahiers* 78 (Fall 1984): 51–58.

————. "L'Alliance Israélite Universelle et la condition sociale des communautés méditerranéennes à la fin du XIXᵉ siècle (1860–1914)." In *L'"Alliance" dans les communautés du bassin méditerranéen à la fin du 19ᵉᵐᵉ siècle et son influence sur la situation sociale et culturelle,* edited by Simon Schwarzfuchs, vii–lii. Jerusalem: Misgav Yerushalayim, 1987.

Zafrani, Haim. *Mille ans de vie juive au Maroc.* Paris: Maisonneuve et Larose, 1983.

Index of Personal Names

Abdul Hamid II, 243*n12,* 263–64
Abensour, Raphaël, 84
Albala, Nissim, 188–95
Alchalel, Aron, 76–77
Antébi, Albert, 100–101, 195–98
Arié, Gabriel, 51, 51*nn22,23,* 96–97, 99, 181–83
Aron, Captain, 45

Béhar, Fortunée, 34, 43
Béhar, Nissim, 34, 43, 51, 137–39, 195–96, 195*n3*
Béhar, Rachel, 34, 43
Bénaroya, Fanny, 89–91
Benbassat, Mr., 52
Benchimol, N., 82–84
Benghiat, Moïse, 186–87, 232–35
Ben-Meir, Mr., 285
Benveniste, Abraham, 133–34, 166–70
Bigart, Jacques, 55, 62–65, 188, 191, 211, 257–59
Bischoffsheim, Mr. Louis Raphaël and Mrs., 13, 44
Bloch, A., 110
Bloch, Félix, 34, 43
Bloch, Florentine, 43
Bloch, Mr. and Mrs., 42
Brasseur, Adolphe, 259–62
Buisson, Ferdinand, 35, 45

Carmona, Elie, 208–11
Carré, I., 35
Cattawi, Moses, 164
Cazès, Abraham, 48
Cazès, David, 14, 34, 51, 51*n23,* 94, 135–37, 156–58, 179–81, 182, 198, 200, 200*n5,* 230–31
Cohen, Moïse, 252–56
Cohen, Y., 75–76, 114–16, 127–28, 144–46
Confino, Albert, 47–48, 52–55, 58, 60–65, 103–4, 153–56, 178
Conquy, Joseph, 211–12
Corcos, [Hayim?], 208
Coriat, Messody, 85–89, 98

Danon, Israël, 40
Danon, Vitalis, 225–28
Deinar, Mr., 249
Dépasse, Dr., 45
Dohm, Wilhelm Christian, 288
Douec, Dj., 91–93

Elmaleh, Amram, 149–50, 187–88
Eskénazi, Mr., 65–67

Falcon, Nissim, 211
Franco, Albert, 263–65
Franco, Moïse, 111–12, 130, 142–44, 164–66, 245–48
Franco, Y., 173–75
Fresco, Moïse, 51, 51*n23,* 116–17, 127, 127*n3,* 130–31

Goldschmidt, Mr. Salomon and Mrs., 13
Graetz, Heinrich, 110
Guéron, Mrs. A., 238–44
Guéron, Lazare, 78–79, 158–62, 213

Hadj-Abd-El-Selam, 207
Halévi, Joseph, 35
Halff, Sylvain, 285–86
Hay, Sir Drummond, 206
Hazan, Behor David, 181
Herzl, Theodor, 259
Hirsch, Baroness Clara de, 13, 35
Hirsch, Baron Maurice de, 13, 95, 95*n4,* 96
Hirsch, Samuel, 94
Hochberg, Samuel, 53–54, 178, 259
Holzmann, Dr., 183–84

Isaac, Mrs., 35

Jabotinsky, Vladimir, 253

Kadoorie, Elly, 191
Kadoorie, Laura, 191
Kann, Sacki, 63, 63*n28*

Laredo, Moïse, 277–78
Lebé, Mr., 266
Lemoine, Mr., 45
Leriche, Mr., 212
Lesseps, Ferdinand de, 189
Lessing, Gotthold Ephraim, 287–88
Levaillant, Isaïe, 35
Leven, Georges, 259, 259n5
Leven, Narcisse, 63, 64, 217n2, 259n5
Lévy, Bernard, 205–6
Lévy, Moïse, 183–85, 206–8
Lévy, Rachel, 51, 51n23
Levy, Shalom, 190
Loeb, Isidore, 45, 63, 63n27
Loria, Jacques, 51n23, 52–53, 61, 250–51, 259
Loria, L., 175–78
Loubaton, Léon, 121–24, 198–200, 265–66
Loupo, Samuel, 47
Lyautey, Maréchal Louis, 188, 217n2

Mangin, Charles, 147
Marx, Maurice, 34, 46, 47
Matalon, Joseph, 139–42
Méana, Mr., 212
Mefano, Robert, 276–77
Melchett, Lord (Sir Alfred Mond), 277
Menda, Ezra, 279–84
Mendelssohn, Moses, 287–88, 289
Montefiore, Sir Moses, 205
Morali, Mr., 110
Moyal, Albert, 150–53
Munk, Salomon, 110

Nahon, Moïse, 51n23, 74–75, 84–85, 107–10, 126–27
Nataf, Elie, 79, 119–21, 131–33, 214–16
Nathan, Elie, 251–52, 273–75
Navon, A. H., 37, 38, 40, 49, 51n23, 65, 118–19, 128–30
Nehama, Joseph, 51n23, 236–38, 248–50
Netter, Charles, 46, 94, 196, 196n4
Niégo, Joseph, 97–98

Oppert, Mr., 260
Ottolenghi, Moses, Rabbi, 248, 248n3
Ouziel, Clément, 222–25, 252, 275–76

Palatche, Abraham, 182
Parienté, Samuel, 95–96, 183
Penso, Elie, 170–72, 284–85
Pisa, Mr., 213
Polako, Dudu de, 182
Poliakoff, Chief Rabbi, 255

Rabban, Joseph, 191
Reinach, Salomon, 260, 260n6
Reinach, Theodore, 110
Ruff, Mrs., 104
Russell, Lord John, 205

Sabbah, Joseph, 51n23
Saguès, Albert, 30–33, 54–55, 57–60, 146–48, 185–86, 212–14, 287–89
Salzer, Hélène, 51
Sasson, Ezechiel, Effendi, 191
Sassoon, David, 191, 278
Schamoon, Ezechiel, 35
Sciuto, Lucien, 250
Sémach, Félicie [Mrs. Weismann], 42–44, 51
Sémach, Yomtov David, 51, 102, 217, 218–22
Se-El-Ar'bi-ben Abbou, 207
Shahebandar, Dr., 280
Slousch, Nahum, 37
Sol, Mrs., 104
Somekh, Samuel, 162–64

Toledo, Mr., 52
Torrès, Si, 207
Trenel, Mr., 45

Ungar, Sara, 51

Valadji, Jacques, 113–14, 148–49
Valensi, Joseph, 160
Valensi, General Gabriel, 160

Weill, Mr., 42
Weill-Kahn, Miss, 35

Zilberstein, A., 266–73

Index of Place Names

(see also table 2)

Acre, 166
Adrianople, 12, 34, 39, 42, 43, 128, 142–44, 165, 166, 168, 198, 231, 238–44
Afrine, 282
Agadir, 265–66
Aleppo, 166, 170–72, 189, 246, 268, 279–84
Alexandretta, 170
Alexandria, 162, 166
Algeria, 4, 47–48, 61–62, 84–85, 103–4, 107–10, 118–19, 128–30, 153–56, 166, 217, 219, 220, 229
Algiers, 47–48, 61–62, 84–85, 103–4, 107–10, 154
Alsace, 34
Alsace-Lorraine, 12, 269
America, 192, 257, 260, 272
Antakya. *See* Antioch
Antioch, 166, 170
Arabia, 191, 270
Australia, 192
Austria, 164, 192, 231
Auteuil, 35, 40, 66
Aydin, 166, 182, 183
Ayn-Teb, 166

Baghdad, 12, 34, 35, 45, 91–93, 172, 188–95, 198, 231, 246, 263–65, 267, 268, 276–78, 281
Basra, 266–68, 278
Beirut, 100, 166, 284–85
Bèja, 180, 181
Bergama. *See* Pergamon
Berlin, 100, 287, 288
Bessarabia, 164
Bitola. *See* Monastir (Macedonia)
Bizerte, 123
Bucovina, 164
Buenos Aires, 100
Bukhara, 166
Bulgaria, 48–49, 166, 230*n5*, 231, 232, 236–44, 248, 251

Burnabat, 182
Bursa, 139–42, 166

Cairo, 101, 162–64, 166
Canada, 261
Casablanca, 57–60, 74–75, 126–27, 146–48, 185–86, 212–14
Cassaba, 140, 183
Chaouia, 213
China, 191
Chios, 183
Cilicia, 172
Constantine, 118–19, 128–30, 281
Constantinople, 25, 34, 45, 52, 63, 63*n26*, 100, 101, 116–17, 130–31, 133–34, 137–39, 140, 143, 165, 166, 195, 198, 216, 231, 250–52, 263–64, 268, 273–75
Crete, 235

Damascus, 12, 76–77, 166, 172, 246, 268–73, 283
Davos, 99
Djedeida, 14, 94, 199, 200
Djerba, 199. *See also* Gerba
Doubnitza, 166

Edirne. *See* Adrianople
Egypt, 4, 100, 162–64, 166, 268, 269, 280
England, 189, 192, 257–58, 261–62, 266–68, 270, 276–77, 280, 281, 283

Fez, 82–84, 89–91, 113–14, 143, 148–50, 166, 187–88
Figuig, 154
France, 7, 10, 11, 11*n12,* 25, 27, 34–36, 143, 206, 217–29, 259, 265–66, 269, 270, 272, 279, 280, 281, 283, 284–85, 287, 288, 289–90

Gabès, 180, 181
Galicia, 164, 165
Gallipoli (Gelibolu), 59, 166

Gaziantep. *See* Ayn-Teb
Gerba, 180, 181. *See also* Djerba
Germany, 12, 260–61, 270, 280, 287, 289
Greece, 14, 49, 99, 186–87, 231, 232–38, 248–50

Hamadan, 53, 131, 177, 178
Hebron, 166
Hille, 191
Hindiya, 191
Hindustan, 166, 267
Hong Kong, 192
Hungary, 164, 165

India, 189, 191, 192, 268, 270
Iran, 14, 52–55, 60–61, 79, 119–21, 131–33, 166, 167–68, 172, 175–78, 193, 214–16, 231, 259–62, 263, 267, 268
Iraq, 51, 91–93, 173–75, 188–95, 263–65,
İskenderun. *See* Alexandretta
Isphahan, 61, 131, 177, 259–62
Israel, 14, 94, 97–98, 100–101, 111–12, 130, 164–70, 175, 195–98, 245–48, 253, 254, 257–58, 261, 268–69, 270, 271, 275, 277, 278, 281, 282, 284, 285, 286, 292
Istanbul. *See* Constantinople
Italy, 12, 142, 143, 157*n6,* 228, 240, 259
İzmir. *See* Smyrna

Jaffa, 14, 166, 197
Jerba. *See* Djerba
Jerusalem, 14, 34, 94, 96, 100–101, 166–70, 195–98, 275–76

Kamishli, 170
Kermanshah, 54–55, 58, 215
Kurdistan, 172, 193

Lebanon, 229, 270, 273, 284–85
Libya, 240*n10*

Macedonia, 232–35, 240
Magnesia, 183
Mahdia, 199
Malabar, 191
Malta, 158, 159
Manisa. *See* Magnesia
Marrakesh, 85–89, 98, 183–85, 206–8
Mascara, 154–55
Meknes, 150–53
Mitylene, 233
Monastir (Macedonia), 166

Monastir (Tunisia), 199
Morocco, 4, 14, 49–50, 50*n20,* 51, 57–60, 74–75, 75–76, 82–91, 98, 102, 113–16, 118, 125, 126–28, 144–53, 154, 166, 183–86, 187–88, 192, 205–14, 217–22, 231, 265–66, 287–89
Mossul, 173–75, 189

New York, 100

Oran, 153–54
Ottoman Empire, 13, 49, 51, 171, 203, 216, 229–30, 230–31, 232, 234–44, 245, 249–50, 251, 263–65, 267, 269, 273, 276

Palmyra, 172
Paris, 5, 7, 11–12, 34–36, 42–47, 96, 100, 240–41
Pergamon, 183
Poland, 164, 165, 240, 257, 258, 261
Port Said, 166
Portugal, 142, 220

Rabat, 211–12, 220–22
Rangoon, 192
Rhodes, 166
Rio de Janeiro, 100
Romania, 164, 198, 230*n5,* 261
Ruse. *See* Rustchuk
Russia, 10, 164, 165, 166, 196, 198, 257, 258, 259, 260, 261
Rustchuk, 45, 231

Safed, 111–12, 130, 164–66, 197, 245–48, 277
Salonica, 25, 34, 45, 99, 165, 166, 186–87, 198, 232–38, 248–50
Samacoff, 231
Seneh, 131, 177, 215
Settat, 213
Sfax, 123, 180, 181, 199, 225–28
Shanghai, 192
Shiraz, 79, 119–21, 131–33, 166, 214–16
Shumla (Shumen), 45, 231
Sicily, 143
Smyrna, 45, 95–97, 135–37, 166, 181–83, 231
Sofia, 166, 241
Somalia, 100
Sousse, 121–24, 180, 181, 198–200, 257–59, 285
Spain, 142, 143, 144, 220
Syria, 76–77, 170–72, 178, 229, 245–46, 245*n1,* 268–73, 279–84, 285

Tafilalet, 154
Tangier, 50, 60, 75–76, 94, 102, 114–16, 127–28, 144–46, 166, 185, 198, 205–6, 207, 209, 210, 218–20, 287–89
Tbilisi. *See* Tiflis
Tedef, 170
Teheran, 52–54, 55, 60–61, 131, 175–78
Tetuan, 12, 34, 45, 50, 127, 154, 192, 198, 208–11
Tiflis, 166
Tireh (Tire), 183
Tlemcen, 155–56
Tunis, 31–33, 60, 75–76, 78–79, 101, 114–15, 123, 156–62, 179–81, 198, 199, 200, 222–25, 226, 230–31, 252–56, 275–76
Tunisia, 4, 14, 30, 33, 78–79, 121–24, 156–62, 166, 179–81, 198–200, 203, 217, 218, 219, 222–28, 229, 230–31, 252–56, 257–59, 275–76, 285
Turgutlu. *See* Cassaba
Turkestan, 166
Turkey, 3, 4, 14, 44, 49, 95–97, 116–17, 129, 130–31, 133–34, 135–44, 165, 166, 167, 180, 181–83, 234–35, 236*n7*, 238–44, 250–52, 269–70, 273–75, 277, 281

Urmia, 177

Varna, 231
Volo (Volos), 12, 14, 45, 94

Widdin, 231

Yemen, 166, 167, 168, 240